PUBLIC HEALTH ONSTAGE
MEDICAL ESSAYS AND ORIGINAL SHORT PLAYS

David J. Holcombe, M.D.

authorHOUSE®

AuthorHouse™
1663 Liberty Drive
Bloomington, IN 47403
www.authorhouse.com
Phone: 1 (800) 839-8640

Published by AuthorHouse 03/07/2017

ISBN: 978-1-5246-7267-6 (sc)
ISBN: 978-1-5246-7266-9 (e)

CONTENTS

INTRODUCTION

PUBLIC HEALTH ONSTAGE represents an attempt to combine two visions of public health, the scientific and the artistic. Cathedral builders of the Middle Ages claimed that visual art adorning the insides and the outsides of the great cathedrals of Europe were an attempt to bring the word of God to the unlettered.

Although we are a literate public, the tolerance for the written word has often descended to the length of a tweet. More complicated exposés cannot hope to compete in the instantaneous social media marketplace. The issues, however, remain complex and the answers often just as complex or completely elusive.

Each one of the short essays deals with some aspect of public health including Human Papilloma Virus vaccination, medication marketing, safe sleep, malpractice, sexual assault, opioid abuse and many more. Paired with each scientific essay are one or more short plays that delve into the same or similar subject matter while exploiting its dramatic potential. This unlikely pairing hopefully stimulates both sides of the reader's brain.

It has been said that genius is the art of putting together different domains that have been mastered by a single creative individual. The resulting synergy exceeds the power of the separate elements. The arid complexity of a scientific analysis suddenly takes on a new dimension when it appears on the stage.

Dr. David Holcombe has taken many of the plays from previous publications including *Beauty and the Botox, Old South, New South, No South, Chateau in Hessmer* and *Why Go All the Way to Fulton, Louisiana?*

Other plays have never appeared in print. Some of the medical essays have been extracted from his previously published *Mendel's Garden: Selected Medical Topics*. Most of these medical essays have already appeared in *CENLA FOCUS*, a regional publication in Central Louisiana, or *Visible Horizon*, another regional publication by the Council on Aging. Some have never been previously published.

Combining the scientific and the artistic can be fraught with peril. Their hoped-for synergy can dissolve into nonsense or, worse yet, alienate the reader who becomes completely unreceptive. My hope is that this volume will break new ground in both public health and theater and appeal to the most discriminating critics. Many famous authors have tackled complex social and medical issues in the past (notably Henrik Ibsen and George Bernard Shaw). Physicians have also distinguished themselves as playwrights while steering clear of medical topics entirely (such as Dr. Anton Chekhov.) But this volume hopes to put the medical and theatrical together for the edification and entertainment of the reader and the potential viewer.

Scientific readers may gain a new appreciation for the persuasive power of the stage and theatre lovers may acquire some unexpected medical information.

ACKNOWLDEGEMENTS
AND DISCLAIMER

Any scientific or artistic work owes a debt of gratitude to all of the precursor works that have gone before. No work springs, as did the goddess Athena, full-grown and clothed in armor from Zeus's forehead. Science is laboriously built on previous discoveries as it lurches toward some perfect truth.

Artistic works, whether they are paintings, sculptures or theater, also evolve from previous attempts to explore reality and translate it into something the general public might understand and enjoy. Novelty on stage is balanced by an appreciation of timeless themes.

Whether it be in science or art, the comprehension and vision of the artist or scientist can leap ahead of general knowledge, often at the creator's peril. Regardless of the risks, however, the truly sustainable works contain something of the immortal, some grain of truth that transcends time and space and offers some consolation to the creator through recognition, sometimes only posthumously.

Many people over decades and across continents have contributed to both the scientific and artistic works in this compilation. To all of them, I owe my thanks. I would especially like to thank Dr. John Hill, who patiently read over the manuscript to verify errors and omissions and offer helpful editorial suggestions.

Finally, these plays, while they may seem to represent familiar characters are, of course, all fictional, as are the character's words and actions. Any resemblance to the living or the dead is strictly fortuitous.

PUBLIC HEALTH:
WHAT HAS IT DONE FOR YOU LATELY?

The general public has a poor understanding of what Public Health does and what it has accomplished. That confusion persists, especially among those over 50, because of the shifts in public health activities over the past decades. Older Louisianans, when asked, "What happens at the health units?" will invariable say "That's where kids get their shots." In fact, two decades ago, 88% of Louisianans did get their shots at a health unit while now the number is closer to 10% or even less.

In Louisiana, public health has traditionally been associated with direct service care, notably immunizations, contraception, STD treatment and surveillance, and WIC (Women, Infants and Children) food supplementation programs. While direct care by public health still serves as a safety net for some services, there are other states that adhere to the classic public health functions (i.e. surveillance, connecting people with services, dissemination of information, enforcement of regulations, development of policies, research and creating a competent public health work force). Providing direct care when no other providers are available (notably for contraception and STD treatment) remains a part of public health, but not a core function in many parts of the U.S.

So what has public health nationally done for our country? Those accomplishments include 10 activities most people will recognize:

1. Reducing disease through vaccine use remains a triumph. There has been huge decreases in all "vaccine preventable disease," more recently rotavirus, meningococcus, pneumococcal pneumonia, as well as the

older childhood diseases: measles, mumps, rubella, polio, diphtheria, whooping cough, chickenpox and hepatitis, both A and B. Many of these diseases are so rare that patients (and even doctors) have never seen them.

2. Prevention and control of infectious diseases through screening, surveillance and treatment, notably with TB and HIV, have resulted in huge improvements in survival through timely treatment.

3. Promotion of tobacco control with increases of tobacco taxes, proliferation of smoke-free ordinances at local and state levels, restricted advertising and aggressive education campaigns, have resulted in a decrease in tobacco use nationally from 42% of adults in 1965 to 20% now.

4. Improving maternal and infant health through the mandated use of folic acid in grains, and the generalized use of neonatal screening for a host of treatable infant disorders have reduced cases of spina bifida and resulted in earlier diagnosis of many genetic disorders.

5. Enhancing motor vehicle safety through mandated seatbelt and child safety seat use and, improving safety by promoting changes in the road construction and signage have resulted in steady declines in motor vehicle death rates.

6. Reducing cardiovascular death by promoting and standardizing treatment for hypertension, cholesterol and tobacco cessation has saved millions of lives.

7. Occupational safety promotion using best practices, notably for lifting and farm equipment use (especially for children), has reduced injuries and workman's compensation cases.

8. Increasing cancer screenings to improve survival following early diagnosis, especially in breast cancer and colon caner has resulted in improved survival rates.

9. Aggressive screening programs have reduced lead poisoning from 88.2% of high-risk children in 2003 to less than 1% in 2008 (notably in minority children in substandard housing.)

10. Development of national and state emergency response systems with the use of the National Incident Management System and improvement in the coordination of state and local resources produced remarkable results in Louisiana's responses to Hurricanes Gustav, Ike and Isaac (and other emergencies nationally.)

Public health, as enigmatic as it seems to the general public, continues to play a role in communities throughout Louisiana. The safety net function of their services depends on the availability of local providers, but the other functions remain, regardless of those circumstances. The collaborations and cooperative efforts generated by public health go a long way in promoting a healthier community even though those efforts may not always be that evident. Whether it's a public health nurse, sanitarian, nutritionist, disease intervention or surveillance specialist or the Regional Administrator/Medical Director, give them a call. They have a wealth of information and experience to share.

VACCINATION FOR HUMAN PAPILLOMA VIRUS

HUMAN PAPILLOMA VIRUS (HPV): THE ENEMY WITHIN

Human Papilloma Virus (HPV) is one of the many viruses that infect humans (and other primates). Viruses are bits of genetic material, housed in a capsule, that inject themselves into their human host. The genetic material is actually incorporated into the cell's genetic material. In essence, the human host cell is hijacked by the virus and turned into a viral replication factory.

There are many strains of HPV, one of which is the HPV-16. Some strains are more virulent than others. The problem with HPV, as with some other viruses, is that once it infects the host, it may remain in the host's cells indefinitely. The important question is, "Once we get hijacked, what harm does this intracellular pirate cause?"

Although you may not have heard of HPV, everyone knows about *verruca vulgaris*, or common skin warts. Common warts can form on any part of the body, but are often located on the hands. They can last for months or years. They can also disappear without treatment if the body's immunity overcomes the invader. Freezing, burning them off with a corrosive agent or use of electrocoagulation, as long as the root is treated, can also result in cure.

Condyloma accuminata, or genital warts, is the same problem, albeit in a different location. Genital warts can be huge and recurrent, despite multiple applications of a corrosive agent, TCA trichloracetic acid (TCA). Burning off the top genital wart sometimes reduces the size, but rarely eliminates the offending virus, which continues to live deep in the tissues and reforms the wart at a later date.

While genital warts are unpleasant, even disfiguring, the virus (especially HPV-16) has the propensity of inhibiting the repair of damaged cellular DNA. Without these protective properties, cells become dysfunctional and can undergo malignant (cancerous) transformation. Through this mechanism, HPV causes both cervical cancer in women and head and neck cancers in both men and women. Over 10,000 women die each year of HPV induced cervical cancer. The cost, both in lives and money, is staggering, all the more so since this is a vaccine-preventable illness.

Some years ago, vaccine became available against HPV. Several vaccines are currently available and they are administered by pediatricians, obstetricians-gynecologists, and through the Office of Public Health. Since HPV is a sexually transmitted disease, which can be treated but not cured, any preventive measures, such as vaccination, must be considered.

To be effective, the HPV vaccine is best administered prior to the initiation of sexual activity. Girls should be vaccinated after they reach 9 years of age, but may be vaccinated later if they have not already done so. The vaccine is given in a series of three intra-muscular shots at 1, 2 and 6 months. If given prior to 15 years of age, only two shots are required. There are many strains of HPV so vaccination, while it will not cure an existing infection, will help prevent other strains, notably the cancer-causing HPV-16.

Boys should be vaccinated as well. Although they are not subject to cervical cancer, they can contract and transmit HPV and are subject to HPV induced head and neck cancer. In addition, an infected person will spread the disease through sexual intercourse to partners. Available without charge from the Office of Public Health to adolescents 19 years or younger, the vaccine is also available through private physicians. It can cost up to $120 per shot at most private providers, although it is usually covered by insurance plans.

Despite HPV vaccine's effectiveness, since it is a "recommended" rather than a "required" vaccination in teens, it is grossly underutilized. While increasing gradually, less than 60% of young women start the HPV series (and only 42% complete it) and less than 50% of young men start the series (and only 28% complete it). National figures resemble those in Louisiana, which is otherwise well known for excellent childhood and adolescent vaccination rates. Baseless apprehension about the vaccines, notably that it increases adolescent sexual activity, have discouraged some parents from insisting on the HPV vaccine for their teens.

In conclusion, HPV represents more than a nuisance and the vaccine should be given to adolescents, especially girls but also to boys, prior to the initiation of sexual intercourse. Help fight HPV, this insidious hijacking pirate. Get your children or grandchildren vaccinated to stop this preventable cancer-inducing virus.

ARRANGING THE SPICES

CHARACTERS

> MARIA: Young woman, granddaughter to Clara. She is dressed in causal, clean Eddie Bauer type clothing.

> CLARA: An older woman, Maria's grandmother. She has her graying hair in a ponytail. She wears some flashy ethnic jewelry. She also looks like an "old hippy." She is a retired English teacher.

SETTING

> There is a kitchen table with a couple of chairs. There is also a cabinet for spices. There are a dozen or more bottles of various spices.

> > *MARIA watches as her grandmother, CLARA, arranges the spices in alphabetical order. All of the bottles were scattered over the counter in total disarray. CLARA picks them up, one by one, and puts order into the chaos.*

CLARA: You need to replace your spices every two years or even less to have a fresh supply. They lose their potency with time, you know.

MARIA: Grandma, I really don't do that much entertaining anymore.

CLARA: (*Stops and stares at MARIA*) Maybe that's why you're not already married and with children at your age . . . .

MARIA: (*Cuts CLARA off*) I bet when you were my age, you didn't have massive genital warts either.

CLARA: (*Stops ordering the spices and looks at MARIA*) You have what?

MARIA: (*Takes a bottle of spice from CLARA's hand and leads her to the kitchen table*) I think you need to sit down for this.

CLARA: Is it so bad that I have to sit down?

MARIA: (*Shrugs*) Maybe.

CLARA: (*Wipes off the table with her hands before folding them in a position of thoughtful prayer*) I'm ready.

MARIA: Grandma, the table's not dirty. And I'm not contagious, unless you are having unprotected sex with me.

CLARA: That's disgusting. (*Pauses and narrows her eyes to slits*) Go on. I'm listening.

MARIA: I have *condyloma accuminata*, genital warts. They look like pink cauliflowers growing out of my vagina.

CLARA: (*Her face remains cold and immobile, devoid of emotion*) How big?

> *MARIA goes over and pulls out a Polaroid picture, tucked between two cookbooks. She hands it to CLARA, who takes the edge with the tips of her fingers as if it, too, was infectious.*

CLARA: (*Examines the photo*) What is it?

MARIA: (*Turns the photo upside down and points to it*) This is my vulva. And this is the top, with my pubic hair. And on the sides, you see all of this tissue. All those little bumps are genital warts.

CLARA: Who took this picture?

MARIA: (*Sighs*) I asked the nurse practitioner at the health unit to take it so I could show you and anyone else who might be interested.

CLARA: It's horrible! How did you get this?

MARIA: (*Takes the picture from between CLARA's fingers and replaces it between the cookbooks. Returns to the table and sits down*) It's a sexually transmitted disease. I think I got it from Greg. Or maybe it was Carl! Or Peter!

CLARA: (*Holds up her hand and cuts off MARIA*) That's enough. Is it gone now? (*Resumes her prayerful position.*)

MARIA: No, it's not gone. It's just a bit less obvious. It lives in the skin cells of my vagina. And I could have gotten from any number of guys.

CLARA: So that's why you're not married?

MARIA does not answer.

CLARA: Can you still have children?

MARIA: Yes.

CLARA: (*Stands up and returns to the spices on the counter where she continues sorting*) We need to get these spices in order. You can't live with this disorder and you have to get rid of those things, whatever they are and whoever gave them to you! How could you do such a thing?

MARIA: Grandma, stop! You make me feel like I'm a child being scolded for a bad grade in English. I'm sexually active and financially independent and have been for years. And I still feel like the victim of your emotional blackmail. I know you raised me when my own mother left. I appreciate it. But can you just sit down so we can discuss this like adults?

CLARA: No! I want to get these spices in order first. How can you find anything in this cabinet? You need to have these all in order. Then we can see what you need and what has to be replaced. Spices are the cornerstone of good cooking.

MARIA: (*Stands up and removes the Hungarian Paprika from CLARA's hand*) Don't you understand? I have enough spice in my life.

CLARA: (*Spins around*) That's not funny! I always warned you, I never liked Greg. I bet he gave you this awful thing.

MARIA: (*Picks up a bottle*) He did give me this freeze-dried dill. I don't know about the genital warts.

CLARA: (*Cringes and pushes a bottle away*) Or Peter? Maybe he was the one. I didn't care for him either. He was a shifty character, with bad grammar.

MARIA: And Carl? What about him? (*Picks up another bottle*) He gave me the saffron from Spain. Very expensive! Maybe he brought a little infection back with him?

CLARA: Well, Carl was okay, as long as he didn't give you these accumulated condylomas or whatever you call them (*ignores MARIA and resumes her work.*)

MARIA: Condyloma accuminata. (*Sighs*) The point is that I can't say who gave me this problem. (*Puts down the bottle and goes over to the bookshelf where she pulls out a little booklet*) Do you know what this is?

CLARA: (*Looks over and shakes her head*) No! It doesn't look familiar.

9

MARIA: (*Flips through the pages*) It's my childhood vaccination booklet.

CLARA: (*Looks more closely*) Yes, it is. I haven't seen that thing in years. (*Returns to the spices*) What of it?

MARIA: (*Speaks loudly and firmly*) Why didn't you let me get the HPV vaccination?

CLARA: What? (*Unscrews a bottle and gives it a whiff.*)

MARIA: HPV.

CLARA: What is that?

MARIA: Human Papilloma Virus. It's sexually transmitted and it's the virus that causes genital warts. (*Pauses*) Grandma, it's a preventable condition.

CLARA: (*Does not seem to notice and continues to sort the bottles*) This nutmeg looks moldy.

MARIA: (*Ignores the remark*) Remember that vaccine? The one they offered when I was 11 or 12 years old?

CLARA: (*Pauses and looks lost in thought. Replaces the dill and takes a bottle of oregano*) That was so many years ago. I do remember, vaguely. There was something about it not being required . . . . (*trails off.*)

MARIA: I remember like it was yesterday. You said you didn't want me to have that vaccine because it was experimental, and chemical and would pollute my pre-adolescent body. You said it wasn't required and you didn't want me to have it. You said that I was too young and it would encourage me to have early sex. That's what you said, early sex.

CLARA: (*Sets the oregano down on the counter*) How do you remember all that?

MARIA: I remember every word! I remember the nurse saying that it was safe and effective and not experimental and that it would protect me from cervical cancer and genital warts. She said it was recommended, but not required. (*Brings her fist down on the kitchen table*) And now I have this shit and I can't get rid of it, ever! It's in me. It's in my cells. It grows and grows and it puts me at risk for cervical cancer.

CLARA: (*Replaces the bottle and comes over to the table. Places her hand gently on MARIA's shoulder*). Maria, please.

MARIA: (*When CLARA's hand touches, her, MARIA shudders and pulls back. Turns and looks into CLARA's eyes, barely a few inches from her own*) Grandma, I hate you!

CLARA: No! You can't hate your own grandmother.

MARIA: Yes! I hate you and your fake hippy naturalistic health crap. I hate you and your fresh spices and organic food and gluten-free bullshit. I know you raised me when Momma left, but she would have got me vaccinated, I know it.

CLARA: (*Pulls away*) I don't know that and, besides, your mother wasn't around to raise you. I stepped in and did the best I could. And as for organic food and vegetables, they're important. Our bodies are a temple that we must cherish and respect.

MARIA: Yes! And so is my vagina! And now it looks like an alien cauliflower garden and it won't ever go away. Do you know how that makes me feel? (*Looks at CLARA intently. Pauses again*) Grandma, all I needed was three lousy shots and you didn't want them to give them to me. It's crazy!

CLARA: (*Comes over and sits beside MARIA at the table*) I didn't know. I didn't understand that it was so important. For me, it was just dangerous chemicals in your body. I didn't want them to pollute your young, beautiful, pure body with an experimental vaccine that . . . . (*voice trails away.*)

MARIA: That promoted sexual promiscuity?

CLARA: Yes.

> *They sit in silence for a few seconds.*

MARIA: Like for Momma?

CLARA: (*Quietly*) Yes.

MARIA: So now I'm sexually promiscuous and I have a cauliflower vagina and I can get cervical cancer, too. Plus I have to warn my boyfriends that they can get this stuff on their dicks. So they have to wear condoms to protect themselves. It's so romantic.

> *Looks over at CLARA, who sits upright, with her hands again folded in a prayer-like position. Gets up and goes behind CLARA, who remains rigid and motionless. Slides her hands over CLARA's shoulder and they come to rest around CLARA's interlaced fingers.*

MARIA (CONT): I know you meant well. I know you raised me the best you could. And I appreciate that. But you were wrong about this and I'll be paying the price for the rest of my life.

CLARA: Maria, (*turns her head and reveals her tear-filled eyes*) I'm so sorry. I was foolish. I didn't understand. (*Pauses*) But I didn't make you sleep with all those men. Any more than I made your mother sleep with anyone. I didn't make you have unprotected sex, either. Don't you have to accept some responsibility for your own actions? (*Clutches MARIA's hand*) Aren't we both to blame here, just a little?

MARIA: All that talk about Woodstock and Free Love. I heard it from you. Momma believed it and I believed you, too. I really did. Did you believe any of that? What were your consequences?

CLARA: I did believe in Free Love. I was lucky not to get genital warts. (*Pauses*) I got your mother. And I would not have traded her or you for all the spices in world. She's gone, but I still love you, warts and all. Please forgive me (*walks over and embraces MARIA.*)

MARIA: (*Kisses CLARA pulls away and sighs*) I guess I am better than genital warts. But I still have to live with this nightmare and you can go on with your macrobiotic food and solar panels. You can shop at Whole Foods and eat organic vegetables and gluten-free bread in peace.

CLARA: How can I be in peace knowing that my own flesh and blood suffers? (*Pauses*) Can I make it up to you somehow? What can I do? And please do it by alphabetical order and not by color.

MARIA: (*Releases CLARA's hands*) Finish arranging the spices. (*Picks up a bottle off the counter and hands it to CLARA*) Here's the curry. It goes after the cumin. I think Peter gave me that one.

BLACKOUT

THE EVOLUTION OF MEDICAL CARE DELIVERY IN LOUISIANA

MEDICAL CARE IN LOUISIANA AND THE GHOST OF HUEY P. LONG

It is said that you cannot understand the present without knowing the past and healthcare is certainly no exception. The State of Louisiana underwent a recent revolution in its healthcare delivery system, precipitated in part by changes at both the local and national level.

Louisiana has long suffered with a significant number of poor and unhealthy citizens. Although rich in natural resources, Louisiana has a long tradition of social inequality, resulting in marked health disparities and poor outcomes. With the discovery of huge oil deposits, companies of that time, notably Standard Oil, converged on Louisiana to extract its black gold. Huey P. Long, a brilliant speaker and savvy politician, recognized the deep-seated resentments of the indigent population, made even worse by the Great Depression, as well as the opportunity to benefit from the oil bonanza.

Huey P. Long ran on a populist platform of "Share the Wealth." He proposed that the resources that left the state must be paid for and that money should, in part, be funneled back into roads, schools, books and medical care for those unable to pay. This position, extremely popular with a large number of Louisiana's destitute citizens, resulted in Huey P. Long's meteoric rise to political power. His populist views and organizational abilities proved an unbeatable combination.

His party apparatus proliferated and he was able to establish effective control over the legislature, State Police, National Guard and civil service structure. Civil servants were obliged to forfeit a portion of their salaries for "voluntary" contributions to the Huey P. Long political machine, the famous "deduct."

One of his goals was the establishment of a world-class medical institution for the poor of Louisiana. The Charity Hospital of New Orleans was the flagship and first of a system of state owned and state operated medical institutions scattered throughout the state. The Office of Public Health also expanded under the same tradition of state delivered medical care, which continued until this decade. This heavily state-driven model is unique in the United States. Most states have county hospitals and county health departments established for the indigent. Their structure and functions vary from county to county depending on their wealth and population. There is always some state component to public health in all states, but the Louisiana model is peculiar in both its regional structure and robust state presence at the local level.

Louisiana's unique model came under critical review with changes in the political climate in the state with the election of Governor Bobby Jindal. The populist state-driven system was labeled as an inefficient, expensive and archaic leftover of a bygone social era. The result has been a rapid dismantling of the state operated system with repercussions to all aspects of the healthcare delivery system. Since many medical providers grew and prospered in collaboration with the state system, a rapid and somewhat chaotic transformation gripped Louisiana. The premise that the private sector can and will deliver better and less expensive care has driven these changes. The charity system, established under Huey P. Long, disappeared, to be replaced by a collection of public-private partnerships that varied from region to region.

At the time of these transformations, the State's population was still made up of over 25% Medicaid recipients and around 20% uninsured, and the State remains 49/50th in its health outcomes. Caring for this mass of indigent patients remains a significant challenge; especially since the then Governor Jindal refused Medicaid expansion. This situation changed dramatically with the election of Governor John Bel Edwards, whose first official act was the expansion of Medicaid, resulting in the prompt enrollment of over 350,000 new individuals.

The verdict is still out as to whether the transformation in healthcare delivery from public to private options can be achieved without a marked deterioration in health outcomes. Since Louisiana has always remained close to or at the bottom for health outcomes, a further drop is not a long way to go, but still undesirable. The ghost of Huey P. Long continues to haunt Louisiana, but perhaps with the dismantling of the state-driven healthcare system, that ghost will, at long last, be put to rest. Ultimately, it will be the improvement in the state's health outcomes that will be the proof of any positive change in our healthcare delivery model.

BIG CHARITY

CAST OF CHARACTERS

HUEY: Governor of a Southern state. Politician with a vision. Speaks with a pronounced Southern rural accent and may be overweight. Dressed in a 30's style white linen suit and a conical straw hat with a band, typical of the deep South.

EDDIE LEBLANC: Assistant to Huey. Speaks with a pronounced Southern accent with Cajun intonations. He is dressed simply, perhaps in some sort of uniform.

DR. CARL WEISS: Speaks with no accent. His grammar and pronunciation are both correct. He is impeccably dressed in a suit and tie from the 30's.

BOBBIE: Governor of a Southern state. The character needs to be slender, well dressed. His speaks correctly, almost as if English is his second language.

TONY: Works with Governor in Scene II. May be the same actor as Eddie LeBlanc, but he speaks without a Southern accent. He is well dressed.

DR. FRED CERISE: Well-dressed and well-spoken younger man. He has no regional accent.

SETTING

Both scenes have minimal, if any set items. There should be an American flag that denote an official event or location in the first two scenes. If it is not clear about the date, there may be a sign marked "1930" for Scene

I and "2012" for Scene II. Scene III should be totally empty, with no suggestion of time or place.

SCENE I – LE DEBUT (THE BEGINNING) (1932)

HUEY: (*Waves his hands in the air and looks around*) Can you see it, Eddie?

EDDIE: (*Looks around*) No, boss.

HUEY: That's cuz you ain't no visionary like me.

EDDIE: What's a visionary?

HUEY: Someone who can see the future before it happens just by usin' their imagination.

EDDIE: No, I guess, I ain't no visionary. I'm just a downed to earth country boy with a sixth grade education, hardly any book learnin' at all.

HUEY: That's the problem. (*Slaps EDDIE on the back*) You never got the benefits of a decent education and I'm goin' change all that.

EDDIE: Boss, we done heard it all before. Every politician promises us books and roads and doctorin' and then they pockets the money and hightails it out of the country before they can git caught.

HUEY: I'm different.

EDDIE: (*Looks skeptical*) Really?

HUEY: I really am different. I come from the backcountry too, them piney woods up North. I know poverty and even hunger. But I got myself through law school and got enough book learning to be elected governor. (*Pauses*) It wasn't easy, no sireebob. I done struggled for every scrap of information and every vote I ever got. (*Pauses*) But once the power and money started to accumulate, then it jus' snowballed. More power, more votes, more money. (*Pauses*) It's been a wild ride to the top and now you all, the people, are gonna benefit from my rise to the top. (*Swings his arms around*) We gonna build the biggest, the best hospital, and fill it with the best doctors in the entire South. I'm gonna fill it with the best professors that money can buy from all of them fancy Eastern schools. It's gonna have the best, shiniest equipment in the country, also the best that money can buy.

EDDIE: Whose money? Not the taxpayers, I hope.

HUEY: No, course not, Standard Oil's money, and lots of it. Those fat cats have been rapin' this state and stealin' us blind. If I could I'd nationalize them sons-of-bitches, but that ain't gonna happen anytime soon. Gotta respect free enterprise and all that.

EDDIE: Them oil companies; they'd just git up and leave and never come back if you taxes 'em like that.

HUEY: (*Laughs*) No, they won't. They ain't goin' nowhere and neither is that oil. They'd squeak and squawk and whine all the way up to Washington D.C. and Wall Street. But in the end, it won't make a bit of damn difference. They gotta come back and take that oil where they can find it and pay a hell of lot more to take it out.

EDDIE: Do you really think it's possible?

HUEY: Possible? It's goin' happen just like this hospital is gonna happen. (*Pauses.*) Big Charity Hospital down here will be the first of many. We can't neglect them poor folks around the rest of the state. We gotta think about them towns up north, damn it! They'll get their new hospitals in every corner of this state.

(*Pauses.*) Maybe not in my lifetime or yours, but sometime in the future it'll happen. By God, it will happen. (*Grabs EDDIE*) We don't have to be the clo-a-ca of the nation, the laughin' stock of them Eastern prep school snobs, them rich bastards with their stock coupons and houses in the Hamptons. We don't have to be the bottom of the barrel for everythin' while all them barrels of oil gettin' pumped out day after day, year after year.

EDDIE: What's a clo-a-ca?

HUEY: Where shit and eggs comes out of the same whole. (*Sees DR. WEISS coming*) Never mind. (*Walks over to DR. WEISS and shakes his hand*) Glad you could make it, doc.

DR. WEISS: Good to see you, sir. Sorry I was late. We had a little emergency at the hospital. So what did you want me to see?

HUEY: (*Waves his hands around and points to the distance*) There! Over there. That's gonna be the new Big Charity Hospital, the biggest and the best hospital in all the South. You gotta believe me, doc. (*Takes DR. WEISS by the shoulders*) This project is gonna happen and it's gonna be so good and so solid that it will still be here in a 1,000 years. Yup, the thousand year Big Charity Hospital! It'll be a testimony to dedicated staff and a fine administrator like you. Dr. Weiss, you gotta help me make this happen. And it's gonna happen because I'm one son-of-a-bitch determined politician and the people want it, too. Them grateful citizens are gonna love the place and wanna vote for someone who finally shows them that he really cares about 'em.

DR. WEISS: Be careful, Governor, you have enemies out there in industry and finance. Wall Street and the White House aren't very excited about your schemes down here. The President thinks you may have just gotten too big for your political britches. Megalomonaical is the term I think I've heard him use.

HUEY: (*Pronounces each syllable*) Mego-al-o-man-ia-cal? What does it mean again? I'm sure I've seen it somewhere before.

DR. WEISS: Delusions of grandeur from a mental disorder. And frankly, I'm not sure it would be a favorable career goal for me to associate with a project that hasn't even left the planning stage. That's just a big, muddy field over there. I'm sure you understand my reticence.

HUEY: (*Explodes. Yells*) Whose side are you on, anyway, doc?

DR. WEISS: Yours, of course, sir. I want to see the Big Charity Hospital materialize and be the site of a worldclass medical school. I want it to be a source of knowledge and medical care for the poor of this state who have nothing, no money, no insurance, not even good health. You are a visionary. I just need to be prudent.

HUEY: (*Calms*) Of course, I do understand. And I do appreciate your support. (*Pauses*) Schools, roads, books, vaccinations, all paid for by the largess of Standard Oil. Them oil companies just won't be able to say no to me. They'll line up with the money in checks and suitcases filled with cash and Big Charity Hospital will become a reality. (*Pauses and slaps DR. WEISS on the back*) And don't forget all that support from them civil servants of mine. I got their deducts to help fund my campaigns. And what with the poor folks, includin' them votin' Negroes, you'll see this buildin' rise from that mud to become a gleamin' monument to me and medicine, the New Jerusalem of learnin' and healin' right here in this amazin' city.

EDDIE: (*Claps*) You tell 'em, boss!

DR. WEISS: Astonishing.

HUEY: Yes, astonishing. (*Slaps DR. WEISS on the back*) And you, doc, are gonna head up this great institution. You are gonna see the building rise up brick by brick from this swampy soil to become a worldclass medical institution, so help me God.

DR. WEISS: I'm a simple ear, nose and throat specialist. I'm not sure I'm up for the task. It's monumental.

HUEY: Of course you are, doc. (*Turns to EDDIE*) Don't you think docs up for it?

EDDIE: Damn right!

HUEY: (*To DR. WEISS*) Yes, sir, even if you're related to that scoundrel judge that gives the boss so much trouble.

DR. WEISS: Don't go there, Governor, please.

HUEY: Of course, let's just let bygones be bygones. A few harsh words spoken in haste and anger from your father-in-law can't keep us from workin' together, can they, doc?

DR. WEISS: No, they shouldn't. Not between gentlemen, anyway, both working for the better health of the people of this state.

HUEY: Yes indeed, gentlemen. (*Takes DR. WEISS by the shoulder and escorts him off stage*) So you go along, doc, and start recruitin' faculty from every distinguished medical school in the country. And remember, spare no expense! We want talent and brains to run this place. And I don't give a damn how much Standard Oil is gonna to pay for it.

DR. WEISS: Thanks. I will do my best, sir. You won't regret it. (*Exits.*)

HUEY: (*To EDDIE*) Now you make sure that the doctor's father-in-law, that sleazy, no good, son-of-bitch judge, gits what he deserves. You tell them over in the Picayune about his affair with that Creole bitch down in them prairies. And don't spare any of the lurid details. I'm sorry for the doc, but that asshole father-in-law of his has gotta go.

EDDIE: Sure thing, boss (*exits.*)

HUEY: (*Turns around. Waves his hands in the air*) It will be a triumph, a perfect success. I will get my glory with the poor, who'll get the hospital they deserve. And Standard Oil gets what they deserve for tryin' to suck this state dry and throw us away on the garbage. Now that's real charity for you, takin' from the undeservin' rich and givin' to the deservin' poor. I can see it now, by God, I can really see it! (*Exits.*)

BLACKOUT

SCENE II – LE DEMANTALEMENT (THE DISMANTELING) (2012)

BOBBIE: The poor! You really think this monstrous system is serving the poor?

TONY: Sir, the press is crucifying you for dismantling the state run healthcare system. They say you have no room in your heart for charity.

BOBBIE: Charity? For whom? For the bloodsucking civil servants who work in it? For the vendors who sell to it? For the people who get second rate medical care in an expensive and antiquated system? Is that what you call charity? We've spent billions over the years, and for what? To be the laughing stock of the Union, the cloaca of the nation? The last in healthcare over and over again, year after year.

TONY: We just don't have the private infrastructure to take on the task of caring for the poor. There are too many sick, indigent people in this state.

BOBBIE: Sick and poor, yes. And too many, yes. You know what Jesus said?

TONY: He said lots of things.

BOBBIE: "The poor you shall always have among you." But those are not the people on which to found a prosperous state. We need to rely on private entrepreneurship, private practices and personal responsibility to pull us out of this morass into which we have sunk over the decades.

TONY: Perhaps with federal help, it might be possible.

BOBBIE: Federal help? Are you crazy? If we ask for federal help, we sacrifice any ideological credibility we might still possess. Can't you smell the hypocrisy of it all? On the one hand, we râle against the excesses of federal government and on the other hand, we take federal handouts in the vain hope that we can somehow spend our way to prosperity and health. There's no way federal assistance can help us. Besides, it would completely sabotage my conservative credentials.

TONY: It's impossible otherwise, sir. The poor don't have the time, money or transportation to get care now, much less if we don't have a safety net system anymore. We're already 48th out of 50 states in our health rankings. How much lower can we get?

BOBBIE: 50th! We can still sink to 50th! And the sick and poor can go elsewhere for help or die in the streets and decrease the excess population.

TONY: That's harsh, sir, even for you. (*Pauses*) My brother had a streak of bad luck and if it weren't for the state run health system he would have died too. He spent almost a month in the ICU. He got good care, too. Without Big Charity Hospital, he would have died.

BOBBIE: I'm sorry for your brother. I'm sorry for everyone's brothers and sisters who are sick and poor and uninsured. But you cannot buy good health, especially with a separate-but-unequal system, born out of the erroneous beliefs of a populist demagogue. *(Pauses)* It's done! That era is finished. And the ghosts of its creator and all of his like-minded believers should stay down in their graves where they belong *(points downward.)*

TONY: Dr. Cerise is here to see you, sir. He's been waiting outside over an hour.

BOBBIE: Show him in, please.

DR. CERISE: Thank you for seeing me, Governor. I hope you have some good news about hospital funding.

BOBBIE: Dr. Cerise, you are a fine, dedicated physician, with a wealth of knowledge and a reputation for personal integrity. But you must realize you are on the wrong side of history. There will be no more funding for the state medical system at this time. It's finished!

DR. CERISE: Sir, there are no viable private alternatives to the state run health system at this time. The private sector is neither interested in nor obliged to see the hordes of poor, sick people that live in this state. They're over 45% of the population.

BOBBIE: *(Menacingly)* Doctor, don't lecture me on statistics in this state. I know them all by heart. And you should know that we have dumped billions of dollars down the rat hole of state-delivered medical care and our health outcomes are abysmal. You should know better than me that insanity is doing the same thing over and over again despite catastrophic results. My predecessors may have been insane, but I am not.

DR. CERISE: University Hospital has been in the black for years and has managed to deliver decent care to everyone, rich and poor, for decades.

BOBBIE: Decent care! And that's how we got to be 48th out of 50 states? (*Pauses*) No! The state system is finished. This army of sullen, inefficient civil servants, sucking off the tit of the state, is going to have to face the music. They can work with the private sector or retire, or just go home and hate me from there. They can't dislike me anymore than they already do. To hell with them all!

DR. CERISE: There are still ways to reform the system, improve it and make it more efficient. We don't want to throw the babies out with the bathwater.

BOBBIE: Clever, Dr. Cerise, but I'm not interested in improving a broken system. I want the state out of the healthcare delivery business. And you, Dr. Cerise, have demonstrated your persistent opposition to change. Since everyone is either part of the solution or part of the problem, you have demonstrated that you are part of the problem. Dr. Cerise, you're fired!

DR. CERISE: But. . . .

BOBBIE: But what? You are an unclassified employee who serves at the discretion of the governor. That's me! And my discretion is that you leave your position immediately.

TONY: Should I call security, sir?

DR. CERISE: Don't bother. It's been my pleasure to serve. I hope my successor will continue to have the best interest of the people of this state at heart.

BOBBIE: (*Laughs*) Like you? Sucking off the tit of the state while cranking out piss-poor health statistics. Give me a break, doctor.

TONY: Should I show the doctor out?

BOBBIE: Please do. (*To DR. CERISE*) The people of this state need jobs, good paying, tax-producing jobs, not charity. Prosperity brings good health, not unemployment. We can never spend our way to good health.

DR. CERISE: Yes, we need good jobs, but companies will come to a state not only because of tax breaks and lax regulations, but also because of a healthy and well-educated workforce, which doesn't exist here at this time.

BOBBIE: (*Yells*) GET OUT!

DR. CERISE: And as the so-called champion of healthcare and education, you have sadly missed the mark.

TONY: I'm calling security.

BOBBIE: (*To TONY*) Do it! And get this radical, tax-and-spend socialist out of my sight!

DR. CERISE: Don't bother to call security. I'm leaving (*exits.*)

TONY: He's a good doctor. He treated my brother, you know, and discovered that he suffered from some rare disease that no one else had diagnosed. My whole family loves the guy.

BOBBIE: That's nice. I'm sure he'll be able to use his talents elsewhere, the further from this state the better.

TONY: I thought you wanted our citizens to be able to get jobs in this state and not have to leave.

BOBBIE: Shut up! Bring me those files about the oil spill, and that damn sinkhole, too. And don't forget those papers about the brain-eating amoebas. Now those are real problems that need looking into.

TONY: Yes, sir.

BOBBIE: And don't forget to bring me that cup of herbal tea. All this arguing gives me a headache. I need something to soothe my nerves.

SCENE III - LE RENCONTRE (THE MEETING)

> *HUEY and BOBBIE enter from opposite sides of an empty stage. They meet in the middle.*

BOBBIE: (*Looks closely at HUEY*) Huey? Huey P. Long?

HUEY: Yes.

BOBBIE: (*Extends his right hand to HUEY*) Nice to meet you. I've read a lot about you. I'm Bobbie.

HUEY: (*Shakes BOBBIE's hand*) Nice to meet you. (*Looks closely at BOBBIE*) Do I know you?

BOBBIE: Probably not. You were way before my time. (*Looks around*) Where are we, anyway?

HUEY: (*Sighs*) I'm not really sure. (*Leans closer to BOBBIE*) I think we're in purgatory.

BOBBIE: Purgatory! (*Looks around*) You've got to be kidding.

HUEY: No, I'm not.

BOBBIE: I can image why you might be here, but me? That's ridiculous. I've been devotedly religious all my life, a very good Catholic, at least since my conversion. There really must be some mistake.

HUEY: What's that supposed to mean?

BOBBIE: Well, you were a philandering, power-hungry, populist prick, and probably agnostic as well. Does that about sum it up?

HUEY: That's harsh. And by the way, I was Southern Baptist, at least officially.

BOBBIE: And you left our state in a hell of a mess. It took me eight years to wipe away all that socialist garbage you started 70 years ago.

HUEY: What exactly did you do?

BOBBIE: What didn't I do? That's more like it. First, I closed Big Charity Hospital, wiped out the state-run health system, well, privatized it is more like it. Second, I fired half of the state's sullen civil servants. And third, I tried to change the pension system that's destroying the state, even though that didn't work out as well as I'd hoped. Oh, and I also helped give school vouchers to poor black kids so they could get out of failing schools. Now that was a catfight.

HUEY: You closed Big Charity Hospital?

BOBBIE: You bet, with a little help from Katrina.

HUEY: Katrina who?

BOBBIE: Hurricane Katrina. It flooded the whole of New Orleans and nearly wiped it out. (*Shrugs.*) That's recent history. You wouldn't know about that, would you?

A silence ensues.

HUEY: (*Attacks BOBBIE and tries to strangle him*) You pompous little son-of-a-bitch! I'll beat the crap outta you.

> *BOBBIE and HUEY struggle. BOBBIE manages to free himself and pulls away.*

BOBBIE: You crazy old man! Leave me alone!

HUEY: Where will they go for care?

BOBBIE: Who?

HUEY: The poor people?

BOBBIE: (*Sighs and shrugs*) To the private sector, of course. The private sector will take care of the poor.

HUEY: (*Shakes his head.*) There weren't enough private doctors to see the poor in my day. I can't imagine that's changed that much since then. Besides, there ain't enough money in the world to make the private docs see the poor. And there are just too many poor people all over the state to be taken care of.

BOBBIE: (*Strikes a pose*) Remember, Jesus said, "The poor ye shall always have among you." (*Pauses*) And they're still there, just more of them than back in your day, lots more.

HUEY: You're cold!

BOBBIE: No, just practical. (*Pauses*) You can't build a prosperous society on the dredges. We have to wager on the strong, the industrious, the entrepreneurial.

HUEY: The rich, you mean.

BOBBIE: Precisely, the rich. And there's nothing wrong with that. We want to build on the wealthy, good companies that bring good jobs, good wages, and insurance coverage. A rising tide floats all ships, you know.

HUEY: Yeah, but it drowns the ones without boats. (*Shakes his head*) How could you close Big Charity Hospital?

BOBBIE: How could I not? You left a cesspool of costly, inefficient, unproductive healthcare delivery. It was separate but unequal care and they got rid of that in the sixties. You might have been able to live with that, but not me! You and I are very different people.

HUEY: No, we're not.

BOBBIE: How so?

HUEY: Because we both wanted the same thing anyway.

BOBBIE: What? The good of the people?

HUEY: No, we wanted power.

BOBBIE: No, I wanted to change society and turn it back to its basic roots: Christian values, industry, thrift, private enterprise and personal responsibility.

HUEY: (*Yells*) You're a liar! You're cynical, immoral and hypocritical, that's what you are! You'll build your fool's paradise on the bones of the poor and helpless and call it progress. Cynical, immoral and hypocritical!

BOBBIE: No, I'm not! And don't you dare use my words against me! Keeping the poor in ignorance, poverty and sickness is really what's cynical, immoral and hypocritical. You were all three, not me! I am the healthcare governor! I am the education governor! I am the savior of the state!

HUEY: Liar! I hear the moans and groans of the people all the way into this God forsaken place. (*Points to BOBBIE*) You're gonna rot here, Bobbie. You're gonna rot here for a millennium while you dwell on your sins.

BOBBIE: Crazy bastard! Shut up! Maybe this is purgatory if I have to listen to the likes of you for days, weeks, years. . . .

HUEY: How about decades, maybe centuries?

BOBBIE: (*Looks around*) Oh shit.

> *BOBBIE and HUEY stand in silence, lost in their thoughts.*

HUEY: Did you finally get it?

BOBBIE: Get what?

HUEY: What you wanted?

BOBBIE: What was that?

HUEY: Power.

BOBBIE: (*Thinks*) Yes, I did get power, lots of it.

HUEY: And money?

BOBBIE: Enough. But that was never the goal, just a means to an end.

HUEY: You see, (*Slaps BOBBIE on the back*) we're not that different. That was my feeling exactly.

BOBBIE: Spare me the details, old man.

HUEY: No, it's true! That's what made me so dangerous to other politicians in my time.

BOBBIE: Yes, destroying free enterprise with your taxes and entitlements.

HUEY: No, not that. I mean our President back in my day, Franklin Delano Roosevelt, wasn't afraid of anyone but me, a Southern populist who wasn't too greedy. (*Spins around*) I never cared about the money. It was just like the Bible says.

BOBBIE: (*Holds up hid hand*) Please, enough pontificating. `

HUEY: No, really! Jesus also said, "Seek you first the Kingdom of Heaven and all things will be given unto you."

BOBBIE: Stop it!

HUEY: Our Kingdom of Heaven was power and we both got everythin' else we needed as an added bonus.

BOBBIE: (*Thinks*) Except perhaps love.

HUEY: The people loved me! There were so many folks at my funeral that they filled the whole huge garden in front of the state buildin'. There were men and women and children, rich ones, poor ones, people in suits and overalls. They cried and wept while they trampled the landscapin' and just about destroyed the place. HUEY, HUEY, HUEY! You should've seen it. It was a real testimony to the love of the people for me.

BOBBIE: I read it was more like a circus.

HUEY: They loved me. I was the governor for the little people from the swamps to the piney woods. I was their governor and the governor of the rich ones, too. Even the fat cats got used to me in the end. (*Pauses*) What about you?

BOBBIE: (*Sadly*) I think I was more feared than loved.

HUEY: A Machiavellian, eh?

BOBBIE: What do you mean?

HUEY: Machiavelli wrote, "It was better to be feared than loved to stay in power." Was that it with you?

BOBBIE: Something like that.

HUEY: Must've been real lonely.

BOBBIE: Sometimes. But power, especially the heights of power, is always lonely. It's the burden of leadership and I was willing to shoulder it.

HUEY: Did you make it?

BOBBIE: Where?

HUEY: To the summit of power, to the presidency?

BOBBIE: No, sadly I did not. (*Pauses*) It surely wasn't for lack of trying. I did everything to follow the pure dogma of the party. I was an unblemished lamb of conservatism, without a trace of personal scandal. I never supported a new tax. I never had an affair. And yet it was not enough, not for the big prize. (*Looks at HUEY*)

What happened? Why did it slip between my fingers when it seemed so close?

HUEY: (*Shrugs*) Don't ask me. (*Pauses*) I built hospitals, roads, schools and the mother of all political power bases and someone killed me anyway.

BOBBIE: Yes, I read about it. A tough way to go.

HUEY: The little shit who killed me was a doctor, no less, an ear, nose and throat doctor of all stupid things. (*Pauses*) You can trust the little people, but you always have to watch out for the educated elites. They'll stab you in the back every time.

BOBBIE: I love the elites. (*Pauses*) Well, maybe not the educated ones, but at least the rich ones, the captains of industry and commerce. I loved them all.

HUEY: But they didn't love your back, did they?

BOBBIE: (*Sighs*) No, they didn't. I always felt just a wee bit on the outside, even in those power-packed back rooms.

HUEY: (*Goes over and give BOBBIE a big hug*) No one loved you, did they?

BOBBIE: My wife and family did.

HUEY: Well that's somethin'. But it doesn't count in politics.

BOBBIE: And God, did he love me? Doesn't he?

HUEY: (*Looks around at the emptiness*) Apparently not. Not if he put you in this place. (*Pauses.*) Hey, since we have gotta lot of time on our hands, how about havin' some fun?

BOBBIE: (*Skeptical*) Like what?

> *HUEY takes BOBBIE in dance position.*

HUEY: Can you dance?

BOBBIE: (*Stammers*) No, no, not really. I never had the time for that.

HUEY: It's easy. A polka step is just one-two-three hop, two-two-three hop. First one way and then the other. And then we can spin around a bit.

> *BOBBIE follows and they begin to dance. They accelerate with time and then stop.*

HUEY: Good! Very good! You're a natural. Now, with music? Ready?

BOBBIE: This isn't very dignified. What if someone sees us dancing? A man with a man might be misinterpreted. It might cause a scandal, show up on YouTube or something, you know.

HUEY: U-tube?

BOBBIE: Cell phones, videos, everyone's always looking. (*Pauses*) Forget it.

HUEY: (*Looks around*) So who's watching? And who cares anyway? (*Swings his arms around*) Not a soul in any direction.

BOBBIE: (*Looks around*) Okay. (*Pause*) And by the way, thanks for teaching me to dance. It's a nice thing to do. I never had a lot of real friends. It might be nice.

HUEY: My pleasure. (*Pauses*) This music was well known, something some governor wrote between you and me. It's just one-two-three-hop. Very easy. (*Shouts*) Start the music!

"You are my Sunshine," starts to play. It is a 4/4 rhythm and is good for a polka. BOBBIE and HUEY dance together. They smile and laugh as the lights dim.

BLACKOUT

PUBLIC OR PRIVATE GOOD IN HEALTHCARE DELIVERY

STATISTICS, RATINGS AND
HALF-TRUTHS: APPLES AND ORANGES

The public often relies on various ratings from official or unofficial sources to make their choices about healthcare facilities and providers. Periodically, hospital ratings appear that are touted to the general public to extol the virtues of one institution or another. Whether these are more or less popularity contests or rigorous objective evaluations, consumer prudence is always required. As the ancient Latin statement goes "Caveat Emptor" (Buyer Beware).

Some surveys, such as patient satisfaction surveys, may be administered to only a small sampling of individuals. Other surveys rely on self-reporting by consumers, thus making any serious conclusions almost impossible. The alert consumer is usually skeptical of such results, and with reason. The worst evaluations, however, from a consumer perspective, are those that appear to be scientific and objective, yet compare apples and oranges, thus distorting the significance and meaning of the results.

A case in point might be a Five Star rating for a hospital. Although such an institution may have definite merit, a closer looks causes one to ponder the significance. Hospitals, whether they are for-profit or not-for-profit, must serve the communities in which they are located. Part of that service includes a functional emergency room that, by law, cannot turn away any patients if they have a true emergency. (These are the famous EMTALA laws that prevent hospitals from steering away non-paying patients to other institutions.) This invariably means that full-service hospitals will be treating a certain percentage of indigent and uninsured patients, depending on their geographical location.

This group of uninsured or underinsured patients includes many with multiple medical problems, often long ignored and exacerbated by non-compliance. These individuals come disproportionately from low-income, poorly educated populations. This same demographic supplies a disproportionate number of people who are also readmitted to the hospital within 30 days of discharge. Many of these people live in specific census tracts characterized by "concentrated disadvantage" and fraught with problems associated with unfavorable social determinants (i.e. poverty, low academic achievement and low social status).

Medical outcomes, of course, correlate directly with the type of population that is served. When a facility does not have an emergency room and most of their affiliated physicians do not accept uninsured or Medicaid patients, the "sampling error" for statistical significance becomes overwhelming. Non-representative sampling gives results that are impossible to interpret or are grossly misleading.

If, as an institution, you only care for those without social disadvantage, then your statistical results are more likely to be much more favorable. The non-medical term for treating only insured patients is "cherry picking." Some institutions can engage in this activity by being situated in high-income areas with few uninsured patients ("concentrated advantage"), definitely not the case in Central Louisiana. Other institutions restrict their activities by not accepted cases with the litany of social issues (uninsured and Medicaid), often the most challenging from a medical, societal and financial perspective.

Is such case selection illegal? No, as long the institution is fully licensed by the federal government from which it derives at least some of its income, notably through CMS (Center for Medicare and Medicaid Services). But licensure of facilities unable or unwilling to operate a full-service emergence room has become increasingly difficult and came to a screeching halt some years ago.

Licensing agencies recognized the deleterious effect of "cherry picking" by limited access institutions on full-service hospitals, especially located in or near low-income areas. All institutions that achieve unusually high quality ratings should be congratulated, of course. It takes careful management and planning to satisfy the criteria of rating agencies. But high rankings alone should not obscure the fact that any rating, to be meaningful, must compare apples and apples, and not apples and oranges.

While the gullible will be impressed by all positive results, astute observers must look beyond the smoke and mirrors to see how such results were obtained and what population is being served and with which specific services.

BUILDING A CASH COW

CHARACTERS

>DONALD HARTFORD: Physician project lead. Middle-aged, well dressed. Not in a white coat.

>PETER (PETE) FRANK: Potential physician investor-partner. Well dressed, perhaps in a suit or sport jacket. Husband of Carlotta.

>CARLOTTA (CHARLIE): Peter's wife. A middle-aged woman in ostentatious clothing, lots of flashy jewelry and a designer handbag, perhaps Louis Vuitton, Gucci or Coach.

SETTING

>There are minimal set elements. There is a an easel with a photo of a surgical center on it.

DONALD: (*Shows PETER the model on the easel*) Look at this beauty! It will have 12 operative suites, a huge clerical area, break rooms, a waiting room with original artwork and electronic announcement boards, all HIPAA compliant, of course.

PETER: Very impressive.

DONALD: And there's a 200-car, landscaped parking lot with security cameras and ten handicapped parking slots. Everything's handicap accessible, of course, because we're bound to have a lot of those folks all the time.

PETER: And an emergency room?

DONALD: (*Stares at PETER*) What! Are you crazy?

PETER: I mean for emergencies, it's a hospital, isn't it?

DONALD: (*Takes PETER by the arm*) Of course it's not a hospital! That's the whole point. This is a for-profit, physician owned and operated investment with no ER.

PETER: So where are the acutely ill patients supposed to go?

DONALD: To the ER, of course, at the real hospitals. (*Pauses*) Pete, that's the beauty of it. We take only the elective cases. Maybe an overnight stay at most. They all have insurance and we pocket the profit.

PETER: Ah, cherry picking.

DONALD: You're damned right! (*Pauses*) Do you really want to take care of those complicated uninsured patients who pay nothing and turn around and sue you because of a bad outcome? Is that what you want?

PETER: No, of course not. I see enough of those folks at the "real" hospitals.

DONALD: Exactly! (*Admires the photo*) In this high-tech cash cow, we treat our own well-paying insured patients and leave the Medicaid and uninsured for the hospitals to worry about. That's what they're there for, right?

PETER: (*Skeptically*) Isn't this all too good to be true? And is it even legal?

DONALD: No, it's not too good to be true. And yes, it is legal, at least for the time being. There's a lot of talk out there about CMS limiting or eliminating licenses for physician-owned surgery centers. Some bullshit about their negative impact on community hospitals. So we have to act fast! I've already got about 100 physician owner-investors signed up. (*Shows him a contract*) So it's time for you to sign up and write a deposit check.

PETER: This is a big decision and a lot of money. I'll have to ask my wife about it.

DONALD: Of course, of course. That's why I invited her to join us down here.

PETER: (*Surprised*) You did?

DONALD: Yes, she's a great gal. Everyone loves her. Your wife and my wife are on several charitable boards together. Besides, to get a loan of this magnitude, you'll need her to co-sign anyway.

CARLOTTA: (*Walks in. Swings her brand name purse and flashes her jewelry*) Am I in the right place?

DONALD: You bet! (*Greets CARLOTTA with a friendly kiss*) You look terrific.

CARLOTTA: (*Goes to PETER and kisses him on the cheek*) Hello, dear. (*Looks at the photo*) So this is the little cash cow you were telling me about.

DONALD: (*Laughs*) No! This is the big cash cow! We expect over 100,000 client visits a year, generating well over 5 million dollars annually in profits after overhead and taxes. Put that in your pipe and smoke it.

CARLOTTA: Smoke it, eh? I'm already high just thinking about it. (*Spins to PETER*) Tuscany, New Zealand, Bali, the Riviera, Aspen, Sedona, Salzburg! (*Clutches PETER*) We can travel the world and leave this miserable place behind.

PETER: My dear, I would still have to work. In fact, I would probably be working even more, not less.

CARLOTTA: Yes, of course you would have to work harder. (*To DONALD*) We all have to make sacrifices on the altar of medicine, don't we Donnie Boy? (*Turns back to PETER*) Well, did you sign yet?

PETER: Not yet. I'm still concerned that this would damage my relationship with the local hospitals.

CARLOTTA: What! Really, honey, they'd throw you under the bus in a New Orleans minute. You're already on every hospital committee known to man or God and for what? So they can piss their profits down the rat hole of indigent care?

DONALD: (*Applauds*) Well said! Right on!

PETER: The hospitals really don't have a choice about indigent care, Charlie. With EMTALA, they have to treat all emergencies cases, insured or not.

DONALD: (*To CARLOTTA*) I thought your name was Carlotta?

CARLOTTA: (*To DONALD*) Technically it is, but Pete calls me Charlie, a friendly little nickname from my student years. (*To PETER*) I don't care about EM-TA-LA. I do care about this cash cow!

DONALD: Well, Charlie, maybe you can just close this deal for the both of you. Peter will be the one hundredth physician and wife investor. Remember, Bali and Salzburg are waiting (*kisses CARLOTTA's hand.*)

CARLOTTA: (*Winks to DONALD*) You little devil, you.

PETER: Can I interrupt this love fest and get back to business?

CARLOTTA and DONALD: Of course, of course (*both laugh.*)

PETER: I thought you didn't really know one another?

DONALD: (*Backs away from CARLOTTA*) We have met at social events, the hospital galas, fundraisers and that sort of thing. My wife introduced us.

PETER: (*To DONALD*) I thought you were separated or divorced?

DONALD: (*Pauses*) Well, technically I am, but my ex and I remain best friends.

CARLOTTA: (*To PETER*) For heaven's sake, can you keep Donnie Boy's personal life out of this? (*Points to the photo*) This is a business discussion, not a social gathering. (*Walks around the model and bumps into DONALD and giggles*) I'm sorry. Clumsy me. I get so carried away sometimes.

PETER: I have misgivings. National law forbids physician-owned labs because of the dangers of self-referral. How can this be any different? We would be self-referring our own patients?

DONALD: It's different because it's not illegal . . .yet.

CARLOTTA: Bobby, sign the damn paper! I certainly will. (*Takes the contract and signs it*) There! It's done. Someone has got to have the balls in the family (*smiles at DONALD.*)

PETER: (*Crosses his arms*) I won't do it! I don't care if it costs me money. It's not right, even if it is legal for the time being. Maybe we all ought to share the burden of indigent care? That's the socially responsible thing to do.

DONALD: We can't, even if we wanted to. The burden is too great. Half the population in this hellhole has no insurance at all, or just has Medicaid and that doesn't pay shit. You couldn't even run an office on that sort of reimbursement. (*Pauses*) Do you even take Medicaid patients in your office?

PETER: Only when I absolutely have to, and that's pretty rare.

DONALD: Exactly! Because you'd go broke and couldn't afford to keep Charlie here livin' in the manner to which she has grown accustomed.

CARLOTTA: Exactly!

PETER: (*To CARLOTTA*) You're living in a 10,000 square foot mansion on a lake with marble floors and a walk-in fireplace.

CARLOTTA: Yes! And remember that I open it up for every charitable board to tour every time they want to hold some reception or concert or fundraiser. That house gets more traffic than Grand Central Station. (*To PETER*) I'm the perfect hostess for you in the perfect location and I'm glad to do it. I want everyone to benefit from our prosperity. (*Pauses*) And there are so many people coming through our home, I don't even know who's coming and going half the time.

PETER: I'm sorry. That's true. You're amazingly generous with your time and our home. (*Pauses*) I just don't feel right about this surgery center deal. There's something dirty and sinister behind the multimillion-dollar façade. How can we build this luxury surgery center and deny it to those hordes that need it the most, just so we can live in a mansion?

DONALD: Which you slave day and night to pay for, I might add. We all do. We all sacrifice family, friends, hobbies, health, free time and sleep and God knows what else, just to take care of the sick. And then they still turn around and sue us (*Pauses.*) Why not live in luxury? Why not be able to send our kids to the finest, most expensive schools in the world and not worry about the cost?

CARLOTTA: (*Looking at PETER. Quietly*) So you'd really rather not sign?

PETER: Can we think about it a little while?

DONALD: NO! You can't. It's now or never! If we let this financing go and miss the application deadline from the regulatory agency, we'll miss our golden opportunity. Peter, you've got to shit or get off the pot! (*To CARLOTTA*) Can't you give your husband some of your balls? You understand! You know the benefits! Get this little dickless wonder to sign the damn paper, now!

CARLOTTA: (*To DONALD. Hits him across the head with her brand-name purse.*) You miserable greedy-ass bully! I can insult my husband, because we love each other. But you can't! (*Throws the contract at DONALD*) Take your contract and shove it up your philandering ass! (*Takes PETER by the hand*) Come on, dear. Maybe I can live without Tuscany or even Bali. (*Sighs.*) But I would at least like to get this really nice looking Mignon Faget necklace and bracelet set down in New Orleans. You know, Mignon's a local Louisiana artist, so we would be supporting the local economy. You would do that for me, wouldn't you? We'd be building social capital, you know.

PETER: (*Pauses*) And you won't hate me forever for not signing on to the golden cash cow?

CARLOTTA: (*Hugs him*) How could I hate an idealistic dreamer? That's the guy I married, isn't it? (*Pulls PETER away*) Let's go. (*To DONALD*) Sorry Donnie Boy, and by the way, you're a prick and don't call me at the house anymore. Nice people don't call other people's wives at their homes when their husbands aren't there.

DONALD and PETER: Really?

CARLOTTA: Yes, really! (*Takes PETER by the arm*) Come on Pete, we need to get you back to the office. Time is money, you know, with or without the cash cow. Don't shirk on your productivity. I still may want to visit Salzburg this winter or maybe do the Doctor's Ball in Vienna on New Year's Eve.

> *CARLOTTA and PETER walk offstage. DONALD is left with the photo.*

DONALD: (*Yells. Shakes his fist*) FOOLS! (*Picks up the papers from the floor*) What a stupid bitch! (*Stands over the model and shakes his head*) They'll come crawling back to me on their hands and knees, both of them.

BLACKOUT

FOOD SAFETY AND INSPECTIONS

KITCHEN ENTREPRENEURS
AND FOOD SAFETY

Part of the mission of the Office of Public Health in Louisiana, as elsewhere in the United States, is to insure that the public is protected, as much as possible, from the ravages caused by dirty water, unsafe food, and infectious diseases. Food and water safety issues fall under the domain of the environmental services, which includes engineering services and sanitarians. Our engineers review plans for larger water systems and other facilities. They also oversee water quality issues by testing water and working closely with local water districts. Our sanitarians issue permits for smaller sewage systems, as well as perform inspections for restaurants, hotels, nursing homes, day care centers, prisons, and many other facilities.

There is a Food and Drug Sanitarian who inspects food processing and storage facilities throughout the region (and in adjacent regions). His work compliments that of the other sanitarians who oversee the final products and how they are prepared and presented.

A couple of articles in the local paper featured some products, by innovative entrepreneurs who want to sell their food to the public. The first example entailed the sale of raccoon meat. Although it is legal to kill, process and eat raccoons, the commercial sale of the meat is illegal. It would be legal if there were a licensed processor for raccoon meat in Louisiana (or elsewhere), but there is not. All processing plants must be inspected to insure that carcasses (whether they are fish, fowl or other meat) are properly handled. Contamination with *Salmonella*, *E. coli*, *Listeria* and other organisms can have deadly consequences.

Contamination occurs periodically, even under the best of circumstances in commercially inspected facilities and results in episodic food recalls, sometimes massive in proportions.

A second article featured various sauces, spices and relishes, all interesting and tasty regional Louisiana products. Rules for the production and sale of homemade products clearly delineate what can and cannot be done. Honey, jams and jellies are considered a "hobby" if the total sales are less than $5000/year. Even then, the product must be correctly labeled with (1) product name, (2) list of ingredients from the largest to the smallest component, (3) manufacturer's address and (4) respective weights (in standard metric equivalents). When sales exceed $5,000/year, the product must be made in a licensed production facility.

Relishes, pickles, and other acidified products, pose special problems. To avoid the dangers of botulism and other food contamination, the canning must adhere to strict standards. First, a "Process Authority" must test the food and determine whether it is low acid food (naturally due to the food itself or artificially acidified). If it is "acidified" (for example, with the addition of vinegar), the producer must have attended a Better Processing Class (offered at LSU or elsewhere). The product must then be made in an approved processing plant, which adheres to the various FDA regulations concerning such products. Most home kitchen cooks do not have the time, money or interest to pursue such commercialization.

Non-meat containing products, such as cakes, breads, cookies and pastries, fall under special rules. They may be sold in famers' markets and other venues, but they most have a label stating that they are "Not made in a commercial kitchen" to warn consumers. Total sales must remain under the $5,000/year threshold as with other homemade products.

None of this is intended to discourage initiative or entrepreneurship, but to insure that the food we eat, like the water we drink, does not pose a health risk to the public. Please feel free to contact the sanitarian services at the Office of Public Health for specific questions about the sale of food products. Your health and safety are our business. Bon appétit!

COONS FOR SALE

CHARACTERS

BRUCE MAYNARD: Young to middle-aged man, dressed in jeans and a bulky hunter's or GI jacket. Speaks with a rural Louisiana accent. Wears a large, visible hunting knife.

THOMAS DUPONT: Young to middle-aged man, dressed in a button-down shirt and slacks. Wears a badge from the Louisiana Office of Public Health. Speaks with a slight Cajun accent.

PETER MANSFIELD: Older man, with shaggy hair and a beard. Dressed in a flannel shirt and overalls or other country apparel. Speaks with a pronounced rural accent. Sports a prominent holster and firearm.

SERGEANT PHILLIP COSTER: Middle-aged man, dressed in a police uniform. Wears a side-arm and the usual other police accouterments, including a Taser.

SETTING

An impromptu stand by the side of the road on a winter afternoon.

> *BRUCE is sitting in a folding chair. Beside him is a big cardboard box (refrigerator size). "COONS FOR SALE" is printed in large unequal letters in red or black paint. He is whittling a piece of wood with his hunting knife. THOMAS*

DUPONT comes up to confront BRUCE about his coon stand.

THOMAS: Are these your coons?

BRUCE: Sure are, best damn coons in all of Tunica Parish. Fat, juicy and ready to roast.

THOMAS: Can I see one?

BRUCE puts his knife away and reaches into the box and pulls out a large, clear plastic bag with a bloody raccoon carcass. It is the size of a small dog. One of the black paws is prominently displayed.

BRUCE: Look at this baby. It must be a twelve pounder. (*Points to the paw*) And you see, there's the paw to prove this is the real thing, not some dog, like other people around here tries to do. I sell a good, clean product. This baby'll cost you ten bucks and that's a real bargain. Cheaper than turkey and twice as good.

THOMAS takes the bag and examines it closely. Then he hands it back to BRUCE.

THOMAS: You can't sell raccoon meat.

BRUCE: What do you mean, I can't sell coon meat. I've been doin' it in this parts for years now. I got regular happy return customers. They wait all year just to buy them a fat coon for Christmas.

THOMAS: I'm sorry. You can't sell raccoon meat.

BRUCE: Who says?

THOMAS: (*Points to his Office of Public Health badge*) I say! I'm Thomas Dupont and I work for the Louisiana Office of Public Health and I'm shutting down your coon sales.

BRUCE: You can't do that. I killed these coons all summer long and now I got fifteen of them left. You can't shut me down like that.

THOMAS: I sure can. And I'm gonna confiscate your coons so you don't sell 'em tomorrow someplace else.

BRUCE: But somebody from Wildlife and Fisheries told me it was okay to kill 'em and sell 'em. And I got me a peddler's permit from the city. Look at it!

> (*BRUCE presents a piece of paper from his jacket pocket. THOMAS examines it and gives it back to BRUCE.*)

THOMAS: They were mistaken. You can kill coons, you can eat coons, but you can't sell 'em to people, even if you have a permit from the city.

> (*THOMAS begins to pull the whole box off stage left. PETER MANSFIELD walks up and assesses the situation.*)

PETER: Hello Bruce. You got any Christmas coons left. I need one for the family.

BRUCE: Yeah, Pete. I had fifteen of 'em left. But I ain't got none left now.

PETER: What's the matter?

BRUCE: Mr. Dupont here from the Health Department is gonna confiscate my coons as a public danger. He says I can't sell coons. It's illegal.

PETER: (*To THOMAS*) What you mean he can't sell his coons?

THOMAS: He's right. You can't sell coon in Louisiana unless it's been slaughtered at a licensed processing plant. And there aren't any in the State of Louisiana, or anyplace else for that matter. There's no way to tell how these animals have been prepared or under what conditions. I gotta shut down this man's operation and I'm goin' have to confiscate his coons.

PETER: (*To BRUCE*) You gonna let this government asshole take your property like that?

BRUCE: What am I supposed to do?

PETER: You got your knife, don't you?

BRUCE: Sure. I always carry one.

PETER: And I got better than that (*shows his sidearm.*)

THOMAS: (*Stops pulling at the box when he sees the gun and backs away*) Hey boys. I'm not interested in any fighting. I'm not armed and I'm not dangerous. (*To PETER*) So maybe you ought to just back away and go on home.

PETER: I ain't goin' home. And I suggest you better leave those coons just like you found 'em and let Mr. Bruce here go about his business.

THOMAS: He can't sell coons. It's a violation of the sanitary code. That means it's against the law.

PETER: (*Threatening THOMAS with the gun*) You little bureaucratic asshole! You think because you work for the Office for Public Health you can go around terrorizing God-fearing, hard-working folks just trying to make themselves a livin'? You think this is Communist China or Russia or someplace like that? We got rights, mister! We got a right to shoot coons and shoot Communist bureaucrats who come and take away our rights. Ain't that so, Bruce?

BRUCE: (*Nods weakly*) Pete, don't go threatenin' this guy. He's just trying to do his job.

PETER: Doin' his job! He's supposed to be workin' for us. He's a God-damned public servant. We pay this man with our taxes. And I say he's not doin' his job. (*To BRUCE*) Why don't you go and shut down some of those guys sellin' dope to the kids down off Parliament Street, eh? (*Swings his gun around as he speaks*) Yeah, go down there and terrorize some real criminals selling somethin' really bad to people instead of botherin' honest country folks tryin' to make an honest livin'.

> SERGEANT PHILLIP COSTER *comes in from stage left. He is looking at THOMAS, the box of coons, BRUCE and PETER. His eyes follow PETER's gun as it swings around the air. He ends up speaking to THOMAS.*

SERGEANT: Hello, Tom. What the hell's goin' on here?

THOMAS: I'm tryin' to shut down the illegal coon sales.

SERGEANT: And this guy? (*To PETER*) Hey, mister, don't you be swingin' a firearm around like that. You got a permit for that pistol?

PETER: I sure as hell do! I got a permit for this baby and a lot more like it at home, too. You wanna see my assault rifle?

SERGEANT: Mister, why don't you put that pistol away and let this man do his job.

PETER: (*Screaming*) Job! Do his job! This is how it starts. (*To BRUCE*) Don't you see? First they take away your coons. Then they take away your guns. Then they take away your wife and children. Don't you see? It's a left wing liberal Communist plot and we gotta draw the line somewhere. Tom, pull out that knife and help me.

SERGEANT: Calm down, mister. Give me that gun and I'll check to see if it's registered. I gotta do that. (*To BRUCE*) And why don't you give me that knife while you're at it.

BRUCE: I don't need a permit for hunting no knife, do I?

SERGEANT: No, I just don't like the look of it right at this minute.

> *BRUCE begins to hand the knife, handle first, to SERGEANT COSTER. PETER rushes over and pushes BRUCE's arm away. The knife falls to the ground.*

PETER: Don't do it, man! Don't give up that knife. We gotta take a stand somewhere and maybe this is as good a spot as any.

THOMAS: At a coon stand? You gotta be kidding. (*To BRUCE*) Keep the damned coons if you want. I'd just have to figure out a way to get rid of 'em anyway.

BRUCE: You mean you would just dump 'em?

THOMAS: Well, actually we pour bleach on 'em, first so nobody goes in the dumpster to retrieve 'em.

BRUCE: That's a terrible waste, a real crime.

THOMAS: That's what I'm tellin' you. Just take the coons away. Give 'em to your friends and family. Eat 'em yourself. Just don't sell 'em on the street. It's not safe and it's not legal.

PETER: It's not about the coon, man! (*To BRUCE*) It's about abuse of authority. It's about preserving our God given personal freedoms preserved in the Constitution of the United States of America. (*Swings the gun around and points to THOMAS and SERGEANT COSTER*) It's about you two Fascist Communist bastards trying to get my coon (*grabs the coon and waves the bag around*) and my gun!

BRUCE: Pete, just let the officer check the registration for your gun. It's no big deal. You can have the coon if you want. It's a gift, from me to you.

PETER: Yes, it's a big deal. (*Stands on the folding chair and continues to swing the raccoon carcass and pistol*) You will have to pry this coon and this gun out of my cold, dead fingers!

> *PETER points the gun at the three others, who duck behind the coon box. SERGEANT COSTER pokes his head about the edge.*

SERGEANT: Gimme that gun, mister! Now!

PETER: NEVER!

SERGEANT: (*On his radio*) Please send some back up down to the corner of Fulton and Evergreen Street. I got an armed crazy.

PETER: (*To BRUCE, who is poking his head up*) Pick up that knife and stab him! Pete, stab 'em both. You're right there. It's our moment of victory. I can smell it.

> *BRUCE shakes his head and ducks back behind the box. THOMAS yells out to PETER.*

THOMAS: That's coon carcass you smell, you old fool!

PETER: Okay. If I'm on my own, I'm on my own. Give me liberty or give me death!

> *PETER points the gun in the direction of the box. SERGEANT COSTER pops up and shoots PETER with a Taser. PETER goes into a shaking fit and falls to the ground. The coon and the gun fall, too. SERGEANT COSTER goes over and picks up the gun. THOMAS goes over and picks up the bloody coon bag, which he gives to BRUCE. BRUCE picks up his knife and tries to give it to SERGEANT COSTER, who refuses.*

SERGEANT: I don't want your damn knife.

BRUCE: (*Looks down at PETER*) Is he dead?

SERGEANT: Nah, he just wishes he were.

BRUCE: What gonna happen to Pete?

SERGEANT: Don't worry about him. He'll be all right by the time he gets out on bail. (*A pause*) Say, how gooda friends are you guys? He's gonna need bail for assaulting a police officer, disturbin' the peace, incitin' rebellion, and threatenin' a Public Health official in the course of his duties. That outta be a few thousand. You wanna put up some bail money for your friend?

PETER: (*Moaning*) What happened? Where am I?

> *Sirens are sounding in the background. SERGEANT COSTER pulls PETER to his feet.*

SERGEANT: You're comin' with me buddy. You have the right to remain silent. Anything you say can and will be used against you in a court of law.

> *SERGEANT COSTER leads PETER off stage right. BRUCE and TOM look at one another. BRUCE looks down at THOMAS's name tag.*

BRUCE: Dupont? Are you from out around Effie?

THOMAS: Yeah, my folks still live out there. What's your last name?

BRUCE: Maynard, Bruce Maynard's the name (*extends his free hand to THOMAS, who shakes it.*)

THOMAS: Are you Cecil and Clara's son?

BRUCE: The same.

THOMAS: Well I'll be damned. We're second cousins.

BRUCE: Ain't that something.

THOMAS: How do you cook them things, anyway?

BRUCE: You bake 'em in an oven at 375 degrees for about four hours. Every few minutes you baste them with the drippings, mixed with butter and a combination of soy-sauce and white wine. It is some kinda good. Serve it with yams and little onions in cream and you got you one heck of a Christmas. (*Hands the coon to THOMAS.*) Wanna keep it?

THOMAS: Nah, but thanks anyway. That's bribing a state official and I don't want any more trouble from you. . .cousin. (*Pause*) You need any help gettin' that box in your truck?

BRUCE: I'd be mighty obliged . . .cuz.

> *BRUCE throws the coon into the box and slaps THOMAS on the back and the two of them pull the box off stage left.*

BLACKOUT

EBOLA: EPIDEMIC CONTROL

EBOLA: JUST A PLANE FLIGHT AWAY

Ebola Viral Disease (or EVD) is one of many RNA (ribonucleic acid) viruses that infect humans. All viruses reproduce by hijacking the cellular machinery and making the cell produce new viruses instead of normal proteins. Ebola is one of a group of filoviruses (string-like viruses) that produce a deadly hemorrhagic fever, resulting in the deaths of over 50% of victims.

Ebola is not new. Periodic epidemics have broken out in West and Central Africa since the 70's, where it is a "zoonosis" or animal-borne disease. The animal hosts include bats, non-human primates (monkeys and chimpanzees) and other creatures, some of which are consumed by humans as "bush meat." Because of this natural reservoir, total eradication of Ebola has proven impossible.

Up until now, the epidemics have had little geographic spread, often being limited to remote villages where the disease infects a few individuals and then dies out. This time, however, Ebola has stricken large urban areas in Guinea, Sierra Leone and Liberia. The latter two countries have been devastated by decades of civil wars, which left their governments and health systems in disarray.

Ebola is not airborne, although it can be transmitted on large droplets. Transmission depends on direct contact with blood, sweat, vomitus, diarrhea, semen and vaginal secretions. Once introduced, the virus invades and destroys epithelial cells, resulting in massive bleeding and diarrhea. As the person becomes sicker, the viral load (the number of viruses) increases, making terminally ill patients particularly dangerous to others. At this time there are no specific proven medications or vaccines against Ebola, although both have been fast-tracked by pharmaceutical companies. An effective vaccine appears to be just on the horizon.

During the most recent epidemic, over 5,000 people died and over 13,000 were infected with Ebola in West Africa. These unprecedented numbers posed an enormous public health challenge. In Africa, the treatment consists of isolation and hydration, often under very primitive condition and mortality rates can exceed 50%. For the U.S. and the rest of the world, infection remains only a plane flight away.

Several notorious cases have been treated in the U.S., eight out of nine of whom have survived. Although not required, specialized biocontainment units (four of which exist around the U.S.) can accommodate up to 12 cases. In the U.S., control measures consist of screenings of visitors from West Africa who have already been screened in their home countries prior to departure. Public health workers will still monitor people who have been to West Africa who are not symptomatic twice daily for 21 days. Quarantine will vary depending on the level of exposure in West Africa.

The first question travelers were asked by a healthcare provider in the U.S. was whether the patient had traveled to West Africa in the last month, specifically to Guinea, Sierra Leone or Liberia. Travelers were then asked if they had been in contact with anyone there who might have had Ebola. Since only symptomatic people can be infectious, travelers from West Africa were then asked if they had fever, nausea, vomiting, diarrhea, joint and muscle pains, headache or unusual fatigue. The extent of fever shifted from 101.5 degrees Fahrenheit to 100.4 and eventually to "subjective fever from baseline." If your travel history and symptoms suggested Ebola, you were isolated and the necessary laboratory work obtained.

Ebola scares the public, and rightfully so. Any disease that kills over 50% of its victims and has no specific treatment must be a source of concern. That being said, actions should be based on science and logic, not on fear. In the end, the development of an effective vaccine and eradication of the disease among humans in West Africa will constitute our best defense in the U.S. Progress in the development of an effective vaccine appears to be well on its way and that will provide the best prevention of all.

EBOLAMANIA

CAST OF CHARACTERS

KATHY: Nurse returning from a mission trip treating Ebola patients in Liberia. Young or not so young, wears casual clothing or scrubs.

ROSCOE: Public Health Official. May be any race or have any accent.

PARAMEDIC: Young man or woman in paramedic's uniform.

SETTING

Apartment living room. Simple, unadorned, a couch, chair and coffee table.

ROSCOE: (*Wearing gloves and a mask. Holds a touchless thermometer and a clipboard*) I'm afraid you will need to be quarantined. And I'm here to take your temperature twice daily. (*Points his touchless thermometer in KATHY's direction*) 98.6 degrees Fahrenheit. No fever.

KATHY: Of course no fever.

ROSCOE: Correct. (*Makes a notation on his clipboard*) Are you having any other symptoms? Nausea? Vomiting? Diarrhea? Muscle aches and pains? Headache? Unusual fatigue?

KATHY: No! Nothing at all. I'm asymptomatic (*begins to leave.*)

ROSCOE: Where are you going?

KATHY: Out. I've been cooped up here ever since I got back from Liberia. I'd like to take a walk.

ROSCOE: (*Blocks her way*) You can't leave!

KATHY: The hell you say! Of course I can!

ROSCOE: (*Continues to block her*) No, you can't. State's orders.

KATHY: Are you the state?

ROSCOE: I'm the delegated representative of the State Medical Officer, who instructed us to quarantine all high-risk persons under investigation for Ebola.

KATHY: That's not what the CDC says. They put me at the "Some Risk" category because I treated Ebola patients, but I wore appropriate personal protective equipment, PPE, you know.

ROSCOE: Of course I know what PPE is, but there is a difference between federal and local recommendations concerning the threshold for quarantining persons under investigation. And you will have to stay put! You can't go out! You can't take public transportation. You can't go into crowds. You are here to stay, with maybe a quick walk outside. And you will be required to maintain a three foot distance from anyone else.

KATHY: Is that all? Just three feet? Why not be in a leper colony or on Devil's Island or in a special prison? Or just stuck in Liberia for the duration.

ROSCOE: No one has recommended those drastic measures.

KATHY: At least not yet.

ROSCOE: We try and stay reasonable.

KATHY: You're not! You're just perpetuating fear. You're panicking and pandering to a paranoid population. It's shameful! It's un-American! (*Stops and stands still*) Excuse me, I feel sick to my stomach (*vomits.*)

ROSCOE: (*Backs up and heads for the door*) You are symptomatic!

KATHY: (*Wipes the vomitus from her mouth*) Just queasy. I have a nervous stomach and you're upsetting me.

ROSCOE: (*Call on his cell phone*) Hello, ID-EPI? (*Pauses*) I have a symptomatic high-risk possible Ebola patient. (*Pauses*) Recently in Liberia treating patients and wearing PPE, but she's vomited all over the place. (*Pauses*) No fever. (*Pauses*) Okay. 2700 Peterman Drive.

KATHY: (*Sits down on the couch*) I'm just a little sick to my stomach. (Vomits again.)

ROSCOE: (*Backs up even further*) The paramedics should be here shortly.

KATHY: I'm not going to the hospital, am I?

ROSCOE: You bet. You need to be isolated and blood tests need to be drawn and you might even get treated with some immunoglobulins or that experimental drug if you're confirmed and lucky.

Sounds of an ambulance approaching.

PARAMEDIC: (*Wears full PPE, perhaps a Tyvek suit if available. Points to KATHY*) Is that the patient?

ROSCOE: Yes, over there on the couch.

KATHY: I don't want to go. I'll stay inside and monitor my temperature. I can still force fluids and take suppositories for nausea. I have everything I need. I'm a nurse, you know.

PARAMEDIC: (*Approaches KATHY*) Come with me, ma'am. The ambulance is waiting for us outside and the biocontainment unit at University Hospital has already been notified. Can you walk?

KATHY: (*Stands up with difficulty*) Barely.

ROSCOE. Can I help?

PARAMEDIC: (*Yells*) Don't touch her! Don't touch anything. Stay back! (*To KATHY*) Do you have a dog or cat?

KATHY: Yes, a dog.

PARAMEDIC: Where is it?

KATHY: In the bedroom. It's old and almost blind.

PARAMEDIC: It's got to be quarantined, too.

KATHY: Quarantined or killed?

PARAMEDIC: Cleaned and quarantined.

KATHY: What happens to my apartment?

PARAMEDIC: It has to be completely disinfected by a special Hazmat team.

KATHY: How?

ROSCOE: Do we really have time for this?

PARAMEDIC: (*To ROSCOE*) Are you still here? Why the hell don't you get out of here? (*To KATHY*) You vomited, so you're a "wet case." That means the rugs need to be ripped up. Any cloth furniture needs to be destroyed. Personal belongings might be contaminated and have to be incinerated as well.

KATHY: (*Screams*) My wedding dress? Incinerated?

ROSCOE: That's harsh.

KATHY and PARAMEDIC: Shut up and leave!

PARAMEDIC: (*To KATHY*) Yes, sorry.

KATHY: Can I bring anything with me?

PARAMEDIC: No! Just come with me now.

KATHY: (*Starts to run*) No! I'm not going.

PARAMEDIC: (*Runs after her. Trips and falls*) Shit.

KATHY: (*Grabs a cushion from the couch and throws it at PARAMEDIC*) Take that! (*Grabs another and throws it*) And that! They're covered with vomit, you asshole.

PARAMEDIC: (*To ROSCOE*) Don't just stand there, grab her!

ROSCOE: Are you crazy? I can't touch her! She might be contagious. She's a wet case. Don't make me touch her.

PARAMEDIC: Then get your ass outside and call for reinforcements. Tell them we've got a Code Blue and send the state police from the HAZMAT unit. Code Blue, do you hear?

ROSCOE: (*Rushes off*) Yes, sir!

KATHY: (*Pushes the PARAMEDIC and grabs his facemask*) Let me get inside your suit. I'll puke in your face, you coward. I'm the one who went to Africa and treated dying people. I heard their moans and groans as they died in excruciating pain. Now you come in here to burn my belongings and incarcerate me. You coward! (*Pulls at the suit.*)

PARAMEDIC: Don't! Don't touch me. I got a wife and kids. I'm just doing my job. They sent me here to escort you out, not kill you. Please be reasonable.

KATHY: (*Calms down and sits on the couch*) So when do the Tasers come out?

PARAMEDIC: (*Sits next to her in his suit*) He won't Taser you. They just want to escort you to the hospital. It'll be fine, really.

KATHY: (*Looks around*) Guess it's all just stuff.

PARAMEDIC: Yes, only stuff. You'll get the best of care. They have a fully staffed biocontainment unit with a full-time dedicated nursing staff, all volunteers.

KATHY: What if you just let me slip out. Who would know?

PARAMEDIC: There are 15 media trucks out there already. We tried to be discrete coming in, but it's impossible. Every one of your neighbors filmed us on their cell phones. Your apartment is already on national news. You're famous. How far do you think you could get? (*Pauses.*) Will you come with me before the police get here?

KATHY: (*Begins to retch*) Watch out!

PARAMEDIC: (*Backs away*) Throw up on the carpet, not on me.

KATHY: (*Vomits*) I think I need to go with you. What's your name?

PARAMEDIC: John.

KATHY: Just like my fiancé.

PARAMEDIC: And yours?

KATHY: Kathy Parmentier (*extends her hand.*)

PARAMEDIC: (*Pulls his back.*) Sorry. Maybe the next time under better circumstances. (*Extends his hands to hold KATHY up*) Let me help you. I think we have a lot of people waiting out there. You'll be famous, Kathy Parmentier.

KATHY: Hopefully only for 15 minutes.

PARAMEDIC: (*Escorts KATHY out*) We'll see. Now smile, there will be a lot of photos and filming.

KATHY: (*Brushes back her hair*) How do I look?

PARAMEDIC: You look just swell. John's a lucky guy, Ebola or not.

KATHY and JOHN exit.

BLACKOUT

TESTOSTERONE USE
FOR IMPOTENCE

DYING TO BE YOUNG AND POTENT

Aging carries with it a host of medical issues for men, among them a gradual reduction in testosterone levels. One of the many consequences of this reduction may be erectile dysfunction ("ED"). It is estimated that around 5% of 40-year-old men and up to 25% of 65-year-old men suffer from erectile dysfunction. A normal man can fail to achieve an erection 20% of the time, but it should not happen over 50% of the time. Fatigue, stress, excess alcohol, arteriosclerosis, hypertension, diabetes, some medications and other factors cause erectile dysfunction. The estimated 5 million men in the U.S. suffering from low testosterone, however, represent an irresistible and lucrative market.

Legitimate concerns about potency, coupled with anxieties associated with aging of the baby boomers, has spawned a multi-billion dollar industry for the treatment of erectile dysfunction. Sales of Viagra and Cialis exceed one billion dollars each. The top 100 most prescribed medications include Viagra (18th), Cialis (21st) and Levitra (96th), all three medications for erectile dysfunction, with total prescriptions of the three exceeding 16 million a year.

Testosterone replacement in gels, patches and injections, all prescribed for decreased potency associated with "Low T", has now achieved sales of 1.6 billion a year. Androgel brought in 1.14 billion in sales in 2013 and Axiron resulted in 168 million in sales (an 85% increase from 2011). Heavy direct-to-consumer (DTC) advertising by pharmaceutical firms has helped boost sales of all such medications significantly, a well-documented phenomena. In fact, sales of testosterone have increased five times from 2000 to 2011, reaching 5.3 million prescriptions. What older man doesn't want to feel a newfound surge of energy, stamina and sexual potency?

Like all medications, however, there is no such thing as a free lunch. While testosterone does increase muscle mass and physical stamina, there is also evidence that it worsens benign prostatic hypertrophy (enlargement of the prostate) and prostate cancer, both contraindications to its use. There is also a question about whether testosterone use may increase rates of heart attacks, although this remains controversial and conflicting data exists. A New England Journal of Medicine study in 2010 reported that testosterone replacement caused a significant increase in cardiac risk. Another more recent study of over 0,000 men by the U.S. Veteran's Administration, published in the Journal of the American Medical Association (JAMA), confirmed a 29% increase in the risk of having a heart attack in the testosterone replacement group. It should be mentioned that many of the men had underlying heart disease or diabetes in that particular elderly population, both conditions that can increase the risk for cardiovascular events.

An associate editor for the JAMA, Anne Cappola, was quoted by Nicole Ostrow at Bloomberg as saying about testosterone replacement use that some "think it's the fountain of youth. It's going to give them back sexual performance, strength and endurance. The direct marketing of testosterone is playing into that. There needs to be that other voice saying there's no medication out there with all benefit and no risk. There's always a tradeoff."

Surgical penile implants and external pumps are erectile dysfunction treatments less commonly used. Surgical procedures always care the cost and risks of any surgical act and the risks and benefits must be carefully weighed for every patient.

As distressing as aging is, especially to those of the baby boomer generation, a decrease in sexual potency may be the price to pay for longevity. Trying to achieve sexual performance through pills, patches, gels or surgical implants may be increasing risk for questionable benefits. Those anxious to sell us the "fountain of youth" need to make it clear that there is always a risk/benefit ratio with all drugs and those risks should never exceed the real or imagined benefits they confer.

GETTING A PENILE IMPLANT

CHARACTERS

> DONALD HARTFORD: Older middle-aged physician. Very articulate but lacks warmth. Well-dressed in a starched white lab coat with a stethoscope hanging pretentiously around his neck. Should wear a tie and polished shoes.

> EDWARD MONCEAUX: Older middle-aged man. A self-important plaintiff's attorney. Articulate but insincere. Impeccably dressed. No particular accent.

> CARLOTTA MONCEAUX: A flamboyant middle-aged woman past her physical prime. Flaunts herself. Uneducated speech pattern with a regional Southern accent.

SETTING

> Varies with the scene.

SCENE ONE

> *DONALD's medical office with a desk and a couple of chairs. There is a laptop and a lamp on the desk. There is a screen, which hides an examination area.*

> *DONALD sits at his desk and is using a laptop computer instead of a written file. EDWARD walks in and DONALD rises to greet him.*

DONALD: Mr. Monceaux. (*Shakes hands with EDWARD*) Have a seat.

> (*An awkward silence ensures. DONALD fumbles with his computer and EDWARD watches him with detached interest.*)

EDWARD: Dr. Hartford, I would understand if you choose not to take me on as a patient. You do remember me?

DONALD: Of course I remember you, Mr. Monceaux, and I do feel awkward. After all, you represented my ex-wife, Christina, in our less-than-amicable divorce proceedings.

EDWARD: Christina, yes, a lovely woman. And I'm so happy you both proved so conciliatory. Nothing like a quick, bloodless divorce to end a doomed relationship, wouldn't you agree? Cut out the infection and move on, just like with an abscess.

DONALD: You might say that. (*Pauses*) Are you sure you trust me to treat you after what we've been through together?

EDWARD: Of course! It's not personal. It's never personal. It's just my job. (*Pauses*) And that's all water under the bridge as far as I'm concerned. Let bygones be bygones, I always say. You're a well-respected physician and that's what I need, someone local who's exceptionally competent.

DONALD: Will I have the necessary empathy to treat you? That's an important question. And will I have the necessary objectivity? Can you even trust my clinical judgment?

EDWARD: Of course I can! You are the man for me and I'm ready to get going in this new doctor-patient relationship, if you agree.

DONALD: Okay. I'm willing to give it a try if you are willing to be a good patient.

EDWARD: What's that mean, "a good patient?"

DONALD: It means you listen to my professional opinion, you follow my recommendations, and you don't sue me . . .ever! If you're not happy, you just move on to another doctor.

EDWARD: That's tough, doc. (*Pauses*) But since I like and respect you, I'll agree.

> *EDWARD and DONALD shake hands.*

DONALD: Now what can I do for you, Mr. Monceaux?

EDWARD: Call me Edward, please! You can start by fixing me up. I don't feel worth a damn!

DONALD: What's the specific problem?

EDWARD: I'm 67 years old and I can't get it up anymore. My penis is softer than a rotten banana.

DONALD: I guess you're talking about erectile dysfunction.

EDWARD: Of course I'm talking about E.D! Carlotta, my third wife, is 20 years younger than me and I just can't satisfy her. It's a real problem, too, because I catch her looking at the Hispanic pool man, really just a kid, with that hungry look, you know?

DONALD: I can imagine. Your current wife and I have crossed paths in social circles along with her former husband, Dr. Peter Frank, my ex-wife's current husband. It's all a bit complicated. Carlotta's a very attractive and charming woman.

EDWARD: Charming, yes, and who the hell knows what she's doing when I'm out of the house, much less out of town?

DONALD: So what exactly can I do for you?

EDWARD: I want a prescription for roll-on testosterone, the stuff I see on the television. I want my "T" up so the rest of me will be up, too. I want the good old days when an all-nighter was a three bang affair and a morning after chaser. My God, those were the days!

DONALD: Let me take a look at you before we go any further. (*Indicates the privacy screen*) Please step behind the screen and drop you shorts. I need to look at your testicles and do a prostate exam.

> *DONALD and EDWARD step behind the screen. They speak loudly enough to be clearly heard by the audience.*

DONALD: Your testicles look like they are normal size. Turn your head to the side and cough.

> *EDWARD coughs.*

DONALD: Now the other side. Turn your head to the other side and cough.

> *EDWARD coughs again.*

DONALD: Now bend over and spread your cheeks.

EDWARD: Ouch! Doc, take your watch off first, damn it!

DONALD: Very funny. (*Pauses*) Mr. Monceaux, your prostate's enlarged. You probably have a lot of trouble urinating. Here's some toilet paper to wipe off the lubricant.

> *DONALD and EDWARD come out from behind the screen and take their seats by the table. DONALD types into the laptop.*

EDWARD: You're right. I can't pee. I can't screw. I can't hear without my hearing aids, which is a real disadvantage in court as you might imagine. And I can't see without my glasses.

DONALD: (*Looking at the laptop*) Your blood PSA level is elevated, too. Not a lot, but certainly above normal. Did you have a prostate biopsy recently?

EDWARD: Yes, indeed! A remarkably painful affair! That urologist shoved some sort of huge tube up my rectum and proceeded to take snippets out of my prostate. Click. Click. Click. I could hear that awful clicking sound, followed by a jolt of pain. It was torture. All that misery, and they didn't even find any cancer. Normal biopsy, he says. I should have sued his socks off.

DONALD: Mr. Monceaux, it sounds like he was doing his job. But, of course, I don't know all the medical details.

EDWARD: Call me Edward, please. I can't stand this formality, especially from someone whose had his finger up my rectum. Don't you agree?

DONALD: Edward, (*pauses*) I can't give you testosterone.

EDWARD: Why not?

DONALD: Because you're prostate's enlarged and your PSA is elevated. And besides, I don't even know if your testosterone level is low.

EDWARD: Then get a blood test and find out. It's got to be low the way I'm performing.

DONALD: It doesn't matter if it's high or low. Testosterone can worsen prostate enlargement and increase your risk for prostate cancer.

EDWARD: You're making this up.

DONALD: No, I'm not.

EDWARD: I've seen roll-on "T" advertised on television. You just smear that stuff on like deodorant and then pop a Viagra or a Cialis and you're good to go. I've seen it.

DONALD: Those are actors. You can't take testosterone. I tell you, it's dangerous for you because of your enlarged prostate.

EDWARD: Don't tell me this stuff.

DONALD: What? The truth.

EDWARD: I don't want to be an impotent old fart with a hot new wife. She'll be out of my life in a heartbeat if I can't perform. I don't want to lose her. I already lost my first wife, a real nice lady.

DONALD: There are penile implants.

EDWARD: Fake penises? (*Pauses*) I'm not into those party favor things. Women don't like them anyway. They never feel right; at least that's what I've heard.

DONALD: No, I mean a real penile implant. The urologist can put something into the shaft of your penis and there's a little pump in the scrotum, with a valve on it. You just pump it up.

EDWARD: Does it work?

DONALD: Apparently it does. At least that's what another one of my patient tells me.

EDWARD: Can I talk to this guy about it?

DONALD: No, that's a HIPAA violation, a breach of confidence.

EDWARD: (*Thinks awhile*) So you just pump it up?

DONALD: Exactly! Either you or your partner.

EDWARD: And when you want it to go back down, what do you do?

DONALD: There's a little valve in the scrotum. You just push it and down it goes.

EDWARD: (*Thinks*) I don't know, doctor, sounds pretty unnatural, very mechanical. (Pauses) I can hear it now, "Honey, wait a minute while I pump myself up or do you want to do it?" (*Pauses*) Doesn't sound very romantic. (*Pauses*) Can I get an implant and not tell my wife?

DONALD: Your wife needs to know. You can't keep something like that secret. And maybe she'll get into it. She'll ask you if she can pump it up for you. That sometimes happens.

EDWARD: Like using a natural pre-heated dildo.

DONALD: Sort of.

EDWARD: But a surgery? I'm not in that good a shape. I had this defibrillator thing put in awhile back. Would it be safe?

DONALD: We'd have your cardiologist give clearance, of course. But it's not a major or complicated a surgery. A simple operation, a new pump and a new sex life. It would certainly be less dangerous than testosterone. And you can't use Viagra or Cialis if you are taking nitroglycerin. You might die from hypotension.

EDWARD: Thank God I don't need that. But the rest of this is all too weird for me. Just give me a script for the "T" and I'll take my chances.

DONALD: No! I can't.

EDWARD: (*Stands*) You don't have a heart, doctor. Life is full of dangers. It's all about taking risks. Every time I take a new case, I take risks. I never know how a case will work out until it's over and done.

DONALD: Yes, but I do, and in this case, your case, the risks clearly outweigh the benefits.

EDWARD: How do you know? You don't know what's really important to me. Maybe I just want to die happy and not be this miserable old wreck you see before you. I've got all the money in the world. I live in a castle in Hessmer. Now I want to buy some youth. I want good, satisfying fornication with Carlotta.

DONALD: I can't prescribe testosterone to you.

EDWARD: No, you won't prescribe it. There's a difference.

DONALD: No, I won't.

EDWARD: And when I die from grief from not satisfying Carlotta, I hope she sues the hell out of you for negligent homicide.

DONALD: That's ridiculous and you know it.

EDWARD: People can sue for anything. Trust me! I do it everyday.

DONALD: Not because I did my job and refused to prescribe something that was dangerous and contraindicated in your particular case.

EDWARD: No, not because you refused to do your job, but because you're depriving me of my God-given chance to be happy.

DONALD: And healthy? What about the healthy part?

EDWARD: What's health without happiness? (*Pauses*) I like you, doctor. But you've got to lighten up.

DONALD: I can't and I won't prescribe testosterone to you, and that's final.

EDWARD: (*Sits down again*) Okay, I'll just have to go online or go to that sleazy doctor down on Fullerton Street that gives anything to anybody for a price.

DONALD: (*Stands*) Mr. Monceaux, Edward, I've enjoyed seeing you again in a non-legal situation, but I can see we have reached a therapeutic impasse. You still have the liberty to go to any doctor of your choosing, even that quack on Fullerton.

EDWARD: Don't lie! You haven't enjoyed seeing me. You can't have. I'm a pain in the ass. I have never met a doctor, especially in a deposition, in court or in divorce proceedings, who enjoyed meeting me. You're a good doctor, just not very accommodating. Can I have my medical records?

DONALD: Sure. They're electronic. I can send them anytime to anyone if I have the appropriate signed permission from you. (*Hands EDWARD a form*) Here's a consent form for a release of information.

EDWARD: (*Sighs*) I'll let you know who needs to get it. If you don't hear from me, then maybe I changed my mind. Or I might come back to you. Life's unpredictable, you know.

DONALD: If we don't see each other again, good luck.

> *EDWARD and the DONALD shake hands. EDWARD exits and the DONALD sits back down and begins to type on the laptop. Lights dim.*

BLACKOUT

SCENE TWO

> *EDWARD and CARLOTTA, both dressed in pajamas, are lying in a bed with a sheet or blanket over them. EDWARD may be bare-chested. One or both may be smoking.*

CARLOTTA: Well, that was big flop.

EDWARD: I know. Can't we try again?

CARLOTTA: Why bother? You're as flabby as a corn dog. Come to think of it, I've eaten harder corn dogs.

EDWARD: Oh, come on, Carlotta. Maybe you could do a hand job. That usually works.

CARLOTTA: In case you didn't notice, I already tried. You must have forgotten already. Maybe your memory's going too.

EDWARD: Please don't make fun of me. That only makes things worse. It effects my self-confidence, my self-esteem.

CARLOTTA: Makes things worse? How can they be worse? You can't hear without your hearing aides. You can't see without your glasses. You can't pee without standing twenty minutes over the toilet. And you have to get up five times at night to do that. And besides all that, you can't even get a hard on, even with that underarm roll-on "T" stuff you got from that quack down on Fullerton Street. What am I supposed to do to get some satisfaction? I got my needs too, you know. I already left a couple of guys who couldn't satisfy me.

EDWARD: Yes, I know. And who beat the hell out of you as well, as I recall. (*Pauses*) What if I got a special pump?

CARLOTTA: (*Laughs*) A pump? What kind of pump?

EDWARD: A little pump for an implant in my penis. You've just got to pump it up each time you want an erection.

CARLOTTA: Like a bicycle pump? What do I have to do, pump you up each time to get a hard on? (*Laughs out loud.*) That's crazy. You've got to be kidding (*laughs again.*)

EDWARD: Stop laughing. It's for real. Dr. Hartford told me about it.

CARLOTTA: Donald? I thought you got mad and left him.

EDWARD: I did. But he's a smart guy and he knows what he's talking about. He'll take me back and get this pump thing arranged. (*Excitedly*) There's a little pump in the scrotum that you pump up and when you're done having sex, you push a little valve and it goes down. Plop, like that. Easy peasy.

CARLOTTA: And oh so romantic! You've got to be kidding.

EDWARD: No, I'm dead serious.

CARLOTTA: Well, that is pretty serious. By the way, is your life insurance paid up if you're dead serious?

EDWARD: Don't change the subject. Donald thinks it would work fine. Besides, he doesn't want me using that "T" stuff anyway. He says it can cause my prostate to grow and maybe even give me prostate cancer.

CARLOTTA: Really? Is your prostate growing?

EDWARD: I don't know. But I can't pee worth a damn and it's gotten worse since I started that underarm "T" stuff.

CARLOTTA: I tried it, too, you know.

EDWARD: What! Don't do that!

CARLOTTA: I thought it might make me hornier. An a-phro-dis-iac, of sorts.

EDWARD: You don't need anything to make you hornier. Besides, that stuff will make you grow a mustache and that's a real turn off.

CARLOTTA: Ugh!

EDWARD: So, what do you think? You want me to give it a try?

CARLOTTA: Try what?

EDWARD: The pump. I can get a penis implant.

CARLOTTA: That's great. You'll have a defibrillator in your heart and a boner implant in your dick. Yes, that'll be great. I'll be afraid to touch you anywhere.

EDWARD: Seriously, it'll help me. It'll help us. I can finally satisfy you. That's what Donald said. I'll be a new man.

CARLOTTA: (*Pauses and sighs*) Why not? I guess I can pump you up. It beats wasted hand jobs. Those were just wearing me out, and giving me carpal tunnel, too. I was wanking you so hard, I nearly lost the feeling in both hands.

EDWARD: You can be so vulgar.

CARLOTTA: (*Caresses EDWARD's chest*) Vulgar, eh? I know you love it, don't you. The vulgarer the better. (*Kisses EDWARD and moves lower*) Maybe something more delicate than my hand will do the job (*puckers up and lifts up the sheet.*)

EDWARD: (*Pushes her away*) Don't bother. It's dead for the time being.

CARLOTTA: Now even a blowjob won't work. Go for the pump! It can't be any worse than what we got now. (*Pauses*) You know that young pool guy?

EDWARD: Yeah, Jason or Jerome or something like that.

CARLOTTA: Jesus is his name. He pronounces it like Hesus. (*Pauses*) He's twenty, maybe even a bit younger and very buff.

EDWARD: So?

CARLOTTA: That kid gets a boner when I walk within ten feet of him.

EDWARD: How do you know?

CARLOTTA: Because I got eyes and I can see just fine, even without glasses.

EDWARD: I hope that's all you do.

CARLOTTA: Sweetie pie, I'm not dumb. Why would I risk my sugar daddy for a Kit Kat bar? (*Pauses*) Anyway, he's poor as dirt and comes from some huge Honduran family. I think he's got a couple of kids already, by a couple of different girls.

EDWARD: So?

CARLOTTA: So, maybe he needs some money.

EDWARD: So? Everyone needs money.

CARLOTTA: So, maybe he'd let them do a penis transplant if you pay him enough. They could graft his dick onto you and you can give him yours.

EDWARD: (*Laughs*) You can be so dumb.

CARLOTTA: Why? They transplant hearts and lungs and kidneys and stuff. I even seen that they transplanted hands and even faces. Why not a penis?

EDWARD: You're not kidding are you?

CARLOTTA: No, I'm not kidding. It's worth a thought.

EDWARD: Well, I don't know if they do that sort of thing. Besides I doubt "Jesus" would be willing to give me his dick for whatever price. And most of the time transplants are from dead people anyway.

CARLOTTA: So? That can be arranged, too. Everything for the right price, you know.

EDWARD: Oh, God! Don't go there! You'd be in prison and I'd have a new penis that I couldn't use. And you would be saving your bananas for your satisfaction in the slammer.

CARLOTTA: Bad idea?

EDWARD: Yes! Very bad.

> *EDWARD and CARLOTTA sit on the bed in silence.*

CARLOTTA: So go ahead and do it! Get the dick implant and the pump. Let's do it.

EDWARD: First I've got to get cleared for surgery. At my age, everything is a risk. I already had a cardiac arrest and now I have that defibrillator. That was a close call.

CARLOTTA: Donald suggested the penile implant, so he must think you're able to get the surgery. He knows about the defibrillator, I suppose.

EDWARD: Of course he knows. (*Kisses CARLOTTA*) Thanks, honey, I worry about you and your needs. I love you and I want to satisfy you.

CARLOTTA: You're my super-sized sugar daddy. And now you'll be my inflatable sugar daddy. (*Claps her hands in excitement. Begins to make pumping motions with her fingers.*)

EDWARD: What are you doing?

CARLOTTA: Practicing.

> *EDWARD and CARLOTTA laugh and fall into one another's arms.*

BLACKOUT

SCENE THREE

> *Back in the DONALD's office some weeks later. CARLOTTA enters. DONALD HARTFORD is working on his laptop at the desk. CARLOTTA is dressed in sexy black dress, something like a Halloween barmaid. CARLOTTA carries some papers.*

DONALD: (*Rises to greet CARLOTTA*) Mrs. Monceaux, this is unexpected. How are you?

CARLOTTA: I fell like shit and this is no pleasure visit. (*Plops some papers on the desk*) And these are for you.

DONALD: (*Picks up the papers and examines them*) It's a lawsuit.

CARLOTTA: You bet your sweet ass, Donnie Boy, it's a lawsuit!

DONALD: (*Frowns*) Usually someone from the sheriff's office delivers these.

CARLOTTA: (*Calmly*) I know. They told me that, but I insisted on doing it myself. They said it was okay because of their respect for my late husband and how important he was and all to the judicial system. And I'm not afraid of you or any of your pseudo-authority.

DONALD: (*Reads the paper*) Failure to exercise due caution. Failure to inform. Failure to perform appropriate testing. Loss of consortium. Mental pain and suffering.

CARLOTTA: Yes, all that and more.

DONALD: I'm sorry about your husband's death. He was never a really great surgical candidate, even for a small surgery and I told him that.

CARLOTTA: Small surgery! You call putting an implant in his dick and a pump in his scrotum under general anesthesia a "small surgery?" You really are a quack! (*Goes into her purse and pulls out a card. Throws the card on the desk*) And here's your so-called sympathy card back.

DONALD: (*Reads the card*) "You murdered him!" You wrote that on my note?

CARLOTTA: Yes, you murdered my Eddie and you're going to pay through the nose.

DONALD: Mrs. Monceaux, we probably should not be communicating under these circumstances. But you need to know that your husband knew the risks, alternatives and benefits of the implant procedure and he chose to proceed. That is all documented in his chart, along with his signed consent form for the surgery. Your suit might prove a long, costly and painful process with no positive outcome.

CARLOTTA: No positive outcome, eh? And what about a million dollars for me and Jesus? (*Pronounced "Hesus" by CARLOTTA.*)

DONALD: Jesus? (*Pronounced "Jesus" by DONALD.*) A son by a previous marriage?

CARLOTTA: No, my pool man.

DONALD: (*Looks heavenward*) Right, of course. I should have guessed.

CARLOTTA: My new lawyer, Mr. Voda, says this is a slam-dunk case. You sent a guy with a bad heart and a defibrillator into a useless, high-risk surgery. That's malpractice!

DONALD: Your husband did not think it was useless. I'm sorry he died. I'm sorry for your loss.

CARLOTTA: (*Weeps and then screams*) You aren't half sorry yet, but you will be! Mr. Voda says this case is worth a ton of money. He says he'll have that jury wrapped around his little finger and you'll be cleaned out, along with your fancy new doctor-owned clinic and that goes for that good-for-nothing surgeon that did the operation, too. I'll get a fortune out of both of you.

DONALD: I'm sure your husband left your well provided for. He was quite a successful plaintiff's attorney.

CARLOTTA: (*Screams*) HE FORGOT TO PAY HIS LIFE INSURANCE PREMIUM! He used the money for this stupid surgery because the damn health insurance company wouldn't pay for an e-lective procedure. He owed a fortune on his stupid castle and he paid a ton of money to his first wife, who already cleaned him out.

DONALD: I'm sorry to hear that.

CARLOTTA: I've got to do this! I've got to sue you. I've got to get some money or I'll have nothing to offer anyone and no money to live off of. (*Weeps and slumps in the chair*) I've got to sue you and I want to sue you.

DONALD: (*Reaches over to comfort CARLOTTA*) Mrs. Monceaux.

CARLOTTA: (*Pulls away*) Call me Carlotta, please! We've known each other a long time. You called me Carlotta when I was married to Peter. Sweet guy when he wasn't drunk and beating me up. I'm sure he and your former wife, Christina, are doing very well together.

DONALD: Please leave Christina and Peter out of this. Besides, this lawsuit is going to go on and on and on and cost a lot of money to the insurance company and to you and to your lawyer. And you may still lose.

CARLOTTA: Yeah, that's what my lawyer, Mr. Voda, said, too. But he's sure they'll want to settle for a fat lump sum so it won't drag on and on and go to court. (*Plays with a letter opener*) This is real nice. Where did it come from, Arabia?

DONALD: Indonesia.

CARLOTTA: That's somewhere in South American, isn't it?

DONALD: No, Southeast Asia.

CARLOTTA: (*Takes a handkerchief out of her purse and blows her nose*) Donald, you've got to pay me. I don't even really hate you. But you got insurance and they have a lot of money.

DONALD: (*Picks up the paper*) This isn't the way. It's not right.

CARLOTTA: You're rich. It's the only way. Besides, I don't pay anything up front.

DONALD: Yeah, no money down and 30% for the lawyer.

CARLOTTA: (*Surprised*) No, 50% for Mr. Voda because he says it's a "complicated case." At least that's what he tells me. (*Opens her bag. Returns the handkerchief*) And I hope your house is paid for, not like Edward and our damn castle.

DONALD: (*Glances into the bag and notices a recording device*) You are recording this conversation, aren't you?

CARLOTTA: Yes, I am.

DONALD: Your idea?

CARLOTTA: Well, mine and Mr. Voda's. We thought you might say something incriminating.

DONALD: Carlotta, I'm going to have to ask you to leave.

CARLOTTA: I'll turn it off. (*Does something in her purse*) There! It's turned off. (*Goes over to DONALD. Hangs over the desk*) I've always liked you, Donnie-Boy. You're handsome and speak really good English. Maybe you want to have some fun? (*Makes a lewd hand gesture.*)

DONALD: I'm happily married.

CARLOTTA: Third time's the charm, eh? And what difference does that make? (*Plays with the DONALD's tie*) I'm a load of fun and I can be very discreet.

DONALD: (Pulls away) Mrs. Monceaux . . . .

CARLOTTA: Carlotta, for heaven's sake! We've known each other for years. (Climbs on to DONALD's lab and begins to gyrate sensually) Eddie used to really like this. (Massages DONALD's neck and chest, working toward the groin) I never met a man who didn't.

DONALD: (Stands and pushes CARLOTTA away) Mrs. Monceaux! Please leave my office right now! If you do not go, I'm calling the police.

CARLOTTA: (Angrily) Do it! Call the police! Call the newspaper! Call the television! I want everyone to know what a quack doctor you are! You're a killer. I already heard about that poor kid who died from an overdose from your prescription! I want everyone in town to know everything. You killed my husband by letting him get operated on for a stupid dick implant and I want to make sure you get what you deserve. (*Pulls a revolver from her purse.*)

DONALD: (*Draws back*) Put that thing away. Don't do anything you'll regret.

CARLOTTA: I already regret just about everything.

DONALD: Carlotta, think of what you're doing.

CARLOTTA: I know what I'm doing. I hate you! You're alive! You're rich! You're happy! And I'm going to be poor and miserable if Mr. Voda doesn't do what he says he's going to do. And that may take years and years. He said it and you said it.

DONALD: (*Approaches CARLOTTA*) Please, give me the gun.

CARLOTTA: Stay back or I'll blow your balls off (*points to DONALD's crotch.*)

DONALD: (*Continues to advance*) Please give me the gun.

CARLOTTA: All for a fake dick! (*Shakes her head*) A fake penis and now he's dead.

DONALD: (*Continues to approach slowly and tries to take the gun*) Give the gun to me, please.

CARLOTTA: Don't! Don't get near me!

DONALD: You're suffering. You're depressed. You need time to grieve, time to figure out your life, to weigh your options.

CARLOTTA: (*Screams*) I DON'T HAVE ANY TIME! YOU FOOL! I don't have any more options! I've got breast cancer and it's already spread everywhere. I'm dying and I'm alone. I don't want to die poor and alone.

DONALD: And Jesus? (*Pronounces "Jesus."*) Your pool boy, what about him?

CARLOTTA: Jesus? (*Pronounces "Hesus."*) He's already gone. He didn't want a dying old lady, especially a poor one. (*Looks back to DONALD*) I don't want to die alone. (*Pauses*) And I don't have to (*shoots DONALD.*)

> *DONALD falls dead to the ground.*

CARLOTTA (CONT): For love? For a fake dick?

> *CARLOTTA looks heavenward and then points the gun at her own head, pulls the trigger and falls over DONALD.*

BLACKOUT

END OF LIFE ISSUES

END-OF-LIFE DECISIONS:
MEDICAL, LEGAL AND FINANCIAL

The end of life is a critical period for patients and for their families. While no one wants to get there, death comes to all of us and our loved ones just as surely as taxes. Discussions surrounding impending death are painful and difficult at any time. The person may or may not realize that they are about to die and the family may or may not be willing to bring the subject up. To make matters worse, the timing of life's end is never an absolute certainty and with few exceptions, no one knows the day and hour of their demise. Some people, who are expected to die in the very near future, will rally and live days, weeks or months more. While some people expected to live months or years may die suddenly.

Complex social and psychological (not to mention financial) issues that have not been addressed suddenly rush to the forefront and demand immediate attention. This is a volatile and potentially explosive period. Guilt, anger, resentment, greed and selfishness can co-exist with love, devotion, appreciation and a genuine desire to be of service. Relatives from near and far may converge on the bedside and long-simmering resentments can bubble up in the exhaustion and confusion of the end-of-life scenario, especially when it is a prolonged process.

None of us want to face our death or anyone else's, but we should all want to make this important life transition as smooth as possible. The patient and family may not want to, but addressing multiple complex decisions prior to death can save an enormous amount of grief for everyone. What are some of these decisions?

One of the first should be having a standard last will and testament. Watching families agonize (or fight) over what their loved one "would have wanted" is a painful experience. A standard last will and testament avoids uncertainty and conflict. A frank discussion of who wants what as an inheritance may seem cold and heartless, but it is even worse when siblings fight over a silver tea set or a piece of furniture. A trust may also be indicated in some circumstances, although it is a more complex document requiring special legal input.

Everyone should also create a living will. That is a document that delineates the level of medical care they want to receive as they approach death. Do they want any resuscitative procedures? CPR? Tube feeding? Use of a breathing machine? Antibiotics? What should be done medically and how far should the doctors go, and under what circumstances? This should all be addressed in the living will. The drama of a distant relative, who insists on prolonged futile care while the rest of the family wants their loved one "just made comfortable," is a formula for disaster. Deciding to place a feeding tube and then deciding not to use it or remove it is traumatic. Artificially supporting life with a ventilator and then having to remove it is equally traumatic, if not more so. Were decisions made in advance, the burden is taken off family members, who are no longer have to guess what the patient wanted.

There are also decisions about who will have financial Power of Attorney when and if the patient becomes physically or mentally unable to make their own decisions. There is also the Medical Power of Attorney, a person designated to make only medical (and not financial) decisions.

Everyone may think they will remain lucid until the point of death, but that is the exception and not the rule. It is estimated that 5.4 million Americans suffer from Alzheimer's disease now and that figure will only increase with the aging population. Such individuals cannot make reasoned decisions despite the best information. Voluntarily designating someone to have Power of Attorney avoids the difficult problem of establishing competency, a complicated legal (not medical) designation.

Doctors often witness horrendous scenes of family conflict, played out at the bedside of a dying family member, just as they are witness to heart-warming scenes of solidarity and love. Addressing a last will and testament, living will, Power of Attorney, Medical Power of Attorney, and if and when and how to initiate hospice care should be made in advance. Such forethought brings peace and closure for loved ones.

David J. Holcombe, M.D.

HANGING BY A THREAD

CHARACTERS

CARL: Mrs. Helen Hampton's son. Middle-aged man. Well dressed and well spoken.

BETTY: Mrs. Helen Hampton's daughter. Middle-aged woman. Somewhat histrionic.

DR. PETER FRANK: Hampton family physician. Older middle-aged man. Well dressed in a white lab coat and a prominent stethoscope.

SETTING

Dr. Frank's medical office. There are three chairs, one, the doctor's, facing the other two.

> *CARL is seated in one of the chairs and BETTY is sitting on the other. PETER is dressed in his tie and white lab coat, not scrubs. He is sitting in a way that faces the siblings.*

CARL: (*Talking loudly to BETTY*) Don't be ridiculous, Betty! Dr. Frank and I are trying to help end mother's useless suffering.

BETTY: (*Jumps up from her chair and starts screaming*) Stop spouting this drivel! You're both trying to kill her and you know it!

PETER: (*To BETTY*) The Hippocratic oath forbids killing. I can't kill people, but I can let nature take its course.

BETTY: Nature! What's natural about starvation? What's natural about euthanasia? What's natural about two men ganging up on a helpless, old woman and snuffing out her life?

PETER: Please. No one is talking about euthanasia.

BETTY: (*Yells at PETER*) God! You're just playing God and you're so full of yourself that you don't even see it.

PETER: Perhaps you're right. But God shows mercy and compassion in the face of suffering. At least I hope he does.

BETTY: Do you? Is killing old ladies showing compassion?

CARL: Betty, would you shut up! You're insulting the doctor and you're insulting me.

BETTY: You! I haven't even started on you. You're nothing more than the sorcerer's apprentice. You don't even have the balls to make the decision yourself. You stir things up and then hide behind Dr. God here. Yes, you're his lapdog. His ball-less little lap dog.

CARL: And you have the balls? Is that it? Is that why you're still an unmarried old maid? Because of your balls?

BETTY: Shut up!

> *BETTY lunges at CARL and begins to pound his chest. CARL does not resist, but keeps his hands and his sides.*

BETTY: You nasty arrogant creep!

> *BETTY continues to pound him, but her blows become weaker and*

weaker. Finally, she stops and CARL puts his arms around her. BETTY pushes CARL away.

BETTY: I'm going out to the waiting room. Call me if you need me.

CARL: You see, Betty is mentally and physically exhausted. Mother's got no quality of life and I can't stand to see her this way. We're prolonging her suffering. Do we have to go on with all these tube feedings? Is it some sort of legal thing about stopping them?

PETER: No, Carl, it's not a legal problem and we don't have to continue the feedings, but your sister wants me to keep them going. If that were not the case, we could convert your mother to comfort care status, get her switched to hospice, and stop the feedings. She'll dwindle away and die peacefully.

CARL: Would that hurt? Would she suffer?

PETER: No. We think in terms of ourselves. She won't suffer; she'll just dwindle away.

CARL: Starving to death? Dying of dehydration?

PETER: It's not painful. Nature will take its course in someone who can no longer eat on their own. We just put water down the tube. She won't die of dehydration, but it would prolong the dying process.

CARL: Can we do it? Stop the feeding?

PETER: Anytime. If you and your sister agree. You can't have one person in the family fighting with another. It's not worth having that kind of disruption and conflict. Your mother would surely not have wanted to be the source of such a terrible controversy between her children. And you don't want a legacy of bitterness to poison your relationship with your sister.

CARL: That's already been poisoned if you haven't noticed. But you are right about Mother; she certainly wouldn't want us fighting. She never did. (*Looks at the doctor*) She really wanted us to get along. As kids, we did, you know. We had a lot of fun together. Then something happened as we got older. The more I succeeded in my own life, the more Betty seemed to resent me. She's so bitter now, so full of guilt. And the weird part is that I don't really know why.

PETER: That happens between siblings. But Betty does appear to sincerely care about your mother and her welfare.

CARL: Care? I don't know who she thinks she's really caring for? It's like she's afraid to let go of mother. Afraid of some awful void. (*Pauses*) Am I some sort of monster to want nature to take it's course with my mother?

PETER: I don't think so. But death is final. No one knows what lies beyond. It's odd, but I've seen believers and non-believers approach death either with dread or total serenity. Their religious feelings didn't seem to matter that much.

CARL: And what do you believe, doctor?

PETER: It doesn't matter what I believe. This is a family decision.

CARL: What you believe does matter, doctor. Here you have all this power in you hands, in your pen. You can keep some patients alive and allow others to die with a stroke of your pen. Such power must be intoxicating.

PETER: It's a huge responsibility, Carl. It's an enormous weight. Sometimes I think I know that a patient is doomed and I turn out to be wrong. I took care of this old man one time and I was trying to help the daughter decide whether to put him on a breathing machine or not. He was lying there on the bed between us and I'm trying to convince the daughter not to be aggressive. And he's dying right there in the bed between us.

CARL: What did she do?

PETER: She decided to intubate him and, against my better judgment, we did it. (*Pauses*) Two months later he walked out of the hospital, and now three years later I still see him in the office as an outpatient. Every time I see him, I think about trying to convince his daughter to let him die. She refused. And she was right.

CARL: You can't be God. You can't foresee the future.

PETER: No, I can't foresee the future. But I do have the power of life and death over people. It's an awesome power. And sometimes I do feel like God. That's when it takes someone like your sister to drag me back to earth.

CARL: So you think that mother is going to wake up like Betty says she will?

PETER: No, not in your mother's case. But I can and do make errors in judgment as much as I try to avoid them.

CARL: I'm not looking for perfection, doctor, just reasonable compassion. Would you talk to my sister again? See's sitting outside in the waiting room.

PETER: Of course.

CARL: I'll bring her back in here, even if I have to drag her in.

PETER: She needs to come in voluntarily. This needs to be a family decision.

> *CARL goes out and gets his sister. BETTY comes in and sits down, but CARL remains standing in back of the other chair.*

PETER: (*To BETTY*) Are you all right? You look tired.

BETTY: I'm fine. I'm really not tired at all (*manages a half-hearted smile.*)

PETER: How many hours of sleep are you getting?

BETTY: Enough. And I appreciate your concern, but this isn't about me. It's about Mother, isn't it?

PETER: Of course. But you don't want to get sick yourself. If you do, who will take care of your mother?

BETTY: Not Carl. That's for sure. He's washed his hands of the problem. (*Looks at CARL, then back to PETER*) He has time for his wife, his kids, his job and his charitable boards, but not for his own mother. He just wants to lead his own selfish life and let mother die in some stinking nursing home.

PETER: Perhaps Carl's not as strong as you.

BETTY: Strong? No. He's not. Carl's weak and spineless and heartless.

PETER: That's very harsh. Don't you think Carl deserves more credit than that?

BETTY: Harsh? What would you say if your sibling left you to make all the decisions, to do all the work?

PETER: Has Carl really done that? Or do you just disagree with his decisions? Maybe you ought to give Carl a chance. It can't be easy for him either.

BETTY: Easy? Who's got the cushy job and the gorgeous, devoted wife, and the brilliant, well-mannered children? Carl's a spoiled brat. And I'm the one doing everything for mother.

PETER: Perhaps you're being too hard on yourself and Carl?

BETTY: Mother's worth it. She raised us almost single-handed. Dad spent most of the time away with his job. Then he died when I was only twelve. After that, mother did it all. She worked, kept house, helped with homework and never missed a softball game. She slaved so Carl and I could go to college. She's a saint. And saints don't deserve to be abandoned like old, sick dogs. *(Glares at CARL, then looks back to PETER)* Dad let her down, Carl wants to let her down, but I'm not going to. Doctor, do you think she's suffering?

PETER: I don't think so.

BETTY: Do you think she feels pain?

PETER: I think she can feel pain, but she probably doesn't recognize it like we do.

BETTY: How can you tell for sure?

PETER: There's no way to be absolutely sure.

BETTY: I would hate it if she were having pain. I would hate myself for causing it.

PETER: Why would you hate yourself?

BETTY: I caused mother so much pain for so long. I said hateful things to her when I was growing up. I do feel guilty and it would kill me if I were just doing all of this for my own selfish reasons. Do you think I'm selfish, doctor?

PETER: No, I don't. I think you hurt to see your mother like this. I think your head tells you one thing while your heart tells you something else. I think you need to put your head and heart in harmony.

BETTY: Put them in harmony. That sounds easy, but it's not. At least not for me *(pauses and sighs.)*

PETER: Let's talk about your mother.

BETTY and CARL nod in agreement.

PETER (CONT): As you've seen, she hasn't shown any sign of improvement over the last months, even after we put in the feeding tube. In fact, I find her less responsive, even to painful stimuli.

BETTY: Painful stimuli? Are you hurting her on purpose?

PETER: Of course not. I just rub her sternum firmly and a normal person would wince. Your mother doesn't react at all.

BETTY: Will she ever get better?

PETER: No, she won't.

BETTY: I've read about these cases where someone's been in a coma for years and then wakes up and asks for a Coke. Why not mother?

PETER: *(After a long silence)* She's not going to wake up. She is not going to get better. She will get pneumonia or a urinary tract infection or bed sores or God knows what other complication. Every patient in her clinical condition worsens; it just depends on when they ultimately die.

BETTY: When?

PETER: I don't know. Days? Weeks? Months?

CARL: This could go on and on?

PETER: Well, yes.

CARL: (*To BETTY*) We can't do that to her. We can't let her lay and rot for God only knows how long.

BETTY: We? Speak for yourself! (*To PETER*) If she were your mother, what would you do?

PETER: Doctors shouldn't treat their own families. I can't answer that question.

BETTY: So if you can't treat your own mother, what if she were a perfect stranger?

PETER: I'd stop the feedings and put her under hospice care to continue to make her as comfortable as possible. (*Pauses and sighs*) I see dozens of these patients in nursing homes. They get started on tube feedings and then they may live for years. Their muscles contract and atrophy so the patients get all twisted up and deformed. They can't talk. They can't move. But they can feel pain. It breaks my heart to see people like that month after month, year after year. We're all getting older. Someday there won't be enough nursing home beds to hold us all. (*Pauses*) Hospice gives comfort care to end-stage patients. They don't force feedings. They don't send the patients back and forth to the hospital. They can help your mother die with some dignity.

BETTY: Die with dignity? That's still death, isn't it?

PETER: Yes, it is still death.

BETTY: And what gives you or Carl or me the right to choose between life and death for my mother?

PETER: Because your mother can't decide herself.

BETTY: So doesn't that make us all the more responsible? Shouldn't we be all the more certain that we are not just snuffing out a life because it is inconvenient, or expensive, or just unnecessary?

CARL: (*To BETTY*) Please! Get off your moral high horse and look at reality down here. Mother's a vegetable, not a person. She's a plant that we're giving food and water to so she just continues. That's selfish and cruel.

BETTY: Cruel! Selfish! Who's selfish here? You, the one who can't stand to see mother suffer? Or me, who has the courage and conviction to stand by her in her most vulnerable hour? (*She stands up and starts yelling.*) I'm not selfish, you are! You're talking about a living, breathing human being as if she were a piece of meat. I can't take it. I can't take it any more.

> *BETTY starts to cry. CARL gets up and takes her in his arms. BETTY resists only weakly and then continues to sob as CARL pats her back.*

CARL: (*To BETTY*) Look at yourself. You're worn out. You're exhausted. You're going to die too if you keep going on like this and I can't stand to lose you both. You're the only family I have and I do care about you.

BETTY: (*Backs up a little and looks up at CARL*) I don't want to lose mother.

CARL: She'll still be here. (*Touches her heart, then his own*) In your heart and in my heart.

BETTY: (*Manages a weak laugh*) You always had a knack for sentimental drivel.

CARL: And you have the hardest head of anyone I know, except perhaps mom.

BETTY: As hard as your heart?

CARL: You're head's harder by far.

PETER: (*Approaches CARL and BETTY*) I'm sorry to push things along, but we should reach some sort of decision.

BETTY: (*Turns to CARL*) Now?

PETER: You have to decide.

BETTY: (*Speaks to CARL*) Am I really being selfish and unreasonable to want her to live?

CARL: No, you're not selfish, nor sanctimonious, nor unreasonable. I just think you're wrong.

BETTY: (*Laughs despite herself*) You're really something. (*Pauses*) My head still tells me one thing, while my heart tells me something else. I have an awful feeling that Mother is hanging to life by a thread and we're going to cut it.

CARL: Yes, we're going to cut the thread to set her free. It's holding her back from God.

PETER: Does this mean we can stop the tube feedings and continue with comfort measures only?

CARL: Betty?

BETTY: I'm tired, Carl. I'm exhausted and I'm ready to see it end. *(Turns to PETER)* I agree. Let's go with hospice and comfort care only.

PETER: Comfort care only. No food. No water. No antibiotics. (*Looks at BETTY and CARL and pauses*) Now you have to decide whether you want to keep her at home or put her in a nursing home.

BETTY: No! No nursing home, please!

PETER: Hospice nurses can provide their services in the nursing home.

BETTY: No! No nursing home. I can bend, but that would break me. (*Turns to CARL and clutches his hand*) Carl, I promised her she'd never have to go into a nursing home.

CARL: She's already left us. Her mind's gone and her body's going. Nursing home, home, what difference does it make at this point?

BETTY: It makes a difference to me. I'd like to keep her home. Please let me have that. It won't affect either of you. Let me at least have that.

CARL: It's already so hard on you trying to take care of mother. It's wearing you out. It's a 24-hour a day job, seven days a week.

BETTY: That's okay. If it kills me, so be it! Please let me keep her at home.

CARL: (*To PETER*) It's okay with me to continue treating her at home if Betty insists. She knows what she's getting into and she knows what it's doing to her. I respect her for that, even if I don't agree.

PETER: You'll both have to sign a DNR, a Do Not Resuscitate form.

BETTY: No resuscitation?

PETER: No chest compressions or intubation when she stops breathing and her heart stops. We just keep her comfortable when that happens.

BETTY: She won't suffer, will she?

PETER: No, I promise.

BETTY: Please, give me your word. I can't stand the thought of her suffering.

PETER: You have my word. She will not suffer.

BLACKOUT

MALPRACTICE AND
TORT REFORM

MEDICAL MALPRACTICE:
THE MOST INSIDIOUS CANCER

The medico-legal climate in the United States defies reason. It is, of course, tied into a whole approach to liability that is, alas, typically American. Although some may cringe when other national solutions are suggested, it is useful to see how other societies handle the universal problem of malpractice. The Belgian model deserves consideration.

First, contingency fees are illegal in Belgium. There is no such thing as a lawyer taking a percentage of an award. Legal fees may be high, but they are hourly fees, much as you would expect from a skilled mechanic or electrician. By removing the motivation of enormous economic windfalls to lawyers, the number of lawsuits drops dramatically. The price of malpractice insurance also drops accordingly (ten times less in Belgium). Removing the insidious practice of contingency fees would remove a good part of the profit incentive from the current American malpractice system.

Some lawyers argue that eliminating contingency fees would deny legal access to the poor. Not so! The issue here is not justice, but greed. And the corrosive effect of unbridled greed poisons the practice of law.

Second, malpractice cases in Belgium are handled by judges specialized in the field of medical malpractice, and never before juries. As noble and as intelligent as the general population may be, the tremendous complexities of modern medicine and the passions whipped up in the jury system in such cases makes trial by jury more of a liability than an asset. Of course, unscrupulous plaintiffs' attorneys thrive on stirring up emotional responses from the jury in the hopes of favorable verdicts. But that hardly serves as a justification for the practice. Using specialized judges, instead of juries, removes the element of public passion, so unhelpful in such complex cases.

Third, specialized malpractice judges in Belgium are appointed for their expertise, and not elected. Although appointing judges does not completely remove the politics from the system in Belgium, it greatly reduces the political and monetary pressures exerted by attorneys on judges. Handsome electoral contributions from plaintiffs' attorneys pervert the objectivity of the judicial process in the United States. Appointed judges remove, or at least reduce, the politics in the judicial process.

Profit, passion and politics all work to made our medico-legal system an unmitigated disaster, a true cancer in our society. The threat of malpractice and the omnipresent tendency to "cover your ass," has gradually infiltrated the process of medical care. The result is that patients are transformed from trusted partners in the doctor-patient relationship to potential litigants to be feared. In no way does this lack of trust enhance patient care. On the contrary, it results in a progressive erosion of trust and a corruption of the patient-doctor relationship, so necessary to effective medical care. It also results in increased medical costs in a system that is already twice as expensive per capita as that of the majority of other developed countries.

The problems of healthcare are universal. Every country has its burden of heart disease, cancer, infectious diseases, and other physical ailments. But medico-legal systems, much like healthcare delivery systems, are man-made. Let us choose wisely when we embark on the challenge of changing our healthcare delivery system and not neglect elements, such as tort reform, that we must address in order to make our system one be of the best and most financially sustainable in the world, not just the most expensive.

HOOK, LINE AND SINKER

CHARACTERS

DR. REGINALD CARDINAL: Older orthopedist. Somewhat pedantic. Obviously beyond his prime. Dressed in a starched lab coat, perhaps a bit wrinkled.

LAURA TATUM: Older woman. Not elegantly dressed, but clean and presentable. Speaks with a noticeable, but mild Southern rural accent.

JONATHAN DAVIS: Plaintiff's attorney. Dressed in a suit and tie. Formal and stiff in his attitude and speech.

DERRICK SHARP: Defense attorney. Dressed in a blazer and grey pants, with a shirt and tie. No regional accent.

SETTING

The setting varies with the scene. Scene I is a doctor's office, with minimal set elements. Scene II is a lawyers' office with minimal set elements. Scene III is a courtroom with only a raised platform with a chair as a "witness stand." Scene IV is a small meeting room with a couple of chairs.

SCENE I

DR. CARDINAL's Office. There is a desk and a couple of books. A stethoscope is casually draped around his neck. He is dressed in a starched lab coat. There is a chair for a guest. Minimal set elements required.

REGINALD: (*Slams down a phone or punches an cell-phone to show it being turned off*) How dare he? How dare he second-guess me? (*Pauses*) And for what? (*Shakes his fist*) Damn that little pipsqueak! (*Stands up and wanders around the stage*) He'll rue the day he ever called me, by God! He'll think twice before he calls and challenges my clinical judgment. And the day before the scheduled surgery no less! God damn him to hell!

(*Buzzer sounds.*)

REGINALD: (*Bangs down on a button*) Okay, okay. Send her in. I'm ready.

LAURA: (*Limps into the room*) Hello Dr. Cardinal.

REGINALD: (*Assists LAURA into a chair*) Sit down, Mrs. Tatum, please. We don't want you on that foot any longer than necessary. Every additional bit of pressure adds to the danger.

LAURA: Well, at least I have two feet. There are enough people around here with only one, or none from what I see in the waiting room. I don't want to end up like that. (*Pauses*) Did you hear from Dr. Frank? Did he clear me for surgery?

REGINALD: (*Scowls*) Yes. That's what I wanted to talk to you about. He called today to express his opinions.

LAURA: So can I undergo the surgery? It is still scheduled for tomorrow?

REGINALD: Yes, he did agree that you could undergo the surgery. That's the good news.

LAURA: And the bad news?

REGINALD: (*Leans forward*) You have a bad doctor!

LAURA: Really?

REGINALD: Mrs. Tatum, may I call you Laura?

LAURA: Of course, although Dr. Frank always calls me Mrs. Tatum for some reason I've never understood. He never calls me Laura. I've always found that odd.

REGINALD: That's not the only thing odd about him. (*Pauses*) Yes, he did clear you for surgery, as I said, but he told me I needed to amputate your foot.

LAURA: Amputate my foot? You mean cut it off entirely?

REGINALD: Yes.

LAURA: Why? Why would he say such a thing?

REGINALD: (*Again leans forward in confidence*) I think he missed your diagnosis over a year ago and now he wants me to amputate your foot to get rid of the evidence of his mistake.

LAURA: Are you sure? Did he tell you that?

REGINALD: Well, he didn't exactly say it in those terms, but I have never had a doctor talk about amputation the way he did. He's a bad doctor, that's all. You'll need to find another one as soon as possible after the surgery.

LAURA: You really think my foot problem is something I had a year ago and Dr. Frank just missed it?

REGINALD: There's no doubt in my mind. Why else would he want me to amputate your foot except to get rid of the evidence?

LAURA: But an amputation, that's so brutal!

REGINALD: Yes, brutal and unreasonable.

LAURA: Is an amputation even a consideration?

REGINALD: Not in the least! I'm going to operate on you, of course, I will save your foot and you're going to do just fine. (*Pats LAURA on the shoulder*) I'll take the very best possible care of you and we will save your foot together, regardless of what your personal doctor recommended.

LAURA: I'm in shock.

REGINALD: Yes, incompetence and deceit are shocking, aren't they?

LAURA: (*Pauses*) Can I sue Dr. Frank?

REGINALD: (*Coyly*) Of course you can and generally I would never suggest such a thing for one of my honored colleagues, but this really deviates from the standard of care. In your case, it might send a message as well as compensate you for your misery. (*Points to LAURA's foot*) If this had been discovered earlier, you may not have even needed this surgery. Now look at your foot: collapsed, destroyed and dysfunctional. It's a real pity, a real avoidable catastrophe. If only there had been a timely diagnosis. (*Pauses*) Yes, in this case, litigation might send a much needed and probably overdue message that such incompetence is not tolerated in the medical profession. Every doctor needs to be held to the highest moral and professional standards and sometimes, as we have here, it is clearly not the case. (*Points to LAURA's foot again*) Now, back to your upcoming surgery.

LAURA: Please, Dr. Cardinal. I'm so upset I'm shaking.

REGINALD: (*Pats LAURA's shoulder*) There, there. I understand. But calm down now so we can discuss your surgery. How do you feel?

LAURA: Nervous.

REGINALD: That's understandable. But I'm talking about your general health? Are you having any health issues I should know about?

LAURA: I guess I feel okay.

REGINALD: Do you have any reservations about the surgery?

LAURA: No! I may have had some before, but now I'm totally committed to the procedure. (*Leans in toward REGINALD*) I have total faith in you and I'm full of gratitude to you for opening up my eyes. I've been blinded by Dr. Frank's personality, his cheerfulness, and his experience, but that's finished.

REGINALD: Knowledge is power, Laura. Sometimes it takes a second look from an outsider to rip away the veil of self-deception.

LAURA: Yes, yes. That's it, the veil of deception! I've been deceived, but now I see clearly. I've been blind, but now I see. It's all coming into focus. (*Pauses*) Dr. Frank will pay! He will pay for hoodwinking me, for making me think he really cared about me. That's a crime; a real crime and it should be punished. And he will be punished, as God is my witness!

REGINALD: I'm just interested in your health and welfare, nothing more. I leave crime and punishment up to others. Now, let's get back to your surgery.

LAURA: All right, Doctor Cardinal.

REGINALD: Call me Reginald, please.

LAURA: Okay, Reginald.

REGINALD: We're a team, you and I, a team that will work together to restore you to optimal health, even if you will experience a reduction in functioning and activity level.

LAURA: Because of Dr. Frank's negligence.

REGINALD: I'll let you reach your own conclusions about that, Laura. Far be it from me to influence you in a legal issue.

LAURA: Of course, I respect your restraint and your professionalism. I'll be handling this in my own way after we finish with the surgery. And I feel fine, just mad as hell at being tricked and betrayed.

REGINALD: As well you should.

LAURA: Are you ready for tomorrow's surgery?

REGINALD: Perfectly! I appreciate your confidence and will work to justify it. I'll see you tomorrow at 6:30 a.m. at the surgery center. Remember, be fasting, and don't take your insulin. We don't want any hypoglycemia complicating things, do we?

LAURA: Thank you so much, Reginald. Thank you for everything. I won't forget your kindness and consideration.

REGINALD: (*Bows slightly*) Thank you. *A demain*!

LAURA: A de-man?

REGINALD: *A demain*, it's French for see you tomorrow.

LAURA: You're so cultivated. *Merci*! That's all the French I know.

REGINALD: That's plenty for me. Your gratitude is all I really want. Now, go get some sleep, we both want to be refreshed and rested for tomorrow's surgery.

BLACKOUT

SCENE II

> *JONATHAN DAVIS'S law office.*
> *There are a couple of chairs, perhaps*
> *a desk with a lamp, and maybe an*
> *oriental area rug. Nothing complex*
> *or fancy. He does have a large silver*
> *crucifix prominently placed on the*
> *wall. That is a necessary element.*

LAURA: I want justice! No, I demand justice!

JONATHAN: And compensation?

LAURA: Of course! My life has been wrecked. I can't walk. I can't stand up to work! I have to use a cane to even get around the house! It's a crime!

JONATHAN: Malpractice is a civil offense, not a criminal matter.

LAURA: Not for me! It's a crime for a doctor to betray a patient's trust. I liked Dr. Frank. He took care of my family members. He chatted with me about all sorts of things. He seemed to care, and then he did this! (*Points to her feet.*) Two collapsed feet and a destroyed life.

JONATHAN: (*Taking notes*) How did you get to me? Were you referred or did you see my ads on TV or see my billboards around town?

LAURA: I asked around for a good lawyer and some people in our church had used you in the past. They said you were very competent and you got them what they deserved.

JONATHAN: Medical malpractice cases are not what I usually do. It's more personal injury and class action.

LAURA: (*Pointing to her feet again*) And this isn't personal injury? Two bad feet caused by a doctor's negligence? (*Pauses*) This is a no-brainer, Mr. Davis, a slam-dunk case, a done deal. Dr. Frank missed the diagnosis a year ago and then asked the surgeon to cut off my foot to get rid of the evidence. That's not just malpractice, that's criminal in my opinion.

JONATHAN: Cut off your foot? Get rid of the evidence? That sounds pretty extreme to me. How do you know this?

LAURA: Because Dr. Reginald Cardinal, the orthopedic surgeon who operated on my foot, told me so. That's the surgeon I went to myself because my foot was getting worse and worse. I had to do something. And Dr. Cardinal said that Dr. Frank was so scared I'd find out he had missed the diagnosis for a year that he wanted the foot removed to get rid of the evidence.

JONATHAN: Did Dr. Frank say that to you directly?

LAURA: Of course not! But that doesn't surprise me. He was ashamed he had missed the diagnosis for a year and he never apologized or told me what happened. He just went behind my back to Dr. Cardinal and demanded an amputation. Can you imagine?

JONATHAN: It does seem awfully egregious. (*Pauses*) Did you go back to Dr. Frank after the surgery?

LAURA: Back to Dr. Frank? Of course not! Why would I want to go back to a doctor that misdiagnosed and then betrayed me? No, never!

JONATHAN: (*Thoughtfully*) You know I will have to do some research on this case. I will need Dr. Frank's records and Dr. Cardinal's and anyone else who has seen you. You will have to sign some releases.

LAURA: Yes, of course.

JOHATHAN: There's a lot of research that needs to be done prior to filing a lawsuit. And, of course, there's the medical review panel.

LAURA: What's that?

JONATHAN: That's a panel formed with three doctors, one from each attorney and one chosen by two others that reviews the case to decide whether there was any "deviation from the standard of care."

LAURA: What does that mean?

JONATHAN: Deviation from the standard of care is just a fancy term for malpractice. (*Pauses.*) And they have to decide whether the deviation from care actually caused any harm, that's what we call a "tort."

LAURA: (*Holds up both legs with special shoes*) Look at these! Look at these feet! They are both crushed. They're destroyed! I can't stand. I can't walk more than a few yards! And then I have to use this cane. You'd have to be blind to not see the damage. Of course there's harm. (*Pauses*) Dr. Frank has destroyed my life by his incompetence. I want revenge! I want justice! I want compensation!

JONATHAN: And hopefully, we'll get all three in a big way.

LAURA: So you'll take my case?

JONATHAN: I think I can commit to you now, although sometimes a lot can change. It seems very straightforward, however.

LAURA: And the medical review panel? What if they disagree?

JONATHAN: No matter. Their decision is not binding. In your case, since it is so egregious, we can easily locate some very competent expert witnesses who will override the panel decision. The review panel is no more than a speed bump in the process. And if they happen to agree with you that there was deviation from the standard of care, it makes things so much easier. Dr. Frank's insurance company will be writing us a hefty check before the ink is dry on the panel's decision.

LAURA: (*Excited*) Do it! Get the information. Start the process! The quicker we start, the quicker justice will be served. (*Grabs JONATHAN's sleeve*) I believe in you. I believe in the justice system. You've got to help me punish Dr. Frank and get the justice and compensation I deserve! You've got to help me, Mr. Davis!

JONATHAN: And so I shall! (*Pat's LAURA's hand*) We are in this together to the end. It will cost some time and money to invest in the case. And there will be the expensive expert witnesses. But that's just more of an investment in your future earnings and mine. Are you willing to make those investments?

LAURA: Anything!

JONATHAN: Even 40% of the eventual award?

LAURA: (*Surprised*) Forty percent? That seems like so much. That might be a lot of money if I get the award I deserve.

JONATHAN: And well it might be. But that's the going rate, Mrs. Tatum.

LAURA: Laura.

JONATHAN: Laura, that's just how the system works. It allows people, such as you, with limited resources, to have full access to the justice system.

LAURA: And hourly fees? Does anyone do that?

JONATHAN: (*Laughs*) Of course not! You would be bankrupt in a matter of weeks and I would be much less motivated to pursue your case. (*Pauses*) Percentages of an eventual award solve all of the problems of access and create built-in incentives for the lawyer. Now let's get back to the case at hand and leave the theoretical considerations of contingency fees. When did Dr. Frank first miss the diagnosis?

LAURA: Well, it all started over a year ago. I came in to see Dr. Frank with swelling, lots of it, for several weeks. And Dr. Frank didn't really know what it was. He was very upset and sent me to the hospital for some X-rays. I thought he X-rayed my foot, but he just did my thigh and leg. And he came to tell me the x-rays were negative.

JONATHAN: Then what?

LAURA: He sent me home and a few days later the swelling was still there, so he sent me to another local doctor for my veins. That doctor even wanted to operate on me.

JONATHAN: And did this other doctor find the diagnosis?

LAURA: He found something, but not the right diagnosis. He found something with the veins or something like that. He was the wrong kind of doctor, that's what Dr. Cardinal said.

JONATHAN: And after that?

LAURA: I still had a lot of swelling and I called Dr. Frank to send me to a big center in Dallas that my family had used. They make diagnoses when no one else can.

JONATHAN: And they made the right diagnosis?

LAURA: No, they didn't because Dr. Frank sent me to the wrong kind of doctor there, too.

JONATHAN: So who finally did make the right diagnosis?

LAURA: Dr. Cardinal, the orthopedist in Dallas.

JONATHAN: How did you get to him?

LAURA: I went myself. Can you believe it? My neighbor saw me limping around and told me about this great foot doctor in Dallas. And that's when I finally got the right diagnosis and I got the truth . . .finally.

JONATHAN: So all the other doctors missed it, including Dr. Frank.

LAURA: Maybe, but they were the wrong kind of doctors. I don't blame them. I only blame Dr. Frank because he wanted to chop off my foot to get rid of the evidence. (*Holds up her feet*) I want him punished! He shouldn't even be a doctor. I'm ashamed that me and my family ever went to see him.

JONATHAN: Why did you?

LAURA: Because he had a good reputation. Little did I know it was all lies, lies and more lies, just a fancy façade hiding an evil and incompetent inside.

JONATHAN: (*Smiles*) We'll get to the truth, Mrs. Tatum, Laura. We'll get to the truth and the truth shall set us free and bring justice and compensation in its wake. I swear to it!

LAURA: (*Grasps JONATHAN's hand*) Oh, thank, you, Mr. Davis. Thank you Jonathan. I can hardly wait.

SCENE III (TEN YEARS LATER)

> *There is a raised platform on the stage with a solitary chair. This is the witness stand. The audience is the jury to which JONATHAN, DERRICK and LAURA both refer from time to time.*

JONATHAN: So you went to Dr. Frank with a swollen right foot.

LAURA: Yes.

JONATHAN: And did he make the diagnosis at that time?

LAURA: No sir, it took him a year and then only when Dr. Cardinal already made the diagnosis.

JONATHAN: Show us you foot, please.

LAURA: The right one?

JONATHAN: Yes.

LAURA: (*Takes off her shoe and pulls off her sock*) Dr. Cardinal says this is something called a rocker foot because of the deformity. See how's there's no arch, but it comes down instead. (*Points to the bottom of her foot*) It makes it hard to walk and it's very easy to get ulcers and other foot problems, too.

JONATHAN: Has this changed your life?

LAURA: Yes, of course. I can't walk, I can't work, I can't go on vacation, and I can't even go to social activities like church anymore. This has destroyed my life and could have been prevented.

JONATHAN: Thank you (*sits down in a chair by the side of the stage.*)

DERRICK: I'm Derrick Sharp and I represent Dr. Frank. Now, you say you went to Dr. Frank with a swollen foot.

LAURA: Yes, sir, I certainly did. My foot was red and hot and swollen.

DERRICK: And yet Dr. Frank's note shows that you complained of swelling to the whole right side of the body. Did you include the foot in your complaints?

LAURA: (*Sticks out her right foot*) Yes, and now it's so damaged that I can barely walk, even with a cane. My life was ruined due to Dr. Frank's negligence. (*Starts to weep and looks at the audience*) Look at this foot! In fact, look at both of my feet! I used to have walks with my husband. I used to work in my garden. Now I can't even get up and around without a cane. (*Pauses*) And Dr. Frank never even looked at my foot. He didn't even take off my shoe to examine me, but he wanted to chop off my foot later on.

DERRICK: (*Calmly*) Let's look at the notes from Dr. Frank's visit on that date. (*Points to a page*) Here is a drawing of your very swollen right thigh, almost 10 centimeters of difference with you left. And here is your swollen right leg, only a couple of centimeters in difference with the left. And here is a drawing of your right foot with a little "plus one" and the word "edema" next to it. Do you know what that means?

LAURA: No.

DERRICK: It means that Dr. Frank had to push with his finger on the top of your foot to see if there was a little indentation. And he wrote that it was "plus one," because it can go up to "plus four" with a lot of edema.

LAURA: So?

DERRICK: So, Dr. Frank had to have taken off your shoes and socks and had to have touched your foot. In fact, your own sworn deposition confirms it. (*Presents LAURA with a binder*) Please read your response here.

LAURA: (*Reads*) "Dr. Frank looked at my whole right side, including my thigh, my lower leg and my foot, which was a little swollen, but not nearly as much as my thigh. He even measured my thigh and leg with a measuring tape and pushed on my foot."

DERRICK: Thank you. (*Takes the binder*) So your recent comments about Dr. Frank not examining your foot were mistaken?

LAURA: No! He never looked at my foot. My foot was swollen and red and hot! My foot was always the problem. Dr. Frank just missed it then and again four months later when I went back to him.

DERRICK: Saying your foot was red, hot and swollen is in contradiction to your sworn testimony at your previous deposition and to Dr. Frank's office note as well. (*Pauses*) When you went to the local specialist, the vein doctor, and then when you went to the specialty center in Dallas. . . .

LAURA: When I saw Dr. Cardinal?

DERRICK: No, the other specialist that Dr. Frank sent you to see, before you went to see Dr. Cardinal yourself.

LAURA: Yes.

DERRICK: Did you complain of your foot to either of those doctors?

LAURA: Of course, my foot was always the problem.

DERRICK: Are you sure, Mrs. Tatum?

LAURA: I am positive.

DERRICK: (*Puts the binder in front of LAURA*) The question here in your deposition was. . . (*DERRICK reads*) "Why did you go to the vascular specialist here locally and to the one in Dallas?" Please read your sworn response.

LAURA: "Because I still had swelling in the whole right side of my body."

DERRICK: The whole right side of the body?

LAURA: Yes, the body included the foot, unless someone chops it off, of course.

DERRICK: And yet we presented the records of both physicians, the local vascular surgeon and the internist in Dallas, and there is NO mention of any complaints of the foot despite a complete exam by both doctors, which included an extensive examination of both feet.

LAURA: They were mistaken.

DERRICK: Who's mistaken?

LAURA: They are!

DERRICK: You mean both doctors, the vascular surgeon and the internist in Dallas, were mistaken and Dr. Frank was also mistaken despite what's documented in their charts, which corresponds with your sworn testimony?

LAURA: I guess so.

DERRICK: And is it possible that you are the one who is mistaken, Mrs. Tatum?

LAURA: No!

DERRICK: Isn't it possible that your memory of events has been distorted with the passage of over ten years of time? And isn't it possible that your self-deluded prevarications have become your own personal reality?

LAURA: What's a prevarication?

DERRICK: Lying.

LAURA: (*Yelling and standing up unsteadily*) No! You're just playing lawyer tricks to get Dr. Frank off the hook. You're the one who's twisting the truth so I look like the guilty one! It's not so! It's just not so! (*Sits down.*)

DERRICK: (*Calmly*) I can understand how you might become unclear about the events after ten years. (*Pauses*) Sometimes I can't even remember what I ate for breakfast, and I'm quite a bit younger than you.

LAURA: (*Yells*) I'm not senile! I'm not mistaken! And I'm not lying!

DERRICK: (*Calmly*) Ten-year-old memories can be muddled, don't you think? That's no crime.

LAURA: Maybe not, but it is a crime to misdiagnose someone and then try to get rid of the evidence with an amputation.

DERRICK: (*Sternly*) Did Dr. Frank say that to you? That he wanted to amputate your foot?

LAURA: No, but Dr. Cardinal said he did.

DERRICK: This is a hypothetical question, but why do your think Dr. Cardinal would say such a thing?

LAURA: Because it was the truth.

DERRICK: And this is also speculation, but perhaps Dr. Cardinal was angry with Dr. Frank for questioning the utility and safety of surgery on a very bad diabetic patient such as yourself? Maybe that questioning was more than Dr. Cardinal could tolerate, especially the day before your proposed surgery. Could that be an explanation, too?

LAURA: No!

DERRICK: No?

LAURA: No, because we have two expert witnesses from Harvard who both said that Dr. Frank missed the diagnosis a year earlier.

DERRICK: (*Sharply*) And we have three expert witnesses who all disagree. And they have just as many qualifications. (*Points to the audience, the "jury"*) So these good people, Dr. Frank's peers, will have to decide. (*Swings his arms to the audience*) And let me remind you that there's not a doctor on this jury. In fact, only three jurors have a higher education. But let me also remind you that three physicians who sat on a medical review panel, certainly Dr. Frank's peers, all agreed that there was no malpractice, no deviation from the standard of care and no evidence of any kind of treatment but competent and compassionate care.

LAURA: (*Coolly*) My attorney said they were mistaken, too.

DERRICK: So Dr. Frank, plus two specialists he sent you to see, plus three physicians on the medical review, plus two eminent academic witnesses we retained are ALL mistaken about your diagnosis and when it was made. But that you are the one who was right? Is that it, Mrs. Tatum?

LAURA: (*Looks a bit shaken*) Yes, that's it. And our two expert witnesses are from Harvard.

DERRICK. Yes, from Harvard. And they are, indeed, highly qualified. But they did not have access to all of the records according to their own depositions.

LAURA: That's not my fault.

DERRICK: No, it's not. (*Pauses*) Do you know how much an expert witness charges?

LAURA: How should I know that?

DERRICK: Between $500 and $700 an hour for around 24 hours of work. Three days of work on over 3,000 pages of evidence in this case. That's a cool $12,000 to $17,000 for their opinions. That's a lot of time and money, and yet there is not a shred of support for your allegations against Dr. Frank from our witnesses or the medical review panel.

LAURA: I don't know anything about what experts charge or what they get.

DERRICK: No, you don't. And I strongly suspect that your attorney, Mr. Davis, has not shared that information with you.

LAURA: No.

DERRICK: Thank you for your testimony, Mrs. Tatum. I have no further questions.

LAURA: (*To DERRICK*) Can you at least help me down from here?

DERRICK: Of course (*takes LAURA's hand and helps her down.*)

LAURA: (*Straightens up and pushes DERRICK away*) I can make it from here. I've had enough of your help. (*Exits limping and using the cane.*)

BLACKOUT

SCENE IV (A FEW MINUTES LATER)

> *Small office with a couple of chairs,*
> *LAURA is seated and JONATHAN*
> *paces back and forth while talking.*

JONATHAN: Laura, it's time to pull the plug on this case.

LAURA: Pull the plug?

JONATHAN: Yes, we need to end this trial, now!

LAURA: Right in the middle of the trial? The jury hasn't even heard all of the evidence?

JONATHAN: There are only two very strong defense witnesses left. It will only get worse for us, not better.

LAURA: We should at least let it go to the end. Those jurors look like nice people.

JONATHAN: Nice or not, they can still tell when a witness has lied.

LAURA: Whose lying?

JONATHAN: Mr. Sharp, Dr. Frank's attorney, impeached you several times, in case you did not notice.

LAURA: Impeached?

JONATHAN: Yes, he demonstrated that you had changed your story over time. You deviated from your previous sworn testimony in your deposition. In the juror's minds there is only one question, Mrs. Tatum, were you lying then or are you lying now? (*Pauses*) We can't win. You've lost all credibility.

LAURA: Let's give it a try, anyway.

JONATHAN: Laura, I already got rid of any prospective jurors who were educated, or had nurses or doctors in their families, or who wouldn't sue their own doctors unless they were deliberately negligent. They were all eliminated! These are simple, poor, uneducated people, but they can understand when someone has lied.

LAURA: I didn't lie! I won't lie! It's a sin and God punishes sinners.

JONATHAN: Yes, and apparently he punishes their attorneys, too. (*Pauses*) We must stop this trial now! I want to petition the court for a dismissal of this case so we can cut our losses.

LAURA: Our losses?

JONATHAN: My losses! Ten years of countless hours of legal work, $50,000 of expert witness testimony, $20,000 in other expenses. The days of travelling and depositions, motions, counter-motions, legal maneuvers. This has consumed my life for the last ten years.

LAURA: And mine? What about the impact this has had on me? Whose lawyer are you, anyway, mine or Dr. Frank's. You're going to let that negligent, lying, incompetent doctor go scot-free. He's going to walk out this courtroom on his two feet while I limp out on mine. It's not right!

JONATHAN: Has it occurred to you, Laura, that we just may have been wrong about this case?

LAURA: WRONG! By God, no! Dr. Cardinal told me to sue Dr. Frank.

JONATHAN: And where is Dr. Cardinal now?

LAURA: I don't know.

JONATHAN: I do. (*Pauses*) He's retired. He retired the year after your case got started and moved to Costa Rica or heaven knows where else. He started this little ten-year forest fire and skipped town while everything burned down.

LAURA: Did he lie?

JONATHAN: I don't know. All I can tell you is that you swallowed his story, hook, line and sinker. I swallowed your story, hook, line and sinker. And that my distinguished Harvard expert witnesses also swallowed the story hook, line and sinker. And maybe, just maybe, it wasn't even true.

LAURA: No! I don't believe that Dr. Cardinal made it up. He told me the truth. He warned me. He said that a doctor like Dr. Frank shouldn't be practicing medicine because he was bad.

JONATHAN: He's not.

LAURA: What? Dr. Frank isn't bad?

JONATHAN: Didn't you listen? Dr. Frank left clinical practice and went into administrative medicine several years ago as some kind of administrative medical director.

LAURA: Good! Good for him. So we did win!

JONATHAN: Did we? Did his other patients win, too? Did the community win by losing a busy, well-respected physician who left clinical practice and went into paper pushing? Maybe he did more good than harm when he was taking care of folks, even you?

LAURA: I don't care! I don't care about the community or his other patients or what he thinks about me. (*Looks at JONATHAN*) Go ahead, pull the plug! Stop the trial! I've already won.

JONATHAN: Did you? Did anyone? Maybe Dr. Frank's attorney did. He won a magnificent case and sent us packing with our tails between our legs. He earned a bucket load of money, so maybe he did win, but I didn't and you didn't and Dr. Frank didn't either. Dr. Frank got dragged through ten years of misery as well.

LAURA: Don't mention that monster's name again in my presence! I hope he burns in hell where he belongs. I hope he suffered each and every day of these ten long years. I hope every one of his patients suffered when he left. It's just a fraction of what I suffered. (*Points to her feet*) Look at these feet! Useless, painful, just waiting to flare up again.

JONATHAN: Maybe diabetes was the enemy all along, just like Mr. Sharp said. Maybe it's the disease and not Dr. Frank that was always the problem.

LAURA: (*Screams*) Don't mention that man's name again or I'll fire you!

JONATHAN: And start over with a new lawyer for another decade? You know you'll have some court costs to pay now, don't you?

LAURA: No.

JONATHAN: You'll have to pay around $3,000 out of pocket, your pocket.

LAURA: You're kidding.

JONATHAN: No, I'm not.

LAURA: I lose, Dr. Frank walks free, and I still have to pay?

JONATHAN: That's better than the $100,000 of my legal labor and my out-of-pocket expenses. But I guess that doesn't matter to you, does it?

LAURA: (*Coolly*) No, it doesn't. And you said no out-of-pocket expenses for me and you would get 40% of this huge settlement. That's what you said. (*Pauses.*) So I guess you lied, too.

JONATHAN: No, I didn't lie. But you did, Mrs. Tatum. You lied on the stand and sunk whatever was left of our sinking case.

LAURA: You lied! You lied, Dr. Cardinal lied, the experts lied and Dr. Frank lied. So where was the truth, Mr. hotshot lawyer? Where was the truth in these halls of justice?

JONATHAN: (*Swings his arms around in the air*) There is no truth or justice here, only settlement. And this time there wasn't even any of that. (*Pauses*) I suggest we go back into that courtroom and finish this drama.

LAURA: And if I refuse?

JONATHAN: You would have to fire me, assume all the court costs, and the bond for the physician panel, and a host of other costs. And then you would have to try and find another sucker lawyer and good luck with that. (*Reaches down and helps LAURA up*) So I suggest we go in there and conclude this tragedy (*shakes his head as he leads LAURA off stage left.*)

Lights dim. There is a solitary pool of light stage where a smiling DR. CARDINAL stands, dressed in a tropical print shirt and white pants. He is smiling and takes a swing at an imaginary golf ball. He yells "FORE!" loudly.

BLACKOUT

THE OPIOID CRISIS

PRESCRIPTION PAINKILLERS IN AMERICA: WHAT A PAIN!

Americans love their pills. The average American spends over $1,000/year on prescription medications every year, about twice that of the average European. This includes pain medications, the use of which has risen steadily since 1999 (increasing 5 times) while deaths from overdoses have followed proportionally. Opioid related deaths now top 22,000/year (2015) or 62 deaths per day. Even within the United States, some places seem to be habitual over-consumers, with painkiller prescriptions three times higher in Florida (reporting the highest use) than in Illinois (reporting the lowest use.) Louisiana is 7th among states for prescriptions of opioid painkillers (over 7 kg/10,000 population) and is in the top third of states for drug overdose death rates (19/100,000 population) in 2015.

The problem, however, is not limited to prescription pain drugs for legitimate use, but spills over into an epidemic of non-medical use as well. In Louisiana, non-medical use of opioids increased over four times from 2004-2011 (from 1.5 to 5.9/100,000). In fact, 12 million Americans engaged in non-medical use of prescription painkillers in 2010, or one out of twenty people over 12 years of age. And ER visits for drug overdoses went up 153% from 2004 to 2011.

The financial cost of opioid use and abuse is substantial. Estimates vary between $25 and $78 billion per year for the U.S. and include 22,000 deaths (2015) and over 500,000 emergency room visits, numbers that have risen annually. Louisiana's costs alone exceed $300 million/year. The phenomenon of overdosing with painkillers strikes certain groups disproportionately. Men die from overdose more often than women. Middle-aged adults overdose more than other age group. Whites and Native Americans overdose more than other ethnic groups. Rural Americans overdose more than twice as often as city dwellers. This is of particular importance to our rural parishes in Central Louisiana.

The availability of painkillers has reached epidemic proportions. "Pill mills," where doctors make easy fortunes by prescribing inappropriate quantities of pain medications to inappropriate clients, have proliferated across the United States, particularly in Florida. Although there have been attempts to better track the use and abuse of painkillers, the creativity of the criminal element, notably among unscrupulous physicians, results in a constant stream of pain pills for recreational use.

What can you do as an individual? Use painkillers only as prescribed, do not share or sell them to others and always keep them locked up. Young people have "pill parties," where they bring assorted medications, notably painkillers, to a party and consume them by the handful along with immoderate amounts of alcohol. The results, of course, can be catastrophic.

Healthcare providers should prescribe painkillers judiciously. Although it often takes more time to explain why addictive pain medications should not be used than to write a prescription, it does no good to add addiction to a patient's list of chronic medical problems. Prescriptions should be limited in time and quantity and habitual users should be drug tested. State governments can improve their prescription monitoring systems, and, with the cooperation of licensing boards such as the Louisiana State Board of Medical Examiners, identify and prosecute those who prescribe inappropriately. States can provide better treatment programs for substance abuse at the community level. The mandatory use of the state's Prescription Monitoring Program (or PMP, sponsored by the Louisiana Board of Pharmacy) by both pharmacists and physicians would help. The Louisiana PMP shares data with surrounding states, which helps eliminate doctor shopping.

Pain medications can be true painkillers, resulting in the death of those who use them. It is the responsibility of individuals, healthcare providers and governmental entities to cooperate in addressing this epidemic. If you have a problem with pain medication, call 1-800-662-HELP. If you want more information about the problem, go to www. cdc.gov/vitalsigns and click on "Prescription Painkiller Overdoses in the US."

HIGH TEA

CHARACTERS

ALICIA MAE BASS: Older woman (may be Black, White, Asian or Hispanic). Joey's grandmother.

JOEY LEE BASS: Young man, older high school. Casually dressed. Casual speech pattern. Alicia's grandson.

FREDDIE: Young friend of JOEY. Casually dressed. Some flashy jewelry or watch. Slick and manipulative.

DONALD HARTFORD: Older middle-aged doctor. Pretentious and overbearing. Casually dressed in chic-casual (i.e. Brooks Brothers shirt and designer jeans.)

CHRISTINA HARTFORD: Donald's wife. Very attractive middle-aged woman, also in casual chic, nice jewelry, perhaps Mignon Faget or David Yurman.

SETTING

Varies with Scene.

SCENE I

Humble home. ALICIA is sorting clothing. JOEY struts around, playing with a cell phone that he looks at from time to time.

JOEY: Why do you even work for those stuck-up people?

ALICIA: The Hartfords pay very well for light work. They treat me nicely and they give us things they don't want or need anymore. Sometimes they're brand new things.

JOEY: Things they don't want any more? Why would you want them either? You can buy nice, new clothes, Grandma. Don't waste your time with hand-me-down trash (*picks up a piece of clothing and throws back down.*)

ALICIA: (*Picks up the clothing*) It is not trash and if we can't use it, I'm sure the folks down at the church can find someone who needs it.

JOEY: For the homeless?

ALICIA: Yes, for the homeless. And what's wrong with that?

JOEY: Because those guys are a bunch of zoned out old drunks with PTSD.

ALICIA: Some are vets, but all the more reason to help them out. They fought for our country and we owe them our respect, even the down-and-out ones.

JOEY: Nobody in their right mind would fight for this country. Black and Hispanic kids get shot every day in Iraq and Afghanistan for nothing. Now, that's a real crime!

ALICIA: (*Sifting through the clothing. Pulls out a designer shirt.*) This shirt is in really good shape. It's a Brooks Brothers shirt. That's not trash.

JOEY: (*Glances at the label*) Bet it cost $200 at least, for a stupid dress shirt. (*Throws it down*) Give it to some homeless drunk down on Lower Third. Maybe he'd appreciate it, but I don't. I can buy that kind of thing if I wanted to, but I'd rather have something else.

ALICIA: What? And with what money?

JOEY: I have lots of money. (*Pulls out a wad of cash.*)

ALICIA: Where did you get that kind of money?

JOEY: (*Puts the money back*) I earned it?

ALICIA: How?

JOEY: None of your business.

ALICIA: Joey Lee Bass, it is my business as long as you're living in my house and eating my food.

JOEY: I'm working part time after school.

ALICIA: Part time? Doing what? Dealing dope with those no good so-called friends of yours.

JOEY: No! I'm tutoring some kids who aren't doing as well as I am in school.

ALICIA: What subject?

JOEY: Math.

ALICIA: Who are you tutoring?

JOEY: Nobody you'd know.

ALICIA: I know everyone in your school and their parents and their grandparents, too. Give me a few names. I'll tell you who they are and how they're related.

JOEY: It's none of your business!

ALICIA: (*Softly*) Don't get involved in dope. We've been down that road with your momma and she's dead. (*Pauses*) Nothing good comes of it. And I'll be damned if I'll watch you go that way, too. (*Hugs JOEY*) You're all I have now, baby, please don't go down that road.

JOEY: (*Hugs her back*) Grandma, you know I love you. I wouldn't do anything to hurt you, not on purpose anyway. I'm smarter than that.

ALICIA: Then stop selling dope or stealing or whatever gives you a heap of money with no work. (*Hugs JOEY again*) I love you too much to lose you. Promise me! Promise me you won't sell dope or take dope or have anything to do with dope. Please, promise me!

JOEY: (*Pulls away*) Okay. I promise. But I don't want to be poor like you and have to clean some rich people's house!

ALICIA: Then study hard and get a college degree. Get some degree employers need all over the country. You can pick your own job and leave this place if you don't want to live here. I'll die one day and you can fly off to Seattle or Houston or Boston or wherever.

JOEY: (*Hugs ALICIA*) Okay, Grandma. I'll be an engineer, or a doctor, or a computer programmer or something really fancy. You'll see. And I won't be leaving anytime soon. You and I are a team. We're as good as married, Grandma, just like husband and wife, 'til death do us part.

ALICIA: Don't talk like that. We're not married. We're not dead and I certainly don't intend to die any time soon. We Basses live a long time, except your momma, of course. Your great grandma lived to be a 102 and she still had all her teeth, all her hair and all her wits.

JOEY: Open your mouth?

ALICIA: Why?

JOEY: I want to see if you still have all of your teeth. Because you sure still have all of your wits.

ALICIA: (*Scoffs*) What a clever boy, you are. Just like your grandpa. Always cracking a joke and making people laugh.

JOEY: Okay, Grandma, is church over? Are you done with your preaching? Can I go now?

ALICIA: Yes, but I want you to take these clothes down to the Salvation Army. They always need clothes for those poor people.

JOEY: (*Takes the bag*) Okay, but I still think you ought to get a better job than cleaning house for the Hartfords. Maybe you should go back to school and be a nurse or a doctor or an engineer. No fooling. You're smart, too.

ALICIA: Get out of here before I smack your behind. And pull up those jeans, too. You are not a hoodlum and you don't live in the hood, by the grace of God and your grandpa's and my hard work.

> *JOEY exits. ALICIA picks up a picture of her dead daughter.*

ALICIA: Such a beautiful girl. Such a terrible waste. (*Looks heavenward*) Jesus, deliver us from evil!

BLACKOUT

SCENE II

An alleyway or park with a bench and garbage can. Minimal set elements. JOEY and FREDDIE are standing and talking. FREDDIE shows JOEY a box.

JOEY: What is it?

FREDDIE: Patches, fentanyl patches.

JOEY: What are they good for?

FREDDIE: This stuff sends you on the highest of highs for a long time. It's Vicodan and Oxycontin and heroin all mixed up into one.

JOEY: I don't know. It's nothing I want to sell, especially if you have to shoot it up.

FREDDIE: It comes in pills, too, but that's a lot harder to get and you don't ever know about the strength. No, this stuff isn't for selling. Hell no! I'm talking about using it for us.

JOEY: How do you use it? Put it on your skin or smoke it or lick it off?

FREDDIE: You can put it on your skin, but that's super slow. Or you melt it off and shoot it up. (*Pauses*) Unbelievable high.

JOEY: I heard about this fentanyl stuff. They mix it up with heroin and it's so strong it sends people straight into a coma. Then they have to inject them with something. Some antidote? Naloxone, maybe? Or something like that so people start breathing again.

FREDDIE: That's a bunch of shit! That happens to people who don't know what they're doing. Besides, you're talking about carfentanil, that's off the street stuff that's a thousand times stronger than fentanyl. They use it for animals, but nobody knows the strength when it comes in the pills. Now these patches, that's another thing entirely. It's a legit prescription medicine and I know the strength. No danger, just a high of a lifetime. You never want to come down.

JOEY: (*Hesitates*) I don't know. I don't want to be a statistic. Besides, I told my grandma I wouldn't do drugs. If something happened to me, she'd die. I swear she'd drop dead. She wants me to be a doctor or a lawyer or an engineer or something.

FREDDIE: An engineer? Like on a train?

JOEY: No, of course not.

FREDDIE: What do you care about what may happen in the distant future? Something you have to work for and study for year after year? You should care about here and now and getting so high it takes a rope to pull you back down to earth. (*Pauses*) What's an engineer do besides drive trains?

JOEY: An engineer is someone who's good with numbers. They design roads and work with machines or computers. I'm good at math. And they make a lot of money too.

FREDDIE: (*Laughs*) Listen to you. Your grandma really has you brainwashed. You're already making a ton of money right here and now. You get the other guys at school to buy and I give you a big cut. No hassle, no risk, no problem. What's there not to like about that? And there's no library, no books, no studying, no exams. It's cool. You don't have to think about some distant future. It's here and now. It's nirvana up there when you're high. (*Pauses*) If you want to use or not, that's your business. I don't force no one to use. But you're really missing something and it's right here, right now, right in front of you.

JOEY: (*Looks at the patches*) Where'd you get these, anyway?

FREDDIE: From a doctor, of course. (*Grabs his knee and starts moaning*) Oh, doctor! I have this awful pain in my knee and it just won't go away. I got injured playing football and I have already tried heat and physical therapy and a knee brace and all of those over-the-counter meds. Doc, you got to help me! I can't sleep. I can't study. I can't even walk around school. It's really effecting my education. You've got to help me, doc. (*Straightens up*) See. It's that easy. Then I go to the next doctor and the next and pretty soon I've got a half a dozen prescriptions. Those doctors are dumb as rock. (*Pauses*) Every once in awhile, one of the docs or the pharmacists checks some sort of electronic list and tells me I've had too many prescriptions. But most of the time, those doctors can't resist a cash paying customer. I pay, I get the prescription, I get the patches. Easy as that! (*Holds up a bag*) Look at them all. This is plenty enough for a high tea. More than enough, in fact.

JOEY: What do you mean? What's a "high tea?"

FREDDIE: (*Laughs*) Just a play on words. The real "high tea" is some stupid charity event my mom goes to every year with her society friends. She pays a bunch of money, too. I wish she'd give me the money instead. I'd know what to do with it.

JOEY: What charity?

FREDDIE: Who cares!

JOEY: I care! My grandma says charity is love incarnate.

FREDDIE: Love incarnate? Wow, you're grandma is something. Didn't know she was a preacher woman. (*Pauses*) Anyway, it's for battered women! Can you believe it? They collect this money and give it to a shelter for all the battered bitches that get beaten up by their husbands or boyfriends. (*Pauses*) I'm sure they all deserve it. Every woman's a prick teaser!

JOEY: Not my grandma.

FREDDIE: Who would want to bang your old grandma? That's perverted.

JOEY: Shut up! She raised me after my momma overdosed and died. I never knew my dad.

FREDDIE: Oh, so that's it? That's why you don't want to get high? You're afraid you'll die like your momma.

JOEY: Shut up! I'm not afraid. Maybe I've just got more sense than you do.

FREDDIE: (*Laughs*) More sense eh? (*Pulls out a wad of bills*) Check this out! Check out these cents, bad boy! There's a thousand in my pocket. Maybe two thousand. (*Stuffs the money back in his pocket*) Who's got the sense now? (*Pauses*) Maybe you have the cents, but I have the dollars. (*Handles the fentanyl patches*) So what do you say? You want to try some or not? You wanna live now, or maybe you just want to wait to be a fucking engineer? (*Pokes JOEY*) Toot! Toot!

JOEY: (*Pulls away*) Stop it!

FREDDIE: A patch in the hand is worth two in the bush. What do you say? Ready for a really high tea? A super high tea? You want to try it, or you just chicken shit?

JOEY: I've never been afraid of anything and I ain't afraid now.

BLACKOUT

SCENE III

> *DONALD and CHRISTINA's lovely upscale home. Oriental carpet. Dining room or card table covered with silverware. CHRISTINA is sorting through the silverware and polishing one or another piece. DONALD is standing nearby.*

DONALD: I really don't want to!

CHRISTINA: Why not?

DONALD: Because we shouldn't be opening our home for a "high tea" so every Tom, Dick and Harry can gawk over our silverware and home furnishings. Carlotta and Peter do that crap all the time and it's disgusting.

CHRISTINA: It's charitable and they're extremely generous with their time and money. (*Pauses*) Besides, there's not likely to be just any Toms, Dicks or Harrys attending a high tea for the battered women's shelter. In fact, I suspect they're will not be any men at all. Also, at $50 a ticket, there are not likely to be any low-life poor white trash, either, if that's what you're worried about.

DONALD: (*Laughs*) Yeah, that's good. You're criticizing the poor white trash and that's who's going to benefit from this event.

CHRISTINA: That's not true! Battered women come from all social classes. Carlotta just got beaten up by her high-minded husband and they can hardly be called poor white trash, now can they?

DONALD: Really? Peter beat up Carlotta? I thought he was such a noble, idealistic guy and they were the perfect couple?

CHRISTINA: He is a noble, idealistic guy, when he's not drunk. And he sure did, and now he's got a court order slapped against him, plus mandated anger management classes. Serves him right, the hypocrite bastard!

DONALD: What did Carlotta do to deserve it?

CHRISTINA: (*Frowns and ignores the question. Hands DONALD some silverware*) Could you look at these and see which ones Alicia needs to polish.

DONALD: (*Takes the silverware and begins to sort it out*) I asked you what Carlotta did to deserve it? She really must have provoked him.

CHRISTINA: (*Angrily*) Why does the woman always have to do something?

DONALD: No one just punches out his wife for the hell of it, especially the saintly Dr. Peter Frank.

CHRISTINA: You'd be surprised.

DONALD: (*Holds up a spoon*) This will be a tempting little souvenir for some tea drinking social climber. By the way, did I ever agree to this high tea fundraiser?

CHRISTINA: I already told the women's shelter committee that we would be delighted to host this worthy event. They're sure to have a sellout and make a bunch of money.

DONALD: (*Slams down the spoon*) I never agreed! I don't care if they are the social elite of this town! They want to see what we have on the walls, our rugs, the furniture, the landscaping. That's all. It's a freak show! Social voyeurism! An open house for the wannabes who never will be!

CHRISTINA: And who wouldn't be proud of a 10,000 square foot mansion, filled with handcrafted furniture, original art and gorgeous antiques? And why shouldn't we be proud of what we have accomplished in this town?

DONALD: We?

CHRISTINA: Yes, we! We're a team, remember?

DONALD: Yeah, one who makes the money and one who spends it!

CHRISTINA: (*Shakes a fork at DONALD*) That's insulting and you know it. I work very hard.

DONALD: (*Looks at the table of silverware*) Lot's of these need polishing.

CHRISTINA: So do you! With wealth comes social obligation. Why do you think I get invited to serve on every charitable board in the city? Why do you think we get invited to exclusive social events and every imaginable fundraiser?

DONALD: Because they all want our money!

CHRISTINA: And we have it! (*Puts a fork in a pile to be polished*) Lord, this stuff tarnishes whatever you do.

DONALD: What about using stainless steel utensils?

CHRISTINA: (*Waves a fork at DONALD*) Don't be ridiculous! This is a high tea in our mansion, not a Piccadilly buffet. We need fifty silver sets, forty at the least for this high tea. Maybe I can borrow a few sets from Carlotta. They won't be doing any entertaining any time soon and she's still in their home, at least for now.

DONALD: You never answered me. Why did she get smacked?

CHRISTINA: Some stupidity about money.

DONALD: Not sex?

CHRISTINA: (*Passing him more silverware*) Do you know something I don't? Did Peter say something to you?

DONALD: No, I just know there are two things that sabotage marriages, sex and money, usually both.

Doorbell rings.

CHRISTINA: Thank God, Alicia is finally here. We have a thousand things to do before the high tea.

DONALD: That I never ever agreed to.

CHRISTINA: But you will . . . . *noblesse oblige.*

DONALD: No Bless O Bleege?

CHRISTINA: Yes, the social responsibility of the aristocracy.

DONALD: Yes, the aristocracy of wealth, the older, the better.

CHRISTINA: Precisely!

Doorbell rings again. CHRISTINA goes to open the door.

DONALD: OKAY! But if so much as one silver butter knife goes missing, I swear I'll never allow this home to be opened again to anyone outside the family. Do you hear me!

CHRISTINA: Coming! Finish sorting that silverware so Alicia can get started.

> *CHRISTINA and ALICIA come in. ALICIA is clutching a handbag and is still wearing a light coat, not working clothing. CHRISTINA and ALICIA come to the table.*

CHRISTINA: Oh Alicia, thank heavens you're here. We have so much to do! That high tea event is this Sunday. You need to polish the silverware, wash the crystal glasses, iron the tableclothes, and clean the bathrooms. It's endless and we only have a couple of days left.

ALICIA: Ma'am, I came here to tell you I'm quitting.

CHRISTINA and DONALD: (*Both stop*) QUITTING?

ALICIA: Yes ma'am, yes sir. You have been very nice to me, but I can't work here any more after what happened.

CHRISTINA: What are you talking about? Aren't we paying you enough? Have you been mistreated in any way? (*Looks at DONALD.*)

ALICIA: No, no! Nothing like that. You've been very generous with me.

DONALD: Then what?

ALICIA: I just can't talk about it.

CHRISTINA: Alicia Mae Bass, four years we've given you steady employment, good wages, enough used clothing to fill a Goodwill store and you "can't talk about it?" (*Pauses*) I'm sorry, but you owe us an explanation.

ALICIA: I'd really rather not talk about it.

DONALD: Alicia, we have a right to know. You've been treated like family and that's not the way family treats family.

ALICIA: No, sir, it is not.

> *CHRISTINA and DONALD put down the silverware and offer ALICIA a chair. CHRISTINA and DONALD remain standing and ALICIA sits down.*

ALICIA: My grandson died.

CHRISTINA: Joey?

ALICIA: (*Nods. Begins to cry*) Yes, ma'am.

DONALD: What happened?

ALICIA: (*Looks at DONALD*) Drug overdose.

CHRISTINA: (*Goes over and comforts ALICIA*) I'm so sorry.

ALICIA: I raised that child since he was a baby. He was a good boy, a hard working boy, a smart boy.

DONALD: Drugs! What a tragedy.

ALICIA: He and a buddy got hold of a bunch of them pain patches, the strong ones. His friend and him figured out how to melt them down and inject them. Joey wasn't used to that. He didn't have any tolerance. He just stopped breathing and that other kid ran away and left him to die.

DONALD: Patches? Fentanyl patches?

ALICIA: Yeah, that's them! They had 20 of those patches.

DONALD: Twenty patches! That's insane. Where'd they get that many pain patches at one time?

ALICIA: (*Pauses*) From you, Dr. Hartford.

DONALD: What! No way! I never prescribe more than a box of three at a time.

ALICIA: That other boy had four boxes of five patches each, all with your name on them.

DONALD: Impossible! There's some mistake.

ALICIA: No, sir! There is no mistake. That boy had prescriptions for so-called sports injuries. He got seen at your fancy new clinic. That kid was dealing and he hooked other kids with your drugs! (*Angrily*) You're no better than those low-life pushers down on Lee Street, but you live in a big fancy house (*swings her arms around*) and have high teas for poor ladies that aren't ever going to amount to anything.

CHRISTINA: Alicia, you're upset. I think you'd better go home. (*Takes a $100 bill out of her purse and hands it to ALICIA*) Here's a hundred dollars. Buy some nice flowers for the funeral.

ALICIA: (*Shakes her head*) I'm not taking any more of your money, ma'am. It's blood money. It's covered with the blood of my Joey and I won't touch it, not here, not anywhere, never so long as I'm breathing.

CHRISTINA: (*To DONALD*) Donald, say something!

DONALD: I follow the strictest professional guidelines for everything I do, especially the prescription of pain medication, Mrs. Bass. I help people. I don't hurt them and I certainly don't kill anyone.

ALICIA: You killed my grandson! You killed Joey. That's all I know. Your drugs killed my boy and I'm never going to forget it for the rest of my life. I hope God forgives you, because I won't.

DONALD: (*Approaches ALICIA*) I'm so sorry for you.

ALICIA: (*Pushes DONALD away*) Not near sorry enough! Don't you dare touch me! I've seen your office, that fancy new building. It looks like the Wal-Mart parking lot, jammed with poor folks, rich folks, kids, adults, old people. All them people wanting their dope and you're in there writing away your prescriptions, making more money than God. You're not a doctor; you're a drug lord! I never want to see you or this monstrous big house ever again. You need to go to hell where you belong! (*Stands to leave.*)

CHRISTINA: Alicia, you're upset. Please let me show you out.

ALICIA: No, ma'am! I can see myself out. I know the way out. I know this place. (*Exits. Door closes.*)

CHRISTINA: (*Looks at the silverware*) I think we need to cancel the event.

DONALD: (*Angrily*) No way in hell! We have got to put this on and show everyone that I run a legitimate business and that business built this house and that we play an important role in this society. No! We are not cancelling the damn high tea. I'll polish the silver myself.

CHRISTINA: Please, I can't do it. All I would think about was Alicia and her grandson.

DONALD: Shut up! That boy took that medication. He took it and he died. He and his grandmother and his family all have to take responsibility for their actions, too. I'm a doctor not a drug lord. What happens to those prescriptions when irresponsible people do crazy things is none of my business. I have safeguards in place against this sort of thing. But clever and unscrupulous people will find a way, regardless of what I do. That's God's truth. (*Picks up a spoon*) Take this spoon and polish it! If Alicia's going to run out on us, then we'll do it ourselves.

CHRISTINA: (*Pushes away the spoon*) Please, leave me alone. This makes me sick to my stomach. She's a lovely lady. I don't know what to think.

DONALD: (*More menacing*) Take this spoon, this rag and polish, damn it! I want this spoon to sparkle. I want this house to sparkle so that every miserable grasping, struggling social climber knows what it means to be rich.

CHRISTINA: What does it mean?

DONALD: You said it. NO BLESS O BLEEGE! That's it, isn't it? The social responsibility of the rich toward the poor! That's what we're doing this for isn't it. NO BLESS O BLEEGE.

CHRISTINA: (*Meekly*) Yes.

DONALD: (*Screaming*) NO BLESS O BLEEGE! Repeat it so I can hear you!

CHRISTINA: Donald, please. You're scaring me.

DONALD: REPEAT IT, DAMN YOU!

CHRISTINA: (*Whimpering*) Noblesse *oblige*.

DONALD: LOUDER!

CHRISTINA: (*Whispers*) Noblesse *oblige*.

DONALD: That's not loud enough, dammit!

> *DONALD strikes CHRISTINA.*
> *CHRISTINA falls to the ground.*
> *DONALD remains standing, a*
> *silver serving spoon in his hands,*
> *held up triumphantly.*

DONALD: (*Continues holding up the spoon up and yells*) NO BLESS O
BLEEGE! (*A spotlight shines on the spoon and then fades.*)

BLACKOUT

SUDDEN INFANT DEATH AND BREAST-FEEDING

SUDDEN UNEXPLAINED INFANT DEATH SYNDROME (SUIDS): AN OFTEN PREVENTABLE TRAGEDY

Sudden Unexplained Infant Death Syndrome (SUIDS) refers to the unexpected death of a child less than one year of age. SUIDS includes SIDS (Sudden Infant Deaths) (45%), unknown causes (31%) and accidental suffocation and strangulation (25%). The loss of a child is a terrible tragedy from which parents never completely recover. It is out of the natural order of things for children to die before their parents, a fact which intensifies both the length and severity of grieving when an infant dies.

SUIDS is not a rare phenomenon, with over 3,500 babies dying each year, 80 in Louisiana alone. Central Louisiana has the sad distinction of being ranked number one in SIDS (1.9/1,000 live births) of all of the Louisiana public health regions. Although it is impossible to completely eliminate sudden infant deaths, there are some clear risk factors that can be reduced or eliminated.

First, babies should be placed to sleep on their backs (not on their stomachs), on a firm mattress, without pillows, cushions, toys or bumper pads. This may seem like a sad and unfriendly sleeping environment for the infant, but it is the best and safest one and has been shown to reduce the risk of SIDS. The infant should be dressed in light clothing in a comfortable (not over-heated) room.

Second, co-sleeping, a tradition in many families, increases the risk of infant death by unintentional smothering. Some well-intentioned mothers will engage in breast-feeding (a very positive action) in bed lying down (a poor location). Falling asleep in such a position by an exhausted mother can prove fatal to your infant.

Third, premature and low birth weight babies are more susceptible to SIDS. Every effort should be made to reduce prematurity through appropriate spacing of children, avoiding teenage pregnancy, and eliminating smoking. Young smoking mothers with multiple children are at higher risk for prematurity and the sudden infant death that might result.

Smoking is an independent risk factor for SIDS, whether it is the mother or others in the household. Smoking cessation will help not only the adults, but also the infant and other children in the household. The state offers a number of programs including the tobacco cessation Quitline (1-800-QUIT-NOW) and www.QuitwithUsLa.org. National programs also exist. While smoking rates in the United States have decreased over the last decades, they still remain high in Louisiana.

Position baby to sleep on the back, no co-sleeping, a firm, empty crib, no smoking, and avoiding teenage pregnancy are the five pillars of reducing SIDS. There will always be the rare infant who dies an unexplained death, but we should do what we can to reduce risk factors that have been shown to increase it. Even one avoidable infant death is too many.

BREAST-FEEDING AND LOUISIANA: ROOM FOR IMPROVEMENT

Whether you are a parent, grandparent, or just a casual observer, nothing evokes the tenderness of motherhood more than breastfeeding. Although not all women succeed in breastfeeding, the benefits for newborns are astonishing. Breastfeeding reduces infections, reduces the risk of sudden infant death, and even reduces the risks of infant and child obesity. It also reduces maternal risks of breast and ovarian cancers.

Despite all of these documented advantages, only around 56% of Louisiana women initiate breastfeeding. Only 20% continue at six months and barely 10% make it to a year. This contrasts with national statistics of 75% initiation, 43% at 6 months and 22% at one year. The statistics for African-American women in Louisiana are disproportionately less. Only 30% of African-American women initiate breastfeeding, while only 13% continue at 6 months and less than 5% continue until a year.

This racial disparity in breastfeeding is not unique to Louisiana. Nationally, only 60% of African-Americans initiate breastfeed, only 28% continue at 6 months and around 13% continue to a year. The reasons for this racial disparity are not clear, but it is worse in Louisiana than in the United States in general. African-Americans in Louisiana breast-feed at only about half the rates of African-Americans nationally.

Breastfeeding, despite its obvious advantages, faces obstacles of social acceptance, workplace accommodations, and inadequate support in the family and at all levels of medical intervention. While Louisiana has five "Baby-Friendly" birthing hospital facilities as of 2015 (as opposed to Nebraska with over 20% of all birthing hospitals) (www. babyfriendlyusa.org), it also has THE GIFT program, which certifies hospitals that implement successful practices related to infant feeding and maternal-infant bonding. There are currently 29 GIFT Certified birthing facilities in 2016 in Louisiana.

To increase the number of mothers who breast-feed, hospitals should have a written breastfeeding policy, with buy-in and training for all personnel. Mothers should be assisted in breastfeeding, initiated within an hour of birth. Mothers and infants should remain together if at all possible and the infant should feed on demand. Supplemental feeding and pacifiers should be avoided. Such a comprehensive program has proven successful in "Baby-Friendly" and GIFT facilities. Support groups for lactating mothers should be encouraged.

Breastfeeding education should also be introduced with pre-natal care and continued through the hospital experience and into the pediatricians' offices or Office of Public Health (or other WIC providers). Persistent, coordinated education and support, especially to better include the African-American community, should help improve breastfeeding statistics in Louisiana. Enhanced infant and maternal health will inevitably follow.

Older adults can play a critical role in encouraging their children and grandchildren to initiate breastfeeding. Once started, supportive family can help to encourage breast feeders to continue as long as possible. Infants, their mothers and our society as a whole are all beneficiaries of breast-feeding. Breast is best!

KNITTING PREMIE CAPS

CAST OF CHARACTERS

PAULA: Young woman with a newborn baby

ELINOR: Paula's mother, a woman in her forties to fifties

NOTE: The ethnicity is not defined and may be any race.

SETTING

There are a couple of chairs and a crib, which is in the center of the stage.

> *PAULA puts the "baby" into the crib on its back. ELINOR is knitting a premie cap for a premature child.*

ELINOR: Well, aren't you going to turn the baby over on its tummy?

PAULA: No, Mama. It's supposed to be on its back.

> *ELINOR stands and reaches in to turn the baby over. PAULA grabs ELINOR's hand and stops her.*

PAULA (CONT): No! It's supposed to be on its back. Back to sleep! That's what the visiting nurse says.

ELINOR: (*Pulls back her hand*) Why I never! Who told you such a silly thing?

PAULA: The visiting nurse, I said.

ELINOR: Well, she's wrong! I raised five children, including you, and they all slept on their stomachs. That's the natural way. It keeps them from spitting up and swallowing their vomit. Everyone knows that.

PAULA: That's changed. Now it's "back to sleep" and the nurse told me so.

ELINOR: You believe some silly stranger over your own mother?

PAULA: (*Hesitates*) Yes, in this case, I do. It's based on research.

ELINOR: I suppose she's told you other lies and misinformation.

PAULA: Like what?

ELINOR: Like you should breast-feed until your tits fall off. And that you shouldn't sleep with your baby.

PAULA: Funny you should mention that. I am breast-feeding and I don't sleep with my baby.

ELINOR: See! I told you!

PAULA: So what?

ELINOR: You've been getting a pack of lies. You need to bond with your baby. Sleeping with it gives you that skin-to-skin touch you both need. And breast-feeding is okay, but not for months. (*Points to her own breasts.*) Look at these disasters! I'm ashamed to go out and when I do, I have to wear some super support bras just to keep these droopers off the floor. It's horrible.

PAULA: You breastfed for a year or more for all us kids, at least that's what you told me.

ELINOR: Yes, because I was too poor to buy formula and they didn't give it out like they do nowadays. Times were tough back then and we didn't have the choice. It was breastfeed or have your baby starve. It's not like that anymore. You got WIC.

PAULA: (*Ignores ELINOR and puts the baby to her breast*) I plan on nursing as long as I possibly can. And I don't care what it does to my breasts.

ELINOR: You may not care, but what about Darren. Do you think he's going to want to stick around and worship your body when you look like some African villager with her floppy boobs hanging down to her belly button?

PAULA: Darren loves me!

ELINOR: That's what your father said, too, until he ran out on all of us.

PAULA: Darren is not like that.

ELINOR: Really, so why hasn't he married you yet. It's his baby, isn't it?

PAULA: Of course it's his! (*Pauses*) He hasn't married me because we both value our independence. He and I want some space in our togetherness, so we can grow.

ELINOR: Yes, and I bet he fills that space with a little something on the side while you're raising his kid.

PAULA: Shut up! You're just jealous because Papa left you.

ELINOR: (*Continues to knit a cap*) Maybe. Maybe not. (*Pauses*) By the way, have you been tested for syphilis and HIV?

PAULA: You are disgusting!

ELINOR: Am I? I just read that the largest group of new HIV cases is in heterosexual women and that we've got the highest rates of HIV and STDs in the whole country right here in Louisiana.

PAULA: Read from where? The Daily Inquirer?

ELINOR: No, from an article in the newspaper, our local newspaper.

PAULA: Mama, don't make me believe you have started reading scientific articles anywhere. You're barely literate.

ELINOR: That's mean and untrue. I got through "Fifty Shades of Gray" and all of the "Twilight" series, too.

PAULA: Right! The movie versions.

ELINOR: Well, I saw them. And I'll be seeing the film of the "Fifty Shades of Gray" as soon as I can.

PAULA: So who told you about the HIV numbers? And anyway, all pregnant women are tested for syphilis and HIV and I'm negative for both, in case you're interested.

ELINOR: Good! I'm glad to hear it. Just make sure Darren gets tested regular, too. You never know what the cat drags home after a night on the town.

PAULA: Speaking of cats, did you every get rid of that horrible yellow cat of yours, the one with a blind eye and the missing right ear?

ELINOR: No, Baxter and I are doing quite well together, thank you for asking.

PAULA: Well, I can't do any more housesitting until you do get rid of him. The litter box might be filled with toxoplasmosis. And I might be getting pregnant again soon.

ELINOR: Why?

PAULA: I like being pregnant. I like breastfeeding. And I like to get my welfare check.

ELINOR: Breastfeeding prevents pregnancy.

PAULA: Not always. Besides, I thought you wanted me to stop so my breasts would stay firm and beautiful.

ELINOR: Honey, birth control pills do the trick or them IUDs, and besides, I did breastfeeding and it didn't stop me from getting pregnant with your brother.

PAULA: Which brother?

ELINOR: The one I aborted.

PAULA: I didn't know you did that.

ELINOR: There are a lot of things you don't know about me. (*Pauses in her knitting*) So what about sharing the bed with the baby. That's bad now, too? Eh?

PAULA: It's a leading cause of infant death, rollovers. We'll second to abortion, of course, but that isn't any accident, is it?

ELINOR: No mother would roll over on her new baby.

PAULA: It happens all the time. Just like abortions, if that's what you really had.

ELINOR: Just like vomiting and aspiration pneumonia when you put babies on their backs. Aspiration, heard of that?

PAULA: Why did you get an abortion?

ELINOR: The child had con-gen-i-tal malformations. It almost didn't have a brain and its heart was malformed. There was no way I was going to inflict that on you or myself. Besides, it was not going to be able to live.

PAULA: Love is not an infliction.

ELINOR: I could not offer that kind of time and energy to a handicapped child at the expense of time I needed to spend with you.

PAULA: He was one of God's children.

ELINOR: Yes, one of God's children. (*Pauses*) But I can't solve the world's problems, face up or face down.

PAULA: (*Looks at what ELINOR is knitting*) What are you knitting? It looks like a sock.

ELINOR: It's a premie cap.

PAULA: What for?

ELINOR: I do it for the children's hospital. It helps those teeny tiny babies who are born premature to keep in their body heat. (*Holds up the cap*) Not much to look at, but they work good and it saves the hospital some money. I can make two or three a day if I'm not doing anything else.

PAULA: That's a nice thing to do.

ELINOR: Thank you. I'm a nice person.

PAULA: (*Hugs ELINOR*) I know, Mama, you mean well, but you just haven't kept up with the times.

ELINOR: Perhaps you're right. Maybe breast-feeding and back to sleep and are both good. Maybe co-sleeping is bad. But I still slept with you, cradled you in my arms and dreamed of the family we were never going to have. I wanted you to have two parents and a stable address and no moving and turbulence and evictions. (*Pauses.*) I wanted you kids to have a better life than I had. And I think you got it, at least most of it.

PAULA: Mama, you gave me a wonderful childhood. I didn't even think about those things then and now I have a baby of my own. Who cares if I'm on welfare?

ELINOR: Lots of people do. When you go to the supermarket and pull out your welfare card. You'll get all those mean, ugly stares. And when you try and get an apartment and you have to live in HUD housing. That ain't no picnic either.

PAULA: I won't care as long as my baby has food and we have a clean, safe place to live. I'll go back to school and get a good job and you can take care of my baby while I get my diploma and a really nice highpaying career.

ELINOR: Yes, that would be right nice. And maybe Darren can marry you and be a decent, God-fearing man who supports his wife and child. Maybe that'll happen, too. (*Pauses.*) You should learn to make these things (*holds up the premie cap.*)

PAULA: Sure, why not? It's a nice thing to do. Give me that. (*Takes the knitting needles and the yarn*) How do you start?

ELINOR: You take the needles like this and catch onto the loops of yarn, like this.

Lights dim.

BLACKOUT

MANAGED CARE:
A BRAVE NEW WORLD

THE ALPHABET SOUP OF CHANGE: ACA, CCN, ACO, CSOC AND MACRA

In this era of dramatic changes in the medical landscape, the average citizen is bombarded with a series of acronyms, all essential to an understanding of our healthcare transformations.

The United States, alone among developed countries, still has a significant percentage of uninsured citizens. Although the number has dropped from 14% of the population to less than 9% with the advent of Obamacare, decreasing the number of uninsured is still a laudable goal, achieved by almost all other developed countries. Yet two major problems arise: First, the cost of medical care in the United States consumes 18% of the gross national product and represents 3 trillion dollars a year. Second, many physicians have been unwilling to accept Medicaid patients, leaving them technically insured, but still without access to regular medical care.

The first acronym is **ACA** or the Affordable Care Act. It is a complex document, referred to as "Obamacare." It does many things, but one of the most important for Louisiana was an increase in the number of insured patients. Provisions for Medicaid expansion, also included in the legislation, resulted in a mammoth increase in the number of patients with that coverage after such expansion was accepted by Governor John Bel Edwards.

Louisiana already had about 25% of the population under Medicaid. We also have around 20% who are uninsured. With the full implementation of the ACA and Medicaid expansion there was an increase of over 400,000 new Medicaid and other ACA insured patients in the state of Louisiana, or a total of around 40% of the population.

That leads us to the second acronym, **CCN** or "Coordinated Care Networks." These are Medicaid managed care organizations (known collectively as "HealthyLouisiana" and formerly "BayouHealth") with affiliated providers that will pick up, at least in theory, the mass of new Medicaid patients. There were two systems, one which was called a "shared savings plan" in which providers benefited from hypothetical savings secondary to improved health among their constituents. The other system is one of capitated payments (so much money received per member per month) in which the profit is derived from reduced expenses secondary to theoretically improved care.

The success of either version of CCNs depended on the level of participation from providers, the inherent efficiencies of the network and the amount the state is willing to devote to Medicaid payments. A successful CNN must have a significant number of affiliated "lives" (enrolled participants) from which it derives a steady income, offsetting expenses. A CNN without "lives" cannot be successful. The shared savings model disappeared after a few years in Louisiana, leaving only the capitated plan in existence.

That brings us to **ACO**s or Accountable Care Organizations. These are national models that combine insurers and providers, whether hospitals or physicians, in a system where the organization is accountable for certain quality results, generated by a more coordinated allocation of resources and services. The better the results, the higher would be the potential reimbursements. Various incentives (and disincentives) would be built into the system to encourage cooperation in the patient's best interest. Theoretically, the cost of care would decrease by improving prevention and decreasing wasteful duplications of services.

That leads us to **CSOC** or "Coordinated Systems of Care." In Louisiana, this initiative to coordinate the care of high risk youths among various providers, including the judicial system, Children and Family Services (formerly Social Services), the educational system and other community providers. Individual cases are managed to reduce the risk of clients falling between the cracks of various agencies. The system would theoretically reduce the cost to society for those few cases that consume inordinate resources.

Finally, and most recently, there is **MACRA** or the Medicare Access and CHIP Reauthorization Act of 2015. This is an initiative to replace the much-maligned Sustainable Growth Rate (**SGR**) formula that threatened reduction in physician payments year after year. **MACRA** actually has two parts, the Merit-based Incentive Payment Systems (or **MIPS**) and the Advanced Alternative Payment Models (or **APM**s). The former is a complex modified fee-for-service model with several components that seeks to pay more for value (and less for lack of value). The Advanced Alternative Payment Models are those in which organizations (notably Accountable Care Organizations as previously mentioned) take on the risk in a managed care, capitated payment model.

Confused yet? Yes, it is confusing. The Affordable Care Act (**ACA**) or Obamacare, Coordinated Care Networks (**CCN**), Accountable Care Organizations (**ACO**), Coordinated Systems of Care (**CSOC**) and **MARCA** are all parts of the complex new wave of healthcare initiatives. The hope is that they will finally begin to bring some sense into an inefficient and expensive system that has left us bankrupt and unhealthy.

National per capita costs for healthcare, as mentioned, still hover around 18% of the Gross Domestic Product (GDP), twice as high as for most developed nations. Although we have leveled off expenditures at about $8,000/person/year for medical costs, or $3 trillion annually, this figure will probably increase for a number of reasons (many linked to technology and medication costs) with no end in sight.

With Obamacare, we achieved, perhaps only temporarily, insurance coverage for over 90% of our citizens, something that had eluded the United States for the proceeding three decades. Despite achieving better coverage, widespread unpopularity of the **ACA** (or Obamacare) may well result in its complete or partial repeal. But the problem of uninsured Americans remains a national disgrace, unparalleled in other developed countries that have achieved nearly 100% coverage for far less cost. We may yet be forced to eat the above-mentioned alphabet soup (as opposed to chicken soup), or some as-yet-to-be-defined alternative to restore some health to an inefficient healthcare delivery system that does not deliver the anticipated bang for our buck.

LIVES

CHARACTERS:

ROBERT VASE: CEO of a small, struggling hospital in rural Louisiana. Dressed in a tie and button-down shirt. Pants are pressed and his shoes shined. Marked Southern rural accent.

ACHILLE PIERRE: Middle-aged country doctor, Robert's friend. Wears a wrinkled lab coat and unshined shoes. Marked Cajun accent.

ALEX TOURNEVISSE: Well dressed corporate attorney type with an eastern accent.

SETTING

Robert Vase's office at the hospital. There is a desk and a couple of chairs. There may be a cheesy hunting picture or Cajun cottage scene on the wall.

SCENE I

ACHILLE: No! No! No! I don't agree! It's just not right. It's not legal.

ROBERT: For heaven's sake, Achille, don't worry about the details. I have all our answers in this little black book (*holds up a black bound book.*)

ACHILLE: A black book. Nice, very nice. Is that all the names of your former girlfriends?

ROBERT: Don't be ridiculous. It's a book full of dead people, taken straight from the obituaries and the graveyard.

ACHILLE: You really are getting morbid in your old age.

ROBERT: No, Achille, I'm just getting practical.

ACHILLE: Collecting dead people's names is practical?

ROBERT: It's not just their names, but also their dates of birth, social security numbers, everything we'll need.

ACHILLE: Need for what?

ROBERT: To enroll them in our Deep South HMO, of course.

ACHILLE: You're kidding. Aren't you?

ROBERT: No, it's the only way out. We have been hemorrhaging enrolled lives from our HMO like crazy. Every month more people leave the Deep South HMO than sign up. (*Holds up a letter*) I'm already getting menacing letters from Corporate. Listen to this. (*Takes a letter and reads*) "Given your declining enrollments at the Tunica-Biloxi divisions of the Deep South HMO, we may be forced to close your institution. Only a drastic improvement in patient numbers will avert a regrettable decision for closure." Etcetera, etcetera. (*Collapses in his executive chair*) They're going to close us if we don't get our numbers up.

ACHILLE: Maybe they should close this place down?

ROBERT: Are you crazy?

ACHILLE: No, I'm not crazy, but I am exhausted. You got me into this mess in the first place. (*Looks over at the liquor cabinet*) I need a drink.

ROBERT offers ACHILLE a drink.

ACHILLE: You told me I would be earning more money while seeing fewer patients. (*Pauses*) You lied! Every deathly ill old maid and widow in this parish signed up to see me. They all want to come in three times a month instead of every three months. I've doubled my paperwork, extended my hours, and earn less than before. You lied!

ROBERT: Let's just say I miscalculated. I thought you were going to get fat monthly checks for doing nothing.

ACHILLE: Well, you did miscalculate . . . badly.

ROBERT: For that, I am truly sorry. But we can't let our personal misfortunes cloud our obligations to the people of Tunica Parish. They need our hospital. They need you! I'm asking you to do this for the good of our parish.

ACHILLE: No! You are asking me to do this for you, personally, because it will save your sorry ass.

ROBERT: And keep this hospital open.

ACHILLE: (*Takes a drink*) Yes, and keep this hospital open. (*Takes another drink*) Okay, what's your latest brainchild?

ROBERT: We sign up the dead. (*Pauses*) It will increase enrollment to the HMO without increasing the costs.

ACHILLE: And what if no one pays for his or her enrollment, of course? They are dead, after all.

ROBERT: That's the beauty. It doesn't matter. (*Pauses*) As long as they aren't consuming my resources or your time, it doesn't make any difference. They certainly won't be coming into the hospital or your office. (*Holds up a black book*) The cemeteries are full of potential enrollees. (*Reads*) Matilda Villemarette, Jeremy Ponthieux, Marie Lemoine, Henry Doucet, Charles Soileau.

It's endless, I tell you. It's a miracle. This book and the names it contains is our salvation.

ACHILLE: And do you think that Corporate is so stupid? Don't you think someone will figure this out?

ROBERT: That's the beauty of it. By the time they get suspicious, we will be able to purge the lists. Yes, it's tricky. Yes, it's unorthodox. . . .

ACHILLE: Yes, it's dishonest, or maybe just illegal.

ROBERT: We need our hospital. I need my job. And you need to lighten up.

ACHILLE: All the way to prison?

ROBERT: Who said anything about prison?

ACHILLE: Illegal activity always leads to prison sooner or later.

ROBERT: No one is going to prison. I tell you, it's just a temporary expedient to get Corporate off my ass. (*Pauses*) If you don't want to do it for the hospital or for the people, then just do it for me. Do it for your sister. She doesn't want me to be unemployed any more than you. I swear, it's just temporary, cross my heart and hope to die.

ACHILLE: I'll do it for you and for my sister, even though I warned her not to marry a sorry ass hospital administrator.

ROBERT: (*Hugs ACHILLE*) You won't regret it, I swear. (*Serves himself a drink and raises his glass*) Here's to our new lives for the Deep South HMO. To their health!

ACHILLE: They're dead.

ROBERT: Okay, to our health!

SCENE II

> *ROBERT is seated at the desk in his office. ACHILLE enters.*

ROBERT: (*Flips through his black book and looks up at ACHILEE, who enters into his office*) Ah, Achille. It's so nice to see you. Thanks so much for dropping by.

ACHILLE: What now? Not enough dead people to sign up for the HMO?

ROBERT: Oh no, plenty of dead people. The obituaries are full and my black book of the dead is almost full as well.

ACHILLE: So what do you need me to do now?

ROBERT: (*Gets up and puts his arm around ACHILLES's shoulders*) You have been our savior, our number one regional HMO doctor.

ACHILLE: With a bunch of dead lives.

ROBERT: And live ones, too.

ACHILLE: Yes, and those are the ones that are killing me. Mrs. D'autremont came in four times last week only. It's amazing. I didn't think you could invent that many diseases.

ROBERT: She won't be coming in any more. Didn't you see?

ACHILLE: See what?

ROBERT: Here (*picks up a newspaper and shows it to ACHILLE.*) Her name is in the obituaries.

ACHILLE: Thank God (*crosses himself.*) And may her soul rest in peace.

ROBERT: I only wish she could.

ACHILLE: Don't tell me she's got to stay on the list of enrollees.

ROBERT: Yes and no. Normally I'd love to leave her on the list of lives, but we have a problem.

ACHILLE: We?

ROBERT: (*Pulls out a letter*) From Corporate, of course. (*Reads out loud*) "Dr. Mr. Robert Vase. Your astonishing increase in HMO enrolled lives has come to the attention of headquarters. We congratulate you on the dramatic turnaround. In an effort to emulate your fine example as a best practice, we are sending Mr. Tournevise down from Corporate to get a better understanding of the functioning of your facility. Enclosed is also a bonus check for you and another for the remarkable Dr. Achille Pierre, internist extraordinaire. Accept them as a token of our appreciation for your remarkable work." (*Extends a check to Achille*) Want it? You earned it.

ACHILLE: Hell no! Where would I spend it? In prison?

ROBERT: (*Shrugs his shoulders and pockets both checks*) Any suggestions?

ACHILLE: When is this guy coming down to do his inspection?

ROBERT: (*Looks at his watch*) He should be driving in just about now.

ACHILLE: (*Looks around in panic*) What! He's coming in today? (*Pauses*) So what have you done to straighten this mess out?

ROBERT: Nothing. I've resigned myself to my fate.

ACHILLE: Nothing! Are you crazy!

ROBERT: No, just depressed.

ACHILLE: (*Comes around the desk and shakes ROBERT by the shoulder*) Snap out of it! Now! I don't care if you go to prison for the rest of your life, but my sister doesn't deserve it and I don't either.

ROBERT: So what do you suggest?

ACHILLE: (*Grabs the black book off the desk*) This is your black book of dead lives, right?

ROBERT: Yes.

ACHILLE: Then dis-enroll them.

ROBERT: When?

ACHILLE: Now!

ROBERT: But I worked so hard putting them all in.

ACHILLE: And now you're going to get rid of them, unless you want to be fired and go to jail for fraud. Your choice!

ROBERT: Okay, give me that damn book. (*Starts typing furiously on his keyboard. Several seconds pass.*) And now?

ACHILLE: Now print out the revised enrollment numbers. Now!

> The printer spits out a bunch of sheets that ROBERT grabs.

ROBERT: (*Pulls out the long list of names*) Ready?

ACHILLE: As ready as we're gong to be.

ROBERT: (*Knock on the door*) Yes? Come on in, the door's open.

ALEX TOURNEVISSE comes in. He is wearing an expensive suit and carrying a brief case. ACHILLE and ROBERT rise to meet the executive.

ROBERT: Mr. Tournevisse, what a pleasant surprise. (*They shake hands*) And this is the remarkable Dr. Achille Pierre.

ALEX: (*Shakes hands with ROBERT and ACHILLE.*) Delighted, to meet you both. I have read about your extensive clientele, Dr. Pierre. You must be very busy, indeed. It's really very impressive.

ACHILLE: Yes, a truly remarkable clientele (*glances at ROBERT and sits down.*)

ALEX: Well, I would like to congratulate you both on some astonishing statistics. We at Corporate have been truly amazed by your increase in enrollment. I've been sent to discover the secret of your success so we could emulate it elsewhere in the system. You are really a shining light to the whole corporate organization.

ROBERT: Thank you, thank you. We're so flattered. (*Goes and takes the printout from his desk*) I do have some updated statistics that you will find of some interest (*hands the sheets to MR. TOURNEVISSE.*)

ALEX: (*Examines the sheets with interest and grimaces*) These are horrible! You've lost half of your enrollment in this fiscal quarter. What on earth has happened?

ROBERT: Uh. . . .

ACHILLE: (*Springs up.*) Let me explain, please. (*Goes to the liquor cabinet and serves a couple of drinks*) Drinks, anyone?

ALEX and ROBERT: No, thank you.

ACHILLE: It's just the usual business cycle, only a bit more dramatic.

ALEX: I'm listening.

ACHILLE: You have your phase of enthusiasm and everything goes up (*gestures upward*). Everyone is excited and interested. They all want to get on the bandwagon of managed care and sign up for the Deep South HMO. Things look wonderful for a while. (*Pauses*) Then there is the phase of disenchantment (*makes a dramatic gesture downward*).

ALEX: Why?

ACHILLE: Because people start to have other options, other HMOs in larger cities. More providers in other plans. Generally more opportunities. You can't blame them. (*Swings his arms around*) Here I am, just one country doctor seeing thousands of patients. In town, with our competition, they have ten or twelve doctors to choose from. They have less waiting times, better customer satisfaction. And voilà, a sudden drop in enrollment, it's as natural as night following day.

ALEX: So what's next?

ROBERT: Uh. . . .

ACHILLE: (*Cuts ROBERT off*) The last phase is the phase of stabilization. Either the plan settles in and reflects its true value to the public or it dies.

ALEX: It dies?

ROBERT: It dies?

ACHILLE: Organizational death, of course. You either stay in the business at some reduced level or you go into oblivion.

ROBERT: Oblivion?

ALEX: Corporate oblivion.

ACHILLE: Precisely. That doom starts here and spreads out like an oil slick in an uncontrollable wave of panic throughout the entire system.

ROBERT and ALEX: Panic?

ACHILLE: Yes, panic! Imagine what happens if the events in this lost village get out to Wall Street? (*Pauses*) Of course it could be the end of the ball game, the collapse of the Deep South HMO. The beginning of the end.

ALEX: (*Concerned*) And how can we stop that malignant contagion? What can we do?

ACHILLE: Nothing.

ROBERT and ALEX: Nothing?

ACHILLE: Yes! You, Robert sit tight and wait for things to stabilize. . .if they do. (*Speaks to ALEX*) And you, Mr. Alex, you go back with this cautionary tale to Corporate. Let them know how volatile success can be. Explain to them how the phase of enthusiasm leads naturally into the phase of disenchantment, something which can occur with dizzying speed and (*bends closer to ALEX*) catastrophic results.

ALEX: (*Clutches his suitcase and stands*) I think I best be going back to Corporate to give them our report.

ROBERT: (*Stands to see ALEX go*) Yes, of course, the quicker the better.

ACHILLE: (*Grabs the famous black book*) And here's a list of people who have left the HMO. You might find it of some interest for your report.

ROBERT: (*Grabs the book*) No, no! That won't be necessary. I'm sure Mr. Tournevisse has quite enough information as it is.

ALEX: Yes, I'm sure I have enough. If I need anything else, I'll let you both know. (*To ACHILLE*) Very informative, Doctor. I'm so glad I got to meet you. (*Turns to ROBERT and shakes his hand*) And very nice to meet you, Mr. Vase. This has been most informative, indeed (*exits.*)

ROBERT: (*Slumps down in his chair and shakes his head*) Thank you, Achille.

ACHILLE: (*Gets two glasses and fills them up*) Here's to all the folks in the black book!

ROBERT: (*Raises his glass*) May they all rest in peace!

BLACKOUT

PHARMACEUTICAL MARKETING AND COST

PHARMACEUTICAL MARKETING
AND MADNESS

Legitimate medications (not illegal drugs) represent a multi-billion dollar industry worldwide. It comprises one aspect of the three trillion dollars spent each year on healthcare in the United States. Advances in pharmacology have resulted in some astonishing improvements in the control of hypertension, hypercholesterolemia, infectious diseases, cancer treatment and other health problems. Decreases in heart disease deaths in the United States and elsewhere are largely a result of improved control of blood pressure, cholesterol and diabetes, thanks to pharmaceutical advances.

Historically, marketing of prescription medications occurred principally through direct contact between pharmaceutical representatives and physicians. Unlike many industries, the products (prescription drugs) require the active participation of the doctor, who holds what is referred to as the "power of the pen" (or the ability to write prescriptions). This power has been absolute and is the reason for the tremendous allocation of personnel and resources by the pharmaceutical industry to influence physician's choice of medications.

This situation began to change in the late seventies with the advent of managed care and HMOs (Health Maintenance Organizations). More and more physicians and patients were confronted with the reality of fixed formularies. A formulary is an approved list of medications from which the physician can choose. The use of generic medications, those that are no longer under patent and usually less expensive, is encouraged through the mechanism of reduced or no co-pays for the consumer. Other more expensive brand name medications may be on the formulary, but are penalized by higher co-payments. Prescribing off-formulary drugs, if permitted at all, might require extensive additional and onerous paperwork by the physician and considerable cost to the patient. Adherence with the formulary list became the path of least resistance for physician and patient alike.

About the same time that managed care and fixed formularies came into existence, a proliferation of direct pharmaceutical advertising to consumers began. This, of course, creates demand and that demand gets transferred to the physician through the patient. The doctor becomes confronted with specific requests for specific medications, a relatively new phenomenon in medical practice. "Doc, could you prescribe me that medication I saw on TV?" is the usual refrain.

The ability to market prescribed medications directly to the general public may seem obvious or even inevitable. In fact, it is rare. Only two countries in the world allow direct marketing of prescription medications: New Zealand and the United States. Why should this be the case? Why does virtually every other country ban direct marketing of prescription drugs and the US does not? The answer is cost.

Publicity enhances demand and demand increases consumption (and hopefully corporate profits). Per capita use of pharmaceuticals in the United States is almost $1,000 per person. In Germany it is only $678/person and in Denmark, it is only $240/person. Are the Germans and Danish dying earlier than Americans because of this reduced medication expense? The answer is no! Life expectance in Germany (81 years) and Denmark (80.6) is longer than in the United States (79.3) and their per capita health spending is considerable less ($5,411/person in Germany and $6,413 in Denmark vs. $9,403 in the U.S. in 2014).

Another phenomenon that has transformed the American legal drug market has been the proliferation of over-the-counter supplements. This might also seem inevitable or even beneficial, but it has not always been the case. Prior to the Hatch Act (Orin Hatch, a politician from Utah) supplements were controlled by the FDA. They were required by the FDA to be proven both "safe and effective." This requirement created two problems for the supplement industry. First, the testing involved is complex, expensive and time consuming. Second, and more important, is that many of these products, if not most, are neither effective nor safe. In fact, many can be useless at best and medically dangerous at worst, although highly profitable to their manufacturers.

With the passage of the Hatch Act, supplements were reclassified as "food supplements" rather than as drugs. The onerous necessity of FDA control suddenly disappeared. What followed was a massive increase in the supplement industry, which just happened to be well represented in Senator Hatch's home state of Utah.

Calls to eliminate direct advertising of prescription drugs and reintroduce FDA control of supplements have both been soundly rejected. The economic pressures have been overwhelming from the pharmaceutical and supplement industries that evoke the merits of free choice and free enterprise.

Another interesting phenomenon has been the internationalization of mail order medications. Drugs, which cost hundreds of dollars in the US, may be sold for pennies on the dollar out of our borders and often with no prescription at all. Efforts to increase the availability of such mail order sources have also met with ferocious resistance. Issues of drug safety are evoked, even if the same company using the same strict quality control standards as in the United States produces the medications. The motivation for the opposition might well be profit margins more than public safety.

While the wonders of the pharmaceutical industry have transformed medical outcomes, the same industries have and continue to influence the medical marketplace. During twenty years of private practice, I was deluged with a constant stream of very affable, very competent pharmaceutical representatives, often several from the same company. Gifts, free lunches and dinners for my staff and me, trips, honorariums for pseudo-research and focus groups all came in an endless and abundant stream. Legislation stopped this flow of goodies in the nineties, but there have always been abundant opportunities to benefit from the pharmaceutical cornucopia.

After changing to a position in public health, whose formulary is determined by state contracts at the state level, the steam of drug representatives stopped abruptly. Having run into one of my former pharmaceutical representatives at a social function, I said, "You folks have all disappeared. No one even drops by to see me now." The representative, a very intelligent and articulate man, replied "Dr. Holcombe, the day you left your private practice, you were removed from our data base. It's only business."

Yes indeed, "only business," but at what cost? And is that cost sustainable?

NO SUCH THING AS A FREE LUNCH

CAST OF CHARACTERS

> DR. PETER FRANK: Physician dressed in white coat or sports coat with stethoscope prominently draped around his neck.

> DR. DONALD HARTFORD: Also a physician with a stethoscope and name badge, perhaps more casually dressed.

SETTING

> Doctor's office with a desk and a couple of chairs. There is an oriental carpet on the floor. There are several boxes of medication samples on the desk.

PETER: We've got to get the pharmaceutical reps out of the clinic.

DONALD: Why? They bring samples. (*Picks up a box and shows it to PETER*) See! They bring lunches. They support educational meetings. They take us to fancy dinners and on trips.

PETER: Sure, they do all that and more. And what do you think they want in return?

DONALD: Nothing! I listen to what they have to say and then I use my own clinical judgment.

PETER: Don, you're a fool. A smart fool, but a fool nonetheless. Nothing in life is free. Nothing is without cost. That's the first rule of ecology. There's no such think as a free lunch (*takes the box out of DONALD's hand and puts it back on the desk.*)

DONALD: Oh, you're just a cynical sourpuss.

PETER: And you're an educated idiot.

DONALD: I thought you just said I was a smart fool. Now I'm just an idiot. (*Laughs*) Anyway, the decision of whether pharmaceutical representatives can come into this clinic is not yours to make. That's a partnership decision. You can't kick them out even if you do think they have a pernicious effect on the choice of which drugs get used.

PETER: I don't think they're intrinsically evil. They're nice ladies and gentlemen. They are just doing their job and their job is not public health. It's sales, sales, and more sales. (*Knocks DONALD on the head*) Can you get that through your thick skull?

DONALD: (*Gets up and walks around*) So you are going to be the valiant doctor, Don Quixote, Man of La Mancha, who goes up against the medico-industrial complex and saves the national debt, one prescription at a time?

PETER: No, you can't eliminate the national debt at the patient's bedside, but you can be aware of the problem.

DONALD: And what if it's not a problem at all? What if them making money and our making money is just a good thing for everyone? It's the American Dream, isn't it? Unbridled capitalism? Getting rich?

PETER: And what happens when there isn't any more money? Whose healthcare is going to suffer? Mine? Yours? Or that poor slob with a minimum wage job who can't even afford medical insurance and can't afford the medication you and I prescribe him?

DONALD: And how does that relate to the question of drug reps inside the clinic?

PETER: Well, for the cost of a few free notepads, a lunch for the staff, a ticket to the baseball game, a trip as a consultant to Florida, plus some golf tournaments thrown in on the side, do you really thing that nothing is expected in return? Do you really think that's not going to influence you when you take out your prescription pad? (*Pauses. Mimics taking out his prescription pad and thinking about what he's going to write.*) Should I prescribe that old cheap generic drug, or that new expensive medication that patients keep asking for because they are bombarded with publicity on the television? (*Picks up a box and shows it to DONALD*) Look at this one, a new immuno-biological drug, genetically engineered and ten times as pricy as the old one. Which one should I prescribe? And besides, that drug rep is so nice and gives me such nice free things and we had such a nice dinner down at the Courtableau (pronounced Court-a-blow) Café.

DONALD: I retain complete freedom and objectivity in my prescribing. Surely you don't think a few baubles or a nice dinner can influence me?

PETER: (*Laughs*) You're lying to yourself. You're lying to me. And you're lying to our patients. (*Drops the box down on the desk*) Drug reps know they can buy a doctor with a free pen.

DONALD: (*Jumps out and shoves PETER*) Peter, that's an insult! I'm a good doctor, a caring doctor, a concerned doctor.

PETER: (*Puts his hand on DONALD's shoulders*) I know. But you're not opening your eyes. Do you really think you can resist that pharmaceutical steamroller? Have your seen those women reps they send. They're beautiful, young, and voluptuous. They hang over your desk with their cleavage inches from your face. (*Imitates a woman's voice. Picks up a couple of boxes and swings them around in a voluptuous way, often circling around the breasts*) Oh, Dr. Hartford, I admire you so much for all the things you do for the community. You are really a role model for us all. Is there anything I can do to make you prescribe more of my product? What can I do to really help you out? What about that favorite charity of yours? What if I give a $1,000 to the museum or maybe Duck's Unlimited, or maybe the community theater, the one you like so much? Of course, I don't expect anything in return, especially from such a popular and well-connected physician with such an enormous clientele. (*Holds the boxes over each breast and hangs them down into DONALD's face*) And you are such a good man and a wonderful doctor and your patients love you so. (*Reverts to his regular voice*) Sound familiar.

DONALD: (*Laughs*) You really do that well. If I didn't know you better, I'd say you'd had some serious practice.

PETER: Sorry to disappoint you, but that's an amateur performance. But seriously, will you help me to get the drug reps out of the office? Men and women?

DONALD: But those lunches? Those treats? The free medical samples? (*Takes a sample box*) And the heartfelt interest in me and my family?

PETER: You know very well that those reps only sample the newest, costliest medications until we start prescribing them and then all those free samples suddenly disappear. And no one even remembers that great drug went generic last year and costs a few pennies a pill. (*Picks up a box*) Look at this! They put two old medications in the same pill together that are about to go off patent and voilà! It suddenly becomes a new miracle pill that just happens to cost ten times as much as the cheap generic components separately. And it just happens to be patented for another 20 years. True or not true?

DONALD: True.

PETER: So, what do you say? Will you help me or not? Just think of the good you'll be doing to your patients, to society, and to yourself.

DONALD: But. . . .

PETER: No buts. You can be part of the problem or part of the solution. Which would you rather be?

DONALD: Didn't Jimi Hendrix say that back in the sixties?

PETER: No, Malcolm X said it and it was true back then and it's still true now (*pushes the boxes of samples into the garbage can.*)

BLACKOUT

EPI-JECTORS FOR SALE

CHARACTERS

> ROGER: Young adult who carries a basket of oversized Epi-jectors.

> MABEL: Early middle-aged woman with casual clothing and an unsophisticated speech pattern

SETTING

> Suggestion of a street or other public outdoor place.

ROGER: (Holds a basket of Epi-jectors. Flourishes a couple of boxes in his hand.) INJECTORS FOR SALE! EPINJECTORS FOR SALE! GET YOUR EPINJECTORS NOW WHILE THEY LAST!

MABEL: (*Stops*) Oh, I need one of those for my daughter. She's so allergic to bee stings, she almost died when she got stung last summer. Can I buy one, please?

ROGER: Sure. (*Hands MABEL a box*) One box or two?

MABEL: I might as well take two since you're here.

ROGER: No problem. (*Hands MABEL another box*) That'll be $1,200, please.

MABEL: What?

ROGER: One thousand two hundred dollars for both boxes, six hundred dollars each.

MABEL: You've got to be kidding.

ROGER: No, ma'am. That's the manufacturers price and I'm just a lowly salesman.

MABEL: (*Hands both boxes back to ROGER*) I don't have that kind of money.

ROGER: We take checks and credit cards, too. I have one of those square things on my phone. It's very handy out in the field.

MABEL: I'm already over my credit limit and there's almost nothing left in my checking account, certainly not $1,200.

ROGER: And what about your daughter? What if she gets a bee sting? Are you going to stand there and watch her die? What kind of a mother are you, anyway?

MABEL: What kind of a drug company are you?

ROGER: I don't make the prices, lady, I just sell the product.

MABEL: Are there any other manufacturers?

ROGER: No.

MABEL: Any cheap generics?

ROGER: No, not yet, and we're the only company who could make one. (*Pauses*) Lady, you're just plain out of luck.

MABEL: (*Pauses*) No, sir. You're the one who's out of luck. (*Pulls a handgun from her purse and points it at ROGER*) Give me an Epi-jector, now!

ROGER: Lady, put that thing down before you hurt someone. These Epi-jectors aren't mine to give away. Taking some would be theft, pure and simple.

MABEL: No, your company's the one stealing from us. You are stealing from people who can't afford it. Now give me an Epi-jector.

ROGER: (*Pulls out a box and hands it to MABEL*) Take it. It's not worth dying for.

MABEL: My daughter might die if she doesn't have one when she needs it. Don't you get it? Thousands of people, thousands of children might die without an Epi-jector. You're a murderer! You and your drug company deserve to die. Give me the whole basket, now! I want them all and I'll give them away to needy parents and their children.

ROGER: (*Hands MABEL the basket*) Like Robin Hood?

MABEL: No, like Robinette Hood, you fool!

ROGER: (*Looks around in the air at what appears to be an insect flying*) Hey! (*Swats the air.*) Get away from me!

MABEL: What's wrong?

ROGER: It's a wasp. I'm allergic to wasp stings.

MABEL: (*Laughs out loud*) You're kidding.

ROGER: (*Swats the air*) No, I'm not.

MABEL: Well, I'll be damned. (*Swats something in the air towards ROGER*) Come on baby. Go to your daddy. (*Swats the air again*) There you go. Right to the neck!

ROGER: (*Screams*) Oh shit! Get away! (*Swats his neck*) Ouch! (*Pauses*) It stung me, by God. The little shit stung me. (Grabs for the basket) Give me one of those pens, now!

MABEL: (*Backs away*) Really? How long do you have before your throat swells up and you can't breathe?

ROGER: Stop it! Stop it right now! I got your point. Now give me an Epi-jector (*lunges toward MABEL but he stops when she points the gun at him.*)

MABEL: Not so fast, cowboy. (*Calmly*) How much are you willing to pay for one, smart ass?

ROGER: Give me one, you idiot. (*Breathes heavily*) I can't breathe. Give me an Epi-jector.

MABEL: (*Steps forward, still brandishing the gun*) How much?

ROGER: (*Gasping*) Everything I got in my wallet. (*Pulls out his wallet and throws the money at MABEL*) Here! Fifty, maybe a hundred bucks and some change. Now, give me that Epi-jector.

MABEL: You don't have $600? That's the retail price, isn't it? That's the price of your life.

ROGER: (*Drops to his knees*) Please, lady. Give me a one. I'll forget all about this: the gun, the theft, the extortion. Keep the rest of them, just give me one now. That basket's worth thousands of dollars. My God! (*Gasping*) You can't just sit there and watch me die, can you?

MABEL: (*Steps back and turns her back*) Of course I can. It's all about the profits, isn't it? Just about making money for your CEO and stockholders. Isn't that all?

ROGER: (*Gasps*) It's about saving my life, for God's sake.

MABEL: Or my daughter's?

ROGER: (*Weakly*) Yes, yes, yes! It's about saving lives. (Drops to his knees.)

MABEL: (*Pulls an Epi-jector out of the basket and steps forward to give a shot to ROGER*) There! For charity and the love of God. That ought to save your sorry ass.

ROGER: (*Continues to gasp*) Thank you! Thank you! (*Starts to breath easier.*)

MABEL: (*Throws down the empty pen.*) There. Take it back. Take them all back except one. I'm saving it for my daughter. I'm no Robinette Hood, just a parent who loves her daughter. And tell your fucking CEO what happened here today.

ROGER: I will. (*Stares at MABEL as she strides off stage*). I swear to God I will.

MABEL: (*Yells over her shoulder*) GOOD! (*Exits.*)

BLACKOUT

CHILD ABUSE AND NEGLECT

CHILD ABUSE AND NEGLECT:
AN ONGOING TRAGEDY

Child "maltreatment", as it is called, remains a serious problem in the United States and in Louisiana. There were 3.4 million referrals to child protective services in the U.S. in 2012 of which over 700,000 (or 9.2/1,000, or about 1%) were confirmed cases of "maltreatment." Most of the victims (78%) were neglected, 9% sexual abused and 11% suffered other forms of maltreatment (i.e. emotional abuse, lack of supervision, parental substance abuse or other.)

Unreported cases vastly outnumber reported cases and child protective services estimates that 25% of all children are maltreated at least once during their childhood. This results in over 1,600 child deaths a year (in 2012), most of these cases being children under the age of 3 years old (27%). More boys than girls die from abuse (2.5 vs. 1.9/100,000) and more African-American children than whites (4.7 vs. 1.6/100,000). The economic cost is also staggering, with an estimated $124 billion dollar in the U.S. and over $2.7 million in Central Louisiana ($1.1 million in Rapides Parish alone.)

Who are the perpetrators of these crimes? Not surprisingly, 80% are parents, and around 6% are other relatives, while 4.2% are unmarried parents of the victim. Most perpetrators are between 18 and 44 years of age (82%) and many are women (54%.)

Risk factors vary for the perpetrators and children. Parental risk factors include depression, domestic violence or history of childhood victimization, substance abuse, separation or divorce, single parent households, social isolation, poverty, unemployment and high-risk neighborhoods. Child Risk factors include prematurity (low birth weights), disability (physical or mental), young age and behavioral issues (sometimes a result of persistent neglect.)

Sadly, only 25% of children report abuse or neglect when it occurs and only another 25% will report it prior to their 18th birthday. That means 50% will never disclose their victimization prior to adulthood, and among those non-reporters, some will continue the cycle of abuse with their own children. Reporting cases by those in contact with victims becomes critical to stopping this destructive cycle.

In Louisiana, there are a host of mandated reporters including: health providers (including mental health), social workers, clergy, child care providers, teachers, law enforcement, mediators, CAS (Child Advocacy Services) and CASA (Court Appointed Special Advocates), youth activity providers, film processors and ALL adults who have witnessed sexual abuse of a child. Cases should be reported immediately, with the name, address, sex and race of the child and what you have witnessed. Reporters are not investigators. In Louisiana, reports should be made at 1-855-4LA-KIDS (1-855-452-5437) available 24 hours a day/7 days a week or call 911.

The assessment of the situation includes an evaluation of the extent of danger (present or impending), the extent of the maltreatment, circumstances, functional capacity of the child and caregiver, parental practices (including discipline). The functional level of the caregiver (intoxication, violence, hostility to intervention and level of control) and child (anxiety, independence, mental and physical state) should both be determined.

In Louisiana, failure to report cases of child sexual abuse by any mandated reporter can result in a $10,000 fine, five years in prison (possibly with hard labor) and felony charges. Worse yet, there is a good chance that victimization will continue, with increasing physical and psychological consequences, possibly resulting in death. Reporters, once they have filed a report, need not inform their supervisors, who cannot prevent reporting under any circumstances. Your name, as a reporter, cannot be released. Should another episode of abuse be witnessed, re-reporting is necessary.

Child maltreatment is pervasive and destructive. Addressing social determinants (income, educational level and social status), as in most issues related to mental and physical health, plays a critical role in prevention and treatment. The psychological scars of victimization last a lifetime and predispose victims to a cycle of repeated abuse. Let's stop the harm now and make Louisiana and the United States a better and safer place for its most vulnerable citizens.

Report child maltreatment (abuse and neglect) to 1-855-452-5437 or 911. Make the call, it's the law!

OH, BABY!

CHARACTERS

WOMAN: A woman in her early thirties. Casual clothing. Nothing fancy. Uneducated speech pattern.

MAN: A man in his early thirties. Casual clothing. Nothing fancy. Uneducated speech pattern.

BOY: A young man in his late teens. Unrefined clothing and speech.

GIRL: A young woman in her late teens. Unrefined clothing and speech.

SETTING

There is no formal setting. The third scene might suggest prison, with some shadows of bars projected on the stage. There may be a couple of chairs.

SCENE I

MAN and WOMAN are confronting one another. WOMAN is very pregnant in this scene.

WOMAN: (*To MAN*) I don't want this baby!

MAN: I don't care what you want; we're keeping this baby.

WOMAN: "We?" Who's this "we?" You don't even live with me anymore. How are you gonna take care of a baby in that dump of an apartment you call home? (*Pauses.*) No, we just need to put this baby up for adoption.

MAN: Like your other babies, with those other guys?

WOMAN: Yeah, like my other ones! And what's it to you, anyway? You weren't the father to any of them other kids.

MAN: Too bad! Maybe I coulda helped take care of them.

WOMAN: But you don't! You don't do a damn thing. I clean, I get up at night, and I feed the babies. What will you do exactly? (*Pauses*) Nothing! Nothing! And nothing!

MAN: That's not true! (*Pauses*) Even if it was true, I won't sign the papers to give this baby up to any strangers.

WOMAN: You don't have to! I'll get the social worker to declare me an unfit mother and then they will take it away whether you want it or not.

MAN: Won't happen! I can tell them that I will be available. I'll pay. I'll get my momma and my sisters to help.

WOMAN: You think you're so smart, real smart. But you don't love this baby. You just hate me and wanna punish me any way you can. That's the truth, isn't it?

MAN: Yeah, I do hate you. But I love my baby and I will find a way to keep it. (*Pauses*) Maybe not at my place, but at least somewhere, somehow. (*Pauses*) I'll win in court and you know it. Those social service people always want the baby to stay with the natural parents, especially the loving mother.

WOMAN: Don't do it! Don't make me do it!

MAN: Make you do what?

WOMAN: Make me kill it! I'll kill it; I swear I'll kill this baby.

MAN: LIAR! No mother kills her own baby.

WOMAN: I will! I swear. The first time it cries all night and all day and has the colic for hours on end, I'll lose my mind and I'll kill it. (*Pauses*) They're fragile, you know. Their skulls aren't fully formed so they're sort of squishy. (*Makes a squeezing gesture with her hands*) Squish, squish, squish!

MAN: Stop it! Just stop it. Don't say things like that. It scares me.

WOMAN: It had better scare you. (*Makes a scary face*) Scary enough?

MAN: You're crazy.

WOMAN: Yes, I am. And you and your baby better not shove me over the edge, because I'm just that close. (*Makes a gesture with her fingers*) Just that close to losing it completely.

> *Lights dim to dark on WOMAN and MAN.*

BLACKOUT

<u>SCENE II</u>

> *Lights come up on BOY and GIRL who are off to stage right.*

BOY: (*Very distraught*) I'm sorry, so sorry!

GIRL: (*Screams*) DEAD!

BOY: (*Tries to comfort the GIRL, who pulls away*) I'm real sorry.

GIRL: (*Starts to pound BOY with her fists*) No! No! No! (*Looks around the room frantically*) Where is she?

BOY: The paramedics came and took her away already.

GIRL: (*Sobs*) No! Not my baby.

BOY: Our baby, honey, our baby, remember. I'm just as busted up as you (*strokes GIRL's hair.*)

GIRL: (*Calming down*) What happened?

BOY: I set her on the couch and she just rolled off and hit the floor. I didn't even notice right away. She was sleepin' so peacefully. Then I went to get a beer and when I come back she's there. (*Points to the floor*) Right there on the floor, cold and dead.

GIRL: Did you try CPR like we learned?

BOY: (*Hesitates*) Yeah, yeah. Just like they taught us, with the fingers over the chest, pushing down a little bit. (*Makes the gesture of infant CPR*) Just like in the parenting class.

GIRL: (*Long pause. Looks at BOY*) I don't believe you.

BOY: No! I did it. I tried to save her.

GIRL: (*Scrutinizing BOY and then screams*) You killed her! YOU KILLED OUR BABY!

BOY: No, I didn't! It just happened. She slipped and fell and hit her head and died.

GIRL: (*Continues to scrutinize BOY*) I know when you're lying. I can see it in your eyes. You did something bad to our baby, didn't you?

BOY: No, I swear to God!

GIRL: Our baby was screaming and you couldn't soother her, could you? You're rough. She knew it wasn't me holding her and you did something bad. That's what happened, isn't it?

BOY: No, nothing like that!

GIRL: And so you threw her against the couch and she bounced back and hit the floor and busted her head. Or maybe you just started to hit her over and over again on the head. That's what happened, isn't it?

BOY: (*Shakes his head nervously*) No! It wasn't like that at all.

GIRL: (*Screams*) You're a murderer! You murdered our baby because you didn't want her in the first place. You never wanted our baby and now you got rid of her.

BOY: No, it's not like that. I loved her. I'd never hurt her or you.

GIRL: (*Quietly*) You told me to get an abortion. You wanted me to kill this baby and now your did it yourself, you selfish, no good, son-of-a-bitch.

BOY: I said that stuff, but I didn't mean it. And then I saw her when she was borned, a cute little pink baby. I just wanted to be a good daddy, a great daddy, just like your dad.

GIRL: But you're not like my dad, are you? You're like your dad: violent, abusive, and short-tempered, a short fused drinker. He beat you and your momma and now you done the same to our baby. (*Drops to the floor and sobs*) No! God in heaven! Strike me dead!

Kill me, too! Go ahead; just beat my brains in so I can join my baby. Do it, please do it.

BOY: (*Leans forward to comfort her*) Come on, honey. We'll get through this, I know we will! We really will.

GIRL: (*Recoils*) Don't touch me! Now or ever again! (*Looks at BOY with contempt*) I hope you go to jail and stay there the rest of your life. I hope you rot in there.

BOY: (*Defensively*) They won't find a thing. You'll see. I'm not gonna go to prison. Not even one day. I ain't done nothing wrong.

GIRL: Maybe you won't go to prison. You know too many people and your folks know too many people, but you'll go to hell some day. And you'll pay for what you did to our sweet little thing. (*Cries again*) Oh God! Strike me down dead.

BOY: (*Knees down*) Let's pray together, please. Let's pray together for our baby. Jesus'll help us get through this.

GIRL: (*Pulls away*) You are the devil. You're the devil incarnate. You don't have an honest bone in your body. (*Stands and moves away*) Get out of my sight! I never wanna see you again, ever!

> *BOY backs away and goes to where the WOMAN is sitting. Lights dim.*

BLACKOUT

SCENE III

> *The WOMAN and the BOY are talking to one another in an ill-defined location. There may be*

the projection of prison bars on the stage. The BOY has a prison guard uniform on and the WOMAN wears a prison jump suit. The WOMAN may be mopping the floor as the BOY looks on.

WOMAN: So you killed your baby, too?

BOY: (*Looks around*) Can I talk to you in confidence?

WOMAN: Confidence in what?

BOY: I mean, can I trust you not to say nothing to nobody?

WOMAN: Who am I gonna talk to? And when? You think they're gonna let me out sooner if I snitch on you? Besides, no one would ever believe anything I say. I killed my baby, remember?

BOY: (*Leans in*) Yeah, I did kill my baby. I didn't really mean to do it. She just started screaming and screaming and screaming and just wouldn't shut up. Nothing I could do would make her be quiet.

WOMAN: So?

BOY: So I threw her across the room onto the sofa and she bounced back and hit the floor (*slams one hand against the other.*)

WOMAN: On her head?

BOY: How'd you know?

WOMAN: Because the same thing happened to me. I just couldn't take it any more. My baby was only 2 pounds and a few ounces when she was born, this little tiny pink thing. They hadda put her in this incubator machine in the NICU (*pronounced nick-you*).

BOY: Nick U?

WOMAN: A special place for premies, them little babies that can't make it on the outside yet.

BOY: Oh.

WOMAN: Then I started to have to take care of her more and more and then I found myself at home with the tiny little baby who was crying all the time. Crying, crying crying, night and day, and nobody to help me. (*Pauses*) And I got sick of it and I couldn't get any sleep at all. Night after night. I tell you, it was hell.

BOY: And the dad?

WOMAN: (*Shrugs*) He's the one who made me keep the baby. He wouldn't let me have an abortion and he wouldn't let me put the baby up for adoption. Oh, no! He was gonna help me and he was gonna do 50-50 and he was gonna get his mom and sisters to help. (*Pauses*) And then he up and disappears. I never saw hide nor hair of him or his money.

BOY: (*Pauses*) My ex-wife was good, real good. But I was the one that got this short fuse. And then we'd been drinking, the first time since the baby came home.

WOMAN: (*Nods*) Drinking, eh? That never helps, especially if you already got a short fuse. (*Pauses*) But at least the mother wanted the baby.

BOY: Oh yeah, she really did. But we was too young. We was barely seventeen.

WOMAN: Yeah, at that age, I already had given up two babies. But this guy, the father of this last baby, he just didn't want to give it up. No, no! He says, I'll take care of the baby, too. (*Pauses*) Yeah, and then he finds this other girl and he disappears and I go day and night with no sleep, no socializing, no one to help and a crying, crying baby with diarrhea and wheezing and screaming.

BOY: That sound's tough.

WOMAN: Yeah, but I shouldn't have killed my baby. You can't kill babies, can you?

BOY: You can, but you shouldn't.

WOMAN: That's what the judge said, too.

> *BOY and WOMAN sit in silence*
> *for a few seconds.*

BOY: So what happened?

WOMAN: Twenty years of hard labor, no parole. That's what happened.

BOY: That's your whole life.

WOMAN: Yes, it is. My whole life in the stinking place! Plenty of time just to think about my baby. And don't think I get any sympathy around here. No one likes a baby killer. (*Pauses.*) So what happened to you?

BOY: Nothing.

WOMAN: Nothing? Why?

BOY: "In-sufficient evi-dence."

WOMAN: A dead baby with a crushed skull?

BOY: Yeah, the coroner called it a hom-o-cide, but not the DA.

WOMAN: And the DA called that insufficient evidence?

BOY: My papa knows the DA and the Coroner and most of our judges. They didn't want to prosecute. I was too young and it was tragic, but not worth wrecking another promising life. That's what the grand jury said.

WOMAN: Young and well connected, I guess.

BOY: Yeah, I guess so.

WOMAN: And the momma?

BOY: We got divorced. After the baby died, the marriage sort of died with it. She went back to school. (*Pauses and speaks to WOMAN*) I got a job in this lousy place. What about your husband?

WOMAN: Boy friend, never my husband. (*Pauses*) He's out screwing around, telling everyone who'll listen what a monster mother I am. And how I deserved the electric chair and how he just loved that poor little baby so much.

BOY: My ex says the same thing about me.

WOMAN: I guess we're both killers.

BOY: Yeah, I guess we are.

WOMAN: Give me hug.

BOY: (*Pulls away*) No, you're way too old for me.

WOMAN: Not that kinda hug. Just a friendly hug, like with family.

> *WOMAN and BOY embrace.*
> *WOMAN pats the BOY on the*

back during a long hug. After a few seconds, they separate.

BOY: My ex said I was gonna burn in hell.

WOMAN: (*Pulls the BOY back*) I think we're there already, don't you?

BOY: Yeah, I think so.

A pool of light turns blood red and dims.

BLACKOUT

SCENE IV

The light goes up on the MAN and GIRL on the stage. GIRL is sitting on a chair. MAN pulls a chair up and sits next to GIRL.)

MAN: Hi, what's your name?

GIRL: Do I know you?

MAN: No, but maybe we can. . . .

GIRL: I really need to go (*stands up.*)

MAN: I wasn't trying to be fresh, just friendly. People can be friendly to one another can't they?

GIRL: (*Relaxes*) I'm sorry. I just don't think I'm ready for flirting yet. I'm still traumatized.

MAN: Sounds serious. What happened?

GIRL: (*Scrutinizes MAN*) Can I really trust you?

MAN: Of course. I can be very trustworthy (*makes a trustworthy face.*)

GIRL: (*Laughs a little and pauses*) My ex-husband killed our baby.

MAN: (*Looks surprised*) Wow! That is bad. I'm so sorry. (*Pauses*) How'd he do it?

GIRL: I don't really know. I came home one night from my momma's place and the baby was dead, gone, taken away by the paramedics. The baby's skull was fractured in five places.

MAN: (*Thoughtful*) My ex-girlfriend did that, too.

GIRL: Killed her baby?

MAN: Yeah, she killed our little baby. She said she never wanted the baby in the first place. And I wouldn't let her put it up for adoption.

GIRL: That's awful. What kind of a mother would kill her own baby?

MAN: That's what I said and the judge, too. (*Looks despondent*) I've never been the same.

GIRL: (*Puts her arm around MAN's shoulder*) You poor man!

MAN: (*Relaxes*) I need that. I really do.

GIRL: (*Pulls away*) I don't mean to get fresh either. I don't know you at all.

MAN: No, no. I understand. I just meant that after our baby died, I never could quite look at a woman in the same way. (*Pauses*)

Every time I see a woman, I think to myself, could she kill her own baby? Would she kill her baby?

GIRL: That's awful! (*Pauses*) But I understand. I start thinking the same thing about men. Is that one a baby killer? Could that one hurt me or my baby? It's like a sickness.

MAN: It's tough when you lose your faith in mankind. I guess all of us could be killers deep down inside under the right conditions.

GIRL: No! Not me! I'd never kill my baby. I'd never kill anyone.

MAN: Me, neither. But I do look at the world different now. It's a darker, unhappier place than before.

GIRL: I understand. I understand completely.

MAN: Sometimes it takes a tragedy to bring people together, like you and me (*moves closer and puts his arm around the GIRL's shoulders.*)

GIRL: (*Recoils at first, but then relaxes*) I guess I am ready for some human warmth and kindness. We've both been wounded, very deeply. Maybe now we can start the healing process.

MAN: (*Moves closer still*) Yes, yes. The healing process. I'm ready for the healing process to start, right here, right now (*leans over to kiss the GIRL.*)

GIRL: (*Pulls away*) Oh!

MAN: Did I hurt you?

GIRL: (*Smiles*) No, it felt good, really good (*leans forward into the MAN.*)

> *MAN and GIRL embrace, first
> tenderly and then passionately. They
> fall to the ground and he paws the
> GIRL while lifting up her skirt.*

MAN: Oh, baby. You're beautiful. You're wounded, but we can make each other whole again. I know how. Relax. Let yourself go (*continues to caress and undress the GIRL.*)

GIRL: Here? Now?

MAN: No one's around. This place is deserted (*unzips his zipper.*)

GIRL: (*Concerned*) Do you have protection?

MAN: No, I ain't got any. And you?

GIRL: No.

MAN: (*Continues*) We don't need that. Let's let nature take its course. This is what life's all about. The healing process.

GIRL: But. . . .

MAN: You need another baby with someone like me, with someone who really loves you and will love a baby, no matter what. (*Mounts GIRL and mimics sex*) Oh, baby! I love you.

GIRL: (*Panting*) Come to me! I'm ready. I need you. Oh, baby, I need you.

> *Panting continues. Lights dim.*

BLACKOUT

THE ENVIRONMENT AND HEALTH OUTCOMES

BAD APPLES AND BAD BARRELS: WHY PLACE MATTERS

Louisiana suffers from a plethora of poor statistics: high obesity, high teenage pregnancy, high infant mortality, high STD (Sexually Transmitted Disease)/HIV rates, high poverty, high incarceration rates and high murder rates. The South, by and large, shares Louisiana's poor outcomes. But even within the region (and the state), the statistics vary greatly from place to place and from group to group.

African-Americans suffer a disproportionate share of our state's poor outcomes, much of which can be attributed to poverty and low educational levels. Well-defined pockets of poverty and poor health outcomes are easily identifiable. While individual choices remain critically important, the environment in which people live has a predictive value on their subsequent behavior and development.

Poor neighborhoods have fewer supermarkets and parks, poorer achieving schools, more crime and correspondingly high rates of STDs, obesity, hypertension, teenage pregnancy, infant mortality, high-school dropouts and crime. The inverse is, of course, true of wealthier neighborhoods creating a disturbing tableau of separate, but unequal communities.

The fact remains that, despite remarkable individual examples of achievement to the contrary, bad barrels generate bad apples and good barrels generate good apples. While not ignoring the individual apple, the trick for improving outcomes appears to be transforming bad barrels.

Pockets of concentrated poverty (sometimes called "concentrated disadvantage" in public health terms) encourage poor outcomes, whether it is a neighborhood, a city, a state or a nation. Professor Zimbardo, in his famous Stanford Prison Experiment, clearly demonstrated that the situation in which people are placed (in his case randomly assigned guards vs. prisoners) can lead to predictable unfavorable results, what he calls "The Lucifer Effect."

People who manage to climb out of poverty by personal initiative should be congratulated. But reducing or eliminating "concentrated disadvantage" should be the goal of city planners, policy makers and community activists. "Bad apples" require disproportionate resources, whether they are medical care, education resources, incarceration or other expensive institutionalization. Resources might be better spent on improving the barrels in order to increase the number of good apples. Place truly matters and both individuals and policy makers can work toward making all the barrels the best possible.

While we all can and should make healthy decisions, it is much easier when the environment in which we live, work, play and worship is conducive to positive choices. Having safe neighborhoods, access to supermarkets and parks, good schools and good, well-paying jobs will all lead to improved health. Hopefully, it will also lead to reductions in the shameful disparities that plague our nation.

Place really does matter.

Zimbardo, Philip. *The Lucifer Effect: Understanding How Good People Turn Evil*, January 2008.

Dannenberg, AL, H Frumpkin and RJ Jackson. *Making Healthy Places*. Island Press, 2011.

PAINTING THE GHETTO

CHARACTERS

> VICTORIA DELAHOUSSAYE: Public health community organizer (white)
>
> DEEJON LA COUR: Young man in gang-like street attire, low-slung pants and lots of flashy jewelry (African-American)
>
> GLADYS HARRIS: Older African-American woman, conservatively dressed

SETTING

> Castlemont Neighborhood, Oakland, California. There is a large wall, covered with gang graffiti, which is partially over painted with bright yellow paint.
>
> > *VICTORIA is painting over the graffiti with yellow paint. DEEJON wanders over and stops to look and comment.*

DEEJON: What are you doing?

VICTORIA: (Stops painting) Good morning to you, too.

DEEJON: I don't need any lessons in manners in my neighborhood from a white outsider.

VICTORIA: Of course not. My apologies. (*Pauses and then resumes painting.*) I'm helping to beautify the neighborhood.

DEEJON: No you're not! You're covering up some of my artwork.

VICTORIA: (*Stands back and examines the wall*) Really?

DEEJON: You bet! Look at that! (*Points to some graffiti*) That's urban art. Now you just take that paint and them brushes and you get back to wherever you come from.

VICTORIA: I live here, on the corner of 8th and Dowling. This is my neighborhood too.

DEEJON: Oh, one of them gen-tree-fied places down toward the end? Running up the property values.

VICTORIA: No, it's a run-down, rodent infested former crack house.

DEEJON: (*Smiles*) Yeah, I know the place. Old Mrs. Bass used to live there 'til she died. (*Pause*) Now stop painting and stop your beau-tee-fi-cation and get going. This is Bancroft and 30th, and this here marks the gang limits.

VICTORIA: NO! I have the authorization of the Castlemont Neighborhood Community Action Committee and I'm not the only one who's painting around this place. We're going to paint all the walls we can. This place is going to sparkle like a new penny. This neighborhood is going to be one that people can be proud to live in and want to live in. That's the goal.

DEEJON: (*Cuts her off*) Can it, bitch! This is our neighborhood, my neighborhood, too, and this here wall marks the line between our gang and those other guys. (*Points disdainfully to the side*) They don't come over here and we don't go over there, get it?

VICTORIA: That's the problem. Gangs, graffiti, guns, murders. How do you think people will escape this cycle of poverty and destruction?

DEEJON: Cycle of poverty? (*Points to his watch and his gold jewelry*) This here watch is a Ro-lex, bitch. This watch costs $3,000 dollars. I'm not poor, far from it. And I get richer every day. Don't pity me with your honky ideas of disadvantage and social justice. Get outta here and leave that yellow paint. I'll get rid of it for you.

VICTORIA: No!

DEEJON: (*Flashes a handgun in his belt*) You don't wanna listen to reason, or maybe you want to listen to the sound of this baby.

VICTORIA: (*Looks alarmed*) You shouldn't be flashing that thing around here.

DEEJON: (*Laughs*) Why? You wanna see my con-cealed weapon permit? (*Flips VICTORIA the bird*) This is power, bitch! This is control. This is fear. This is the only thing that evens out the playing field in this place. Now get! Get outta here and stay over in your ex-crack house. Paint that place if you want to.

> GLADYS enters *holding a couple of shopping bags. Slightly stooped, but obviously alert. GLADYS looks at DEEJON and VICTORIA who look back at GLADYS.*

GLADYS: What's gonna on here? (*Looks at DEEJON*) What you been bothering this lady about?

DEEJON: You stay outta this, Gramma. Just keep moving along. I got it under control.

GLADYS: (*Sets down her bags*) I certainly will not. And I'm not your grandma either. (*To VICTORIA*) Aren't you one of them ladies from the public health?

VICTORIA: (*Extends her hand*) Yes, ma'am. I'm Victoria Delahoussaye. Pleased to meet you.

GLADYS: My name is Gladys Harris. (*Shakes hand*) I know you already. Seen you at the community meeting. (*Looks at the wall*) This looks right nice now. A very cheerful color. I always liked yellow. Lot nicer than them gang symbols.

DEEJON: Both you ladies gotta go. Gramma, you get going, too. This is our wall, our graffiti, our art and no white bitch from Berkeley's gonna tell us what to do in our place.

GLADYS: Aren't you Deejon LaCour from over on 94th Street?

DEEJON: (*Obviously embarrassed*) What's it to you?

GLADYS: I know your mama and your aunties and a couple of your uncles. Their folks all came from Mon-roe, Louisiana a long while back, didn't they? All of them came from there.

DEEJON: (*Taken aback*) You know alla them people?

GLADYS: You bet! And I knew them really good and I know their folks, too, from back in Mon-Roe a whole long time ago. Good people, them LaCours.

VICTORIA: (*To GLADYS*) Thanks for your help. You wanna stop and paint a little bit?

GLADYS: No, I'm not dressed for painting. Besides, I'm not sure I really believe in this beau-ti-fi-cation project. If rents around here get much higher, then no black folks are gonna be able to live here anymore.

DEEJON: (*Decides to leave*) I got more important things to do than listen to two bitches talking nonsense.

GLADYS: (*To DEEJON*) You clean your mouth up, Mr. Deejon! Your mama taught you better than that! We are ladies, I'm Mrs. Harris and this is Miss. . . .

VICTORIA: Delahoussaye.

GLADYS: Dee-la-hous-see. (*To DEEJON*) Now, you can help us or you can move on outta here. Your choice, Mr. LaCour!

DEEJON: Just Deejon. And I'm no mister.

GLADYS: Deejon. (*Pauses*) That's true, you look like a kid. Why aren't you in school, anyway? What you doing down here in the middle of the day at your age?

DEEJON: I don't need any fucking school. That place is so bad that nobody with any sense stays there. Besides, I make more money in a day than my dad did in a month.

GLADYS: Dope! Dealing dope! Aren't you ashamed? Don't you want to get outta this place some day? And don't you use that sorta language around ladies.

VICTORIA: (*A bit perplexed*) We're trying to make this into a livable community, a desirable place to live.

GLADYS: Castlemont isn't desirable. (*To VICTORIA sharply*) Walnut Creek is desirable. Orinda is desirable. Lafayette and Danville are desirable. (*Swings her arms around*) This place crawls with drugs, with sexual transmitted disease, with murder, poverty, bad schools, and unemployment. What's livable about that?

VICTORIA: No! It's more than that. It's a vibrant community full of good people like you, working together to make a better life. That's good, very good! That's something to be proud of.

GLADYS: Proud? Dying babies, drug wars, prostitutes, girls pregnant at fourteen, men and boys hanging around on street corners selling dope or doing nothing at all. No future. What's that, Victoria? What's that Mrs. Public Health? That's a ghetto. It's nothing but a miserable ghetto and you and a lotta other folks make a living off it. You may be another one of them poverty whores.

DEEJON: You got it, Gramma. Right on! We live in a ghetto, but at least it's ours.

VICTORIA: No! This is a neighborhood. And I'm certainly no poverty whore, even if I do work for the Public Health Department. I want to help. I want to live here and be part of the community.

GLADYS: You think people living here want to live here?

VICTORIA: (*Surprised*) Of course!

> *DEEJON and GLADYS laugh after exchanging a knowing glance.*

GLADYS: No we don't. We live here because we can't live anyplace else. A miserable little 1000 square foot ranch style house in beautiful Walnut Creek costs a million dollars. A house there where the streets are clean and parks are man-ee-cured and schools crank out college-bound kids by the thousands rents for $4000 a month. What the heck you think that means for us folks?

VICTORIA: I'm sorry. I'm being culturally insensitive.

GLADYS: (*Sighs. To DEEJON*) What are you still standing here for? I thought you had important things to do, important people to meet, important deals to finish. I thought you wanted to be in this place where you'll die young and not necessarily happy. That's what you want, isn't, Deejon!

DEEJON: (*Looks thoughtful*) I don't wanna be here either, Miss Gladys. I don't wanna see my friends killed or go to prison. I wanna live in Orinda, too, where the schools are the best in the state and nobody is killing each other over a few blocks of dirty asphalt. What kinda life is this? (*Swings his arms around*) I watched my brother get his brains blown out in front of our house. And my sister's got a baby at fourteen. What kinda life is that, anyway? Yeah, I make a lot of money now, but for how long? (*Pauses*) I heard alla them kids from Orinda get to go to college and get a scholarship to go from their PTA. Every one of them! I heard it from a teacher at our school who lives in Orinda.

GLADYS: And that fancy watch and that big gun? And all the money you're making? You want that, too, don't you?

DEEJON: You think I got a whole lot of choice here? Really?

GLADYS: We always gotta choice.

DEEJON: No! I have to go to the school where there aren't three people gonna go on to college and most of the others will drop out, get pregnant, be killed or stuck in prison before graduation. Kids all wanna go and deal dope where they can make a killing and then get killed. A short, rich life, that's what they want.

GLADYS: Like you?

DEEJON: I don't like this either, Miss Gladys. (*Looks ashamed*) I gotta do this to survive. How am I ever gonna get outta this place without money, a whole lotta money?

VICTORIA: Studying!

DEEJON: How can I study when we got three generations stuffed in an apartment meant for one family? There's noise and smells and strangers coming and going all day and all night 'til I just wanna scream. How could I study if I even wanted to?

VICTORIA: They have great study rooms down at the library. It's quiet there.

DEEJON: I can't even get there. It's across the way into their turf. (*Points off-stage*) I'd get killed trying to get there.

GLADYS: (*Puts down her bags*) Gimmie a brush, Victoria, I wanna paint, too. I wanna paint this wall with you. (*Takes a brush and hands it to DEEJON*) You take this one, Deejon. (*To VICTORIA*) I'll take the other one, please. We all need to paint.

All paint in silence.

GLADYS (CONT): Maybe we can all paint our way outta this place.

DEEJON: No, we aren't doing that. We're just making the ghetto prettier. We're just beau-ti-fying the ghetto.

VICTORIA: Isn't that something at least?

GLADYS: Painting the ghetto. Is that all we can hope for? Can we ever move to that Walnut Creek place, with those hanging flower baskets and I-talian music playing in the streets from loud speakers?

VICTORIA: No, you can't! I understand that. Not even if you make a bundle of money on drugs, much less by working at low paying, dead end jobs.

GLADYS: Like cleaning? Cleaning white people's houses over them hills (points offstage). Like I did all my life?

VICTORIA: Yes, like cleaning. There's nothing dishonorable about that, but you really didn't have any choices back then. You are smart, and Deejon here is smart, too. He could work hard and study hard and be a doctor or a lawyer or an engineer, something important.

GLADYS: (*To DEEJON*) Yeah, something nice. And maybe you can move to Orinda or Lafayette or Danville and raise your kids in a nice neighborhood with nice schools and with real supermarkets and nice parks. That'd be real nice.

A gunshot rings out.

DEEJON: (*Drops his brush*) Oh shit! I gotta hide somewhere. Those gang members are gonna kill me for sure. I'm way outta our territory. Bancroft Avenue's no man's land, a war zone, and it's open season for me.

GLADYS: You pick up that brush and you just continue painting here between Victoria and me. Right here (points to the wall).

DEEJON: You don't understand. If they even see me, I'll be dead.

GLADYS: (*Hands him the brush*) You just keep painting!

VICTORIA: Shouldn't we call the police?

DEEJON: With an illegal gun on me? Are you crazy?

GLADYS: (*Calmly*) Keep painting. Up and down. Up and down. Stay between us, Deejon.

All paint. Another shot rings out.
Louder and closer.

257

GLADYS: (*Looks stricken. Drops her brush and falls to the ground.*) God in heaven! I've been shot (*blood saturates her blouse.*) Jesus, sweet Jesus!

DEEJON: (*Kneels down and takes GLADY in his arms*) Miss Gladys, hang in there. You can make it. You gonna be all right.

GLADYS: No, I'm not. I'm gonna die right here under this yellow wall. I wanted to get out of this ghetto, too, one way or another, but dying here on the street. . . .

DEEJON: You aren't gonna die, Miss Gladys. You're tough. You're a survivor. You survived this place.

GLADYS: Just be quiet. Pray with me! (*Looks at VICTORIA*) You, too.

> *VICTORIA kneels and they form a tight triangle. Blood continues to pour out of GLADYS.*

GLADYS: Sweet Jesus, sweet, sweet Jesus. Take your servant to your bosom. Protect this young man and this young lady from evil, let them paint this whole sinful place so bright and yellow I can see it from heaven. Don't let them stray from the righteous path, they be following for your name's sake. Your Kingdom come, your will be done.

DEEJON: No, ma'am! You can't die. No old lady's gonna die for me.

GLADYS: Sush! You hush now, boy.

VICTORIA: (*Takes her phone and calls 911*) Yes, a shooting at the corner of 22nd and MacArthur. A woman is shot and bleeding. (*Pause. Turns to GLADYS*) They'll be here in a minute. (*Puts away her phone and tries to staunch the bleeding*) Just hang in there. Please don't die. I didn't what this. I never wanted this (*starts to cry.*)

GLADYS: Stop that crying, Miss Victoria. I wanna go up to Jesus where I'll listen to angels singing, not moaning white girls. I wanna rise above this place of work and worry and sail right over Walnut Creek and them flowers and I-talian music on my way to heaven. Sing with me.

DEEJON: I can't sing.

GLADYS: SING! Both of you sing with me. (*Begins to sing in a slow resonate voice.*)

Holy, holy, holy,
Lord God Almighty!
Early in the morning
Our song shall rise to Thee.

(*Stops singing*) Jesus Christ, have mercy on my soul! (*Stares at the wall*) It really does looks better painted. (*To DEEJON*) You promise me you gonna help this white lady paint this whole wicked place.

DEEJON: Yes, ma'am. I promise.

GLADYS: (*To VICTORIA.*) And you promise me you gonna paint every last wall in Castlemont and when those walls get spoiled with them gangs signs, you gonna paint over and over and over until no one even remembers alla that ugliness. You promise?

VICTORIA: Yes, yes, of course.

GLADYS: And when it be beautiful, can you hang some of them flower baskets with them pink flowers like they have in Walnut Creek?

VICTORIA: Yes, of course, and Italian music, too.

GLADYS: (*Thinks.*) No. No I-talian music. I want hymns. I want the word of God to rising up in song from this here ghetto until it

259

reaches to heaven and I can hear it. And I wanna see the place shining yellow and bright like a field of sunflowers.

> *Ambulance siren sounds in the distance.*

DEEJON: Just a couple of minutes, Miss Gladys. Please, just a couple of minutes. They're almost here.

GLADYS: Too late, boy. It's too late for me, but not for you (*turns her head to the yellow wall and dies.*)

VICTORIA: (*Screams*) NO! (*Grasps her hands to her mouth and then clutches the limp body and weeps.*)

DEEJON: (*Moans audibly*) Oh my God! (*Shakes his head. Pulls the gun from his belt and throws it across the stage.*)

> *Ambulance siren rises to a crescendo and then goes silent as the lights dim to dark on the three figures against the yellow background.*

BLACKOUT

EVACUATIONS AND SHELTERING

EVACUATION AND SHELTERING
IN LOUISIANA

Louisiana, with its extensive coastline and geographical location on the Gulf, remains vulnerable to devastating hurricanes. No one can forget the destruction wrought by Katrina, but there has also been Rita, Gustav, Ike and Isaac, to name but a few more recent storms. In response to this constant threat, Louisiana has developed a complex system of sheltering for its coastal residents. This becomes a huge issue since almost half of the state population lives near or below I-10, in New Orleans, Baton Rouge, Lafayette and Lake Charles.

There are, in fact, several types of different shelters: General Shelters, Critical Transportation Needs Shelters, Medical Special Needs Shelters, a Sex Offenders Shelter, an Unaccompanied Minor Shelter and Ambulatory Elderly Shelters. General Shelters are those open to anyone driving up from South Louisiana. These are most often run by the American Red Cross, but can be opened by churches and other private organizations. Some parishes in South Louisiana make individual arrangements with parishes in Central and North Louisiana in what is called a "point to point" sheltering system.

Critical Transportation Needs Shelters (CTNS), managed by the Department of Children and Family Services or DCFS (formerly Social Services), are also established in Central and North Louisiana. These are dedicated to people who do not have transportation for self-evacuation. Parish pick up points are established in key locations in South Louisiana and transportation is provided by buses, arranged with cooperation of the Department of Transportation. These evacuees are triaged (sorted) either on spot or subsequently in Baton Rouge to separate those who are medically fragile and would need to go to a Medical Special Needs Shelter.

Medical Special Needs Shelters (MSNS) are manned with providers from the Office of Public Health, in collaboration with other state agencies, and are also located around the state, but principally in Central and North Louisiana. The evacuees in these shelters require complex medical care and are usually accompanied by a caregiver. It is often patients who are benefiting from home health services and may include those with wound care issues, dialysis, tube feeding oxygen therapy or other medical issues. Patients in nursing homes, hospitals and other institutions are evacuated to equivalent institutions and not into a MSNS. Each of these medical institutions must have an evacuation plan with a designated institutional recipient.

Central Louisiana is blessed with a unique asset, the State Shelter at Alexandria (also know as the "MegaShelter.") This is a 206,000 square foot facility, located on the LSU-Ag Center property adjacent to LSU-Alexandria. It can house up to 2,500 Critical Transportation Needs evacuees and up to 450 Medical Special Needs evacuees. The logistics of operating such a facility are staggering and require the cooperation not only of the Department of Children and Family Services and the Department of Health and Hospitals (including the Office of Public Health, Behavioral Health and Medicaid), but also the Louisiana State Police, National Guard, Department of Transportation, Bureau of Emergency Medical Services and many others. Food services, laundry, waste disposal, oxygen and other necessities need to be pre-arranged, a responsibility of DCFS, the "shelter managers."

The state has also established some small, specialized shelters of sex offenders and unaccompanied minors. Some parishes, mostly in South Louisiana, have also established plans for "ambulatory elderly" shelters, for older people with minimal medical needs, but who need some assistance nonetheless.

Pets posed a particular problem during Hurricane Katrina and prompted the passage of federal legislation mandating the establishment of pet shelters. These shelters, one of which is located at the LSU

Ag Center in Alexandria, adjacent to the MegaShelter, is run by the Louisiana Department of Fisheries and Wildlife (LDFW). Pets, like people, are registered at parish pick up points. Smaller pets, if they can fit in a small animal carrier, may accompany their owners on buses destined for Critical Transportation Need Shelters (such as in the MegaShelter). This was not the case during Hurricane Katrina and caused much consternation during that complex and prolonged evacuation and sheltering. Larger animals are registered and loaded onto special trucks to be delivered at one of the two large pet shelters in the state (Alexandria and Shreveport).

Louisiana, by choice and necessity, has become a leader in the development of plans for evacuation and sheltering for people and animals. Central Louisiana has become not only the state's geographic hub, but also the location of Louisiana's only dedicated sheltering facility. The "Heart of Louisiana" has long been known for its hospitality and now we are also known for our sheltering capacity. This being said, every individual still needs to have their own evacuation and sheltering plans since there is not only a collective, but also an individual responsibility for preparedness. With all of its resources, the state can still not shelter each and every individual and their pet.

Know who and what needs to be evacuated and have a preplanned destination. Since disasters can strike anywhere, anytime, always have a plan! Your life may depend on it.

GIVE ME SHELTER! (PETS, PEDOPHILES AND POLITICIANS)

CHARACTERS

> CAROLINE SMITH: An older woman in neat, but shabby, clothing. She is holding a pet carrying cage in her lap. She is wearing a white wristband. There does not have to be a dog in the cage.

> STEVE MILLER: A young man, casually dressed in a leather jacket, which covers his red wristband.

> BUS DRIVER: May be black or white. He has a cap or something to indicate his job.

> POLICE OFFICER: A uniformed police officer.

> NATHAN LANDRY: Louisiana state representative, dressed in a shirt and slacks.

> RICHARD WALLACE: Shelter manager. He is casually dressed.

SCENE I

SETTING

> The set is very simple. There are a few chairs or benches lined up to look like seats on a bus. They are facing the audience. CAROLINE is sitting near STEVE on adjacent seats. CAROLINE holds a small animal cage on her lap.

BUS DRIVER: (*Comes down the aisle and looks at the cage*) You gotta get rid of that animal, lady.

CAROLINE: I can't. This is my dog, Carrie, and she's my life. She's my only friend, my only family. I can't leave Carrie behind to die in the hurricane.

DRIVER: Listen, lady. I don't care. They told us there wasn't supposed to be any animals on this bus, just people goin' to the shelter. And this is my bus and we can't have any animals stinkin' up this bus any more than it already is.

CAROLINE: Carrie doesn't smell. She's a very clean dog. (*Sniffs the cage*) Here, smell. (*Lifts up the cage to the driver.*)

DRIVER: (*Sniffs*) Smells like a dog to me, a wet one. (*Shakes his head*) The rules is the rules. No animals on this bus or I ain't leavin'. No one goes anywhere until your dog is outta here. If you wanna get off with your mutt, that's your business, but do it now.

STEVE: Leave the lady alone!

DRIVER: Keep your nose outta this, mister, or you're gettin' off too.

STEVE: (*Stands up and confronts the DRIVER*) I said leave her alone! That dog ain't bothering anybody.

DRIVER: It's against the rules, it's botherin' me!

STEVE: Then we'll move back a few rows and you won't have to deal with it so close up and personal. How about that?

DRIVER: Front, back, it don't make no difference. I'm not leavin' until that dog's outta here and I want it off now!

CAROLINE: Please, mister. I can't leave Carrie behind. I'll get off. We'll stay behind. I don't care if we both drown.

STEVE: (*Pushes CAROLINE gently back down in her seat*) Sit down! You can't stay behind. You might not even have a house to go back to. We gotta evacuate and we're leaving together, dog and all.

DRIVER: Are you guys related?

CAROLINE: No.

STEVE: (*Interrupts CAROLINE*) Yes, this is my auntie. And I'm taking responsibility for her and her dog. (*Reaches in his wallet and pulls out some bills. Presents them to the DRIVER.*) And maybe this'll make you forget that the dog's on this bus.

DRIVER: (*Looks at the money. Hesitates and then takes it and stuffs it in his pocket*) Move back a few rows and don't let nobody see that damned dog.

> CAROLINE and STEVE move
> back a couple of rows and settle in.

CAROLINE: Thank you, young man.

STEVE: It's okay. (*Looks at the cage.*) What kinda of a dog is it?

CAROLINE: (*Opens the cage*) Carrie's a Pekinese-mix. (*Looks at STEVE*) You wanna pet her?

STEVE: Does she bite?

CAROLINE: No, she's as gentle as a lamb. Besides, she doesn't have any teeth any more. Like me. (*Shows her dentures*) They're fake.

STEVE: (*Ignores the dentures and puts his hand in the cage. Appears to be stroking the dog.*) Wow. She's so nice and soft. (*Closes his eyes and continues to stroke*) Hmmm. Soft as a baby's hair.

CAROLINE: (*Looks a little alarmed*) That's enough. (*Closes the door to the cage*) She gets a little nervous if she gets too much petting. (*Notices he has a red wristband*) What's that?

STEVE: My ID wristband, just like yours.

CAROLINE: But it's red. Mine's white (*shows STEVE her wrist band.*)

STEVE: Yeah (*takes out a pocketknife and cuts off the band, then puts the knife and the band in his jacket pocket.*)

CAROLINE: I thought we were supposed to keep them bands on the whole trip, to keep track of everyone. That's what they said at the registration desk.

STEVE: Yeah.

CAROLINE: Why's yours red?

STEVE: (*Shrugs his shoulders*) Does it matter?

CAROLINE: Are you some sorta criminal?

STEVE: No.

CAROLINE: Then what are you?

STEVE: Do you really wanna know?

CAROLINE: (*Pauses*) Yes, I really do.

STEVE: I'm a registered sex offender.

CAROLINE: (*Backs away*) Really? (*Clutches her cage and starts to stand up.*)

STEVE: Don't worry; it's just with children.

CAROLINE: (*Raises her voice*) Just with children!

STEVE: Shhhhhh! Not so loud, please.

CAROLINE: But that's terrible.

STEVE: That's what my momma says, too, when she kicked me out of the house. Go ahead. You can move away from me. I'm used to it.

CAROLINE: (*Starts to move, then hesitates and sits down*) But children?

STEVE: It was mostly pictures and videos and that sort of thing. I never really touched any kids. Not to say I didn't want to. But I got my principles, too.

CAROLINE: So your family rejected you.

STEVE: (*Sighs*) My momma did. I never knew my dad. When she found my pictures and videos, she kicked me outta the house. So I moved in with this guy who let me stay as long as he could molest me. At first it really bothered me, but after awhile I got used to it. He even got me hooked on kiddy porn and some other stuff, too. (*Stops.*) I swear I never touched any kids. I just kind of got addicted to them pictures. Maybe I was just looking for something innocent and pure. Nothing like I'd ever known in my life. I finally wised up and got away from that guy. He was a real predator! (*Pauses*) Can I pet your dog again?

CAROLINE: (*Looks back and forth between STEVE and the cage*) Okay, but not for too long and not too hard.

STEVE: (*Puts his hand in the cage and puts the dog*) So soft. So fluffy. Very clean.

CAROLINE: (*Slams the door shut*) Okay, that's enough.

CAROLINE and STEVE sit in silence for a few seconds.

STEVE: Are you gonna turn me in?

CAROLINE: I should turn you in.

STEVE: Why?

CAROLINE: Because you might pose a danger to the children at the shelter where we're going to.

STEVE: I'm not dangerous. But if you think I am, I'll turn myself in. (*Starts to stand up.*)

CAROLINE: (*Pulls him down*) No, don't go. I won't say anything.

STEVE: (Drops back down in his seat) Why'd you change your mind?

CAROLINE: Because you look a lot like my nephew. You got the same eyes and the same mouth. I thought about him when I saw you. I just couldn't let you get sent down there with all those perverts. I know what they do to young men in them places.

STEVE: You're right about that. It can be tough. The first time I went to jail, I got raped in the first 6 hours.

CAROLINE: That's awful.

STEVE: Yeah, it was awful. But it taught me a lot, too.

CAROLINE: Like what?

STEVE: Like who and what you need to know to survive. Which guys could offer you protection in return for, you know.

CAROLINE: Know what?

STEVE: You know (*makes a pumping gesture near his crotch with his hand.*)

CAROLINE: (*Turns away briefly*) I think we need to change the subject.

STEVE: Okay, but can I pet your puppy one more time?

CAROLINE: (*Hesitates again*) Her name is Carrie. (*Looks at STEVE*) Okay, but not too hard and not for too long, and just on the top, okay?

STEVE: Okay. (*Puts in his hand and begins to pet. Closes his eyes*) So soft and gentle. You gotta nice dog lady. And you're a nice person, too. (*To CAROLINE*) What's your name?

CAROLINE: Caroline Delacroix. And yours?

STEVE: Steve Miller. Nice to meet you (*pulls his hand out of the cage and shakes CAROLINE's hand.*)

CAROLINE: Nice meeting you. Just sorry it has to be under these conditions. But I guess it's okay if we're both refugees.

STEVE: I think they prefer "evacuees." It sounds better. (*Pauses*) Have you ever been to Fulton before?

CAROLINE: No. Lived in Louisiana 74 years and never been outta New Orleans. It's kinda exciting in a weird sorta way, I guess (*pulls a couple of bottles of water out of a bag. Gives one to STEVE.*)

STEVE: Yes, very exciting. I went through Fulton once on my way to the prison in Winnfield, but we didn't stop.

CAROLINE: Here's to sheltering in Fulton!

> *STEVE and CAROLINE touch bottles.*

STEVE and CAROLINE: Cheers!

BLACKOUT

SCENE II

> *Same bus, a few hours later. CAROLINE appears to be sleeping, her head against STEVE's shoulder. The OFFICER comes down the aisle of the bus and checks the passengers. STEVE sees the OFFICER approaching down the aisle and pulls his red arm band out of his pocket and stuffs it into CAROLINE's jacket pocket. CAROLINE wakes and notices what STEVE has done, but does not react. CAROLINE listens to the OFFICER.*

OFFICER: (*To STEVE*) Where's your wristband?

STEVE: It musta fell off at the parish pick-up point.

OFFICER: What's your name?

STEVE: Brian. Brian Hill.

OFFICER: (*Uses a hand held device and checks for the name*) I don't see anyone by that name in the system. (*Studies STEVE's face*) In fact, I think I saw you earlier in the group supposed to be goin' to the Gonzales shelter.

CAROLINE: (*CAROLINE looks at the OFFICER*) What's the Gonzales Shelter? If it's closer, can I go there, too? Fulton's so far away.

OFFICER: You don't want to go there, ma'am.

CAROLINE: Why not?

OFFICER: It's reserved for perverts.

CAROLINE: Perverts?

OFFICER: Yeah, sex offenders: pedophiles, domestic abusers, and those types. I think this guy next to you may be one of them.

CAROLINE: (*Looks astonished*) Really? I don't believe it!

OFFICER: Why not? Those kinda folks can be sittin' right next to you and you'd never know it.

CAROLINE: Well, this time I do know it, 'cause he's my nephew and his name is Brian, Brian Hill, just like he said.

OFFICER: Really?

CAROLINE: Yes, he's been staying with me since my daughter died of breast cancer a few months ago. Her death has been so hard on all of us. And Brian has been so wonderful. He stayed with me and helped until she died. I don't know what I would have done without him. He's been taking care of me and Carrie. (*Shows the OFFICER the cage*) Carrie's my Pekinese mix. You want see her?

OFFICER: (*Glances briefly at the dog cage, and then continues speaking to STEVE*) So what exactly happened to your wristband?

STEVE: I don't know. It must have fallen off back in New Orleans.

OFFICER: (*Looks skeptical*) Okay. (*To CAROLINE*) Now, what about that dog? I thought there weren't supposed to be any animals on these buses.

STEVE: That's none of your business. Go look for some perverts, not pets.

OFFICER: (*Frowns*) Okay kid. But I got my eye on you (*points at STEVE and then walks away.*)

STEVE: (*Turns to CAROLINE*) Thank you.

CAROLINE: No problem.

STEVE: You didn't have to stick up for me. Why'd you do that?

CAROLINE: You helped me with my dog. And, like I said, you remind me of my nephew. He died of AIDS back in the 80's. I never accepted it back then. And I never said anything nice to him before he died. (*Pauses*) I didn't think much of his lifestyle, but he didn't deserve to die, especially sick and alone like he did. He was always kind to me and to Carrie, like you are. He had his own dog, an ugly little mutt named Staccato, but they made him give it away when his immune system got real bad. It nearly broke his heart. And I never stuck up for him or his dog. I let 'em take the dog to the pound and I wouldn't take it. I thought the dog might have AIDS, too, and infect Carrie.

STEVE: Dogs can't get AIDS. They get rabies and things like that. Dog diseases. And I don't have AIDS, if that's what you think. At least not that I know of.

CAROLINE: I know about dogs and AIDS, but back then I was afraid. I don't know what you have and I don't care. You've been kind to Carrie and kind to me. They wanted to kick Carrie off, too. (*Pauses*) You really don't hurt children, do you?

STEVE: No, just pictures, like I said. I just look at pictures and videos. And I don't take them pictures of kids myself either. You know, I just look, for the pleasure. I look and I don't touch real kids, I swear to God.

CAROLINE: It still hurts them, you know. Someone else has to take them pictures. So it hurts the kids just the same.

STEVE: I know. But I can't help myself. It's stronger than me. I just look at them sweet little kids and it makes me so excited I can burst.

CAROLINE: Stop!

STEVE: Stop what?

CAROLINE: I don't want to hear any more about it. I just want you to sit here next to me and drive on up to Fulton together to that shelter. And don't you be thinking of doing anything bad to any children up there either. I got my eye on you!

STEVE: I wouldn't do that.

CAROLINE: Cross your heart and hope to die?

STEVE: (*Crosses his heart with a simple back and forth gesture*) Cross my heart.

CAROLINE: (*Crosses herself, too, according to the Catholic tradition*) Me, too.

OFFICER: (*The OFFICER returns and addresses CAROLINE*) Ma'am, with all due respect, I think this guy is Steve Miller, a registered sex offender, and I'm taking him off this bus, right now! (*Grabs STEVE.*)

CAROLINE: (*Pulls on STEVE's other arm*) No you can't! I'll scream (*screams very loudly.*) AHHHHHHH!

OFFICER: (*Continues to pull on STEVE*) Don't you be screamin' or I'll arrest the both of you for resisting arrest. I swear to God I will.

CAROLINE: (*Starts to hit at the officer's arm*) Leave him alone! Leave him alone!

STEVE: (*To CAROLINE*) It's okay. I'll go. Don't get in trouble and thanks for trying to help me.

CAROLINE: (*Grabs her cage.*) I'll let my dog out and he'll bite your leg, you bully!

OFFICER: Don't try it, lady, or I'll shoot that dog dead and Taser you!

CAROLINE: (*Sits back down and starts to cry. To STEVE*) Take care of yourself.

STEVE: I will. And you take care of Carrie, too.

CAROLINE: I will. Good luck. (*Reaches in her pocket and pulls out the red wristband. Puts it around her wrist and stands up, still clutching her cage*) Take me! Take me, too! I'm a pervert, too. See my armband. It's a red one.

OFFICER: (*Examines the band*) Yeah, and I guess your name's Steve Miller, too. (*Laughs and throws the arm band on the floor*) Nice try, lady. Now sit down. This bus is taking off to the shelter in Fulton any minute.

CAROLINE: (*She jumps up*) No!

OFFICER: Sit down, lady! I'm just doin' my job. We've got strict orders, right from the governor's office.

CAROLINE: No! I'm not sitting down!

OFFICER: Okay, that's it, you crazy old loon! You're comin' with me, too (*grabs her with his free hand.*)

CAROLINE: Good! And you better put me with Steve so we can look out for one another (*clutches the cage as she is being pulled up.*)

OFFICER: (*Leads them both away*) With Steve? You wanna be with this creep so you can look out after each other? With all them perverts (*laughs.*) Right!

> The OFFICER drags CAROLINE
> and STEVE off the bus. Lights dim.

BLACKOUT

SCENE III

> There are a few cots that suggest a larger building, full of cots and evacuees. CAROLINE is lying on her cot. There is one that is empty next to hers. The cage is discreetly tucked under the cot, but still visible. NATHAN enters the stage, followed by RICHARD, who holds a clipboard.

NATHAN: (*Surveys the scene*) Don't these poor people even have real beds?

RICHARD: No sir, they just have cots.

NATHAN: Cots can't be that comfortable for some of these people. I've had several complaints from my constituents about this very issue.

RICHARD: This isn't a resort, sir; it's just an evacuee shelter.

NATHAN: No, of course it's not a resort. I'm not foolish. But we still have an obligation to our constituents. Can you imagine sleeping on something like this? (*Lies down on the empty cot next to CAROLINE's*) My God, it's as hard as a rock.

RICHARD: Yes, they are firm. They have to support up to 350 pounds.

NATHAN: Wow, a lotta fat people, I guess. (*Pauses*) These poor folks need some comfort, not this kind of torture.

RICHARD: We can't buy beds, sir. It's totally out of our budget. This is the best we can do with the limited money we have.

NATHAN: Can we at least buy some of the egg crate mattress as an overlay at least?

RICHARD: That's not in the budget either.

NATHAN: Whose budget?

RICHARD: The State's budget, sir.

NATHAN: And who was so cruel as to not give you adequate funds for this important humanitarian service?

RICHARD: You, sir.

NATHAN: Me?

RICHARD: Yes. Well, maybe not you personally, but the legislature refused to match funds from the Federal government, so we lost several million dollars. It was taken out of the disaster preparedness funding. You remember?

NATHAN: Ah yes. Perhaps I do. (*Looks down at CAROLINE, who is lying on her cot*) What's your name, dear?

CAROLINE: Caroline Smith.

NATHAN: (*Extends his hand*) Hi, I'm Nathan Landry, state representative. I'm here checking on the conditions in the shelter. Are you doing okay?

CAROLINE: (*Stands up*) No, I'm not okay. (*Points to her cot*) This thing is as hard as a rock. And there's no one to take care of my dog. We can't get a decent snack and there's no dog food.

NATHAN: You eat dog food?

CAROLINE: No, silly. It's for my dog, Carrie. (*Pulls her dog carrier out from under her cot and shows it to NATHAN*) They wanted to take her away from me on the bus, but a nice young man, Mr. Steve Miller, made them leave me alone.

NATHAN: (*Leans toward RICHARD.*) Are they supposed to let dogs into the shelter?

RICHARD: No.

NATHAN: Then why did this one get in here?

RICHARD: (*Shrugs his shoulders*) I don't know. Must have slipped through the cracks.

CAROLINE: I'll tell you. This nice young man by the name of Steve Miller made them let me keep Carrie on the bus.

NATHAN: Steve Miller, a young man around twenty-three years old, with brown hair and brown eyes, medium build? (*This description may be altered to reflect the actor portraying STEVE.*)

CAROLINE: Yeah, that's the one. I told them I was his aunt so they wouldn't take him off the bus.

NATHAN: Take him off the bus? Where? Why?

CAROLINE: (*Leans forward in confidence*) Because he had a red wristband.

NATHAN: (*Leans toward RICHARD*) What does that mean?

RICHARD: (*RICHARD half whispers to NATHAN*) Pedophile or other sex offender.

NATHAN: What? I can't hear a word you're saying in this noisy place.

CAROLINE: Steve said it meant he was a child molester, a sex offender! But he told me he never touched children. He only looked at pictures.

NATHAN: You're lying! Steve Miller would never do anything like that. You're mistaken.

CAROLINE: I am not!

NATHAN: This woman is lying.

CAROLINE: NO! And here's his red wristband with his name on it. I kept it from the bus.

NATHAN: (*Looks at the band and hands it back to CAROLINE*) What is this all about?

RICHARD: (*Shrugs his shoulders*) I don't know anything about this, sir, except that this dog shouldn't be here. This is a people shelter, not a pet shelter. And there is a designated shelter for sex offenders as well somewhere else.

CAROLINE: In Gonzales. I heard the officer say it.

NATHAN: (*Points to the cage*) Then get that thing out of here and take this lady, too.

CAROLINE: I tried to keep them from taking Steve. I tried to go with him, 'cause he protected my dog and he reminded me of my own nephew who died of AIDS.

NATHAN: This woman and her dog have got to go.

RICHARD: We can't kick her out, sir.

NATHAN: The rules are the rules. No animals in a people shelter.

CAROLINE: And no perverts with children!

NATHAN: There has to have been some sort of mistake. That young man could not have been the Steve Miller I knew. He's the son of Margaret Miller from Pointe Coupée, a charming Christian woman from a very good family. I knew her very well, very well.

CAROLINE: Steve tried to help me, I tell you. He tried to help me and my dog. He didn't do anything wrong and they still took him away.

NATHAN: (*Speaks to RICHARD*) Where would they have taken him?

RICHARD: To Gonzales. The lady's right. There's a special shelter there for that kind of evacuee.

NATHAN: Who made that decision? It's segregation. It's discrimination.

RICHARD: It's a question of safety, sir. We try and make sure sexual predators are not mixed with children in the general shelters.

CAROLINE: He said he never touched the children. He just looked at the pictures. I told him that was still wrong, but he said it was stronger than him.

NATHAN: (*To CAROLINE*) Thank you for the details. (*To RICHARD*) Shipping off pedophiles to special camps. It's like the Nazis. Who decided on such a thing?

RICHARD: You did?

NATHAN: I did?

RICHARD: Yes, sir. The legislature passed the law last session after incidents that took place in the shelters a couple of years ago during that evacuation. You know, at the shelter near Monroe.

NATHAN: Oh yes, I remember. (*Pauses*) But Steve was such a nice boy, a good young man with a very Christian mother. I really admired his mother, a real looker, beautiful and very kind. And I would have married her, too, if she hadn't gone and married that good-for-nothing scoundrel down there from St. Francisville.

CAROLINE: I thought he was a nice boy, too. I said he was my nephew so they wouldn't take him or my dog away.

NATHAN: (*Looks at the cage*) Yes, of course, the dog.

RICHARD: Yes, sir, the one that should be in a special pet shelter someplace else.

NATHAN: (*To CAROLINE*) Did Steve seem upset when they took him away?

CAROLINE: No, not at the end. He just let them lead him away. He looked kinda sad, but not really upset. Like he kinda half expected it. He still didn't want to go, 'cause he said the other guys might take advantage of him. I wanted them to take me too, but they just put me back on another bus headed for this shelter in Fulton.

RICHARD: (*Picks up the dog carrier*) Ma'am, we gotta get rid of this dog. Not permanently, just for a little while. He needs to go in a special shelter for pets.

CAROLINE: (*Starts to cry*) Don't take my puppy away. Carrie's all I got. I can't stand to be without her. Please, mister. Don't take Carrie away from me.

NATHAN: Leave the dog alone!

RICHARD: But you said it had to go.

NATHAN: I know what I said. And I can also change my mind and often do. So leave the dog here. And get me the numbers of that special shelter down in Gonzales. I've got to get Steve out of there.

RICHARD: But he's there because he's supposed to be. They're just following the rules.

NATHAN: Damn the rules!

RICHARD: I'm paid to follow the rules you made, sir.

NATHAN: Well, I'm telling you to let the dog stay! And get this woman a decent mattress or an egg crate, or anything to soften this cot. Who could sleep on something like this, anyway? Get going!

RICHARD: Yes, sir.

NATHAN: And don't forget to get me the name and address of the person in charge down in Gonzales. I've got to make a trip down there, too.

RICHARD: Yes, sir. Right away, sir.

NATHAN: (*NATHAN returns the cage to CAROLINE*) Here, lady. Take your dog and keep it quiet. And thank you for trying to help out Steve. He's a good boy. And I really liked his mother. A really special lady. (*Turns and walks briskly away with RICHARD trailing along*) And don't forget to remind me to talk about keeping people and their pets together from now on. It's inhumane to separate a person from their pet. They've already lost everything and we make them give up their pets, too? It's inhumane. It's anti-American! It's an outrage and I intend to change the policy as soon as I get back to Baton Rouge. (*Strides off the stage.*)

BLACKOUT

DOMESTIC VIOLENCE AND SEXUAL ASSAULT: STRATEGIES FOR IMPROVEMENT

DOMESTIC VIOLENCE IN LOUISIANA

For reasons probably related to poverty and low educational attainment, Louisiana has been plagued by a persistent problem of domestic violence. In this respect, it is no different than the United States as a whole where 1 in 3 women in the U.S. report being victims of domestic violence at least once in their lifetime. This comes to over 5,000,000 individuals a year (larger than the entire population of Louisiana). Rape is one manifestation of domestic violence and 20% of women and one in 70 men have reported being raped in their lifetime. Women between the ages of 16 to 24 are four times more likely to be raped than other age groups. Of these rapes, more than half were acquaintances (especially dates, when 57% of rapes occur). Around 27% of the victims did not realize they were raped and 42% did not report the episode.

Sadly, domestic violence, which represents 21% of all reported crimes in Louisiana, can escalate to murder. Louisiana was the 2nd highest in its partner murder rates in 2014 (30.3/100,000 inhabitants). One domestic violence murder has occurred in every parish (county) in Louisiana from 1997 to 2009 and they continue to occur. In Central Louisiana, the Rapides Foundations reported that 13.8% of adults had been "hit, slapped, pushed, kicked, or hurt in some way by an intimate partner." This happened least in Catahoula, Allen and Winn Parishes (6.5 to 8.1%), and most in LaSalle and Natchitoches, Rapides and Vernon Parishes (14.9 to 16.3%). Among all victims, low income, African-American women suffered the highest levels (although paradoxically

LaSalle and Vernon Parishes have the lowest percentage of African-Americans in our region, 11% and 14% respectively).

The cycle of violence is especially severe among women and girls who are vulnerable due to endemic dependence and cultural stereotypes of male dominance. Violence tends to spill over to other family members and can include child abuse or elderly abuse.

Beyond the obvious medical costs of domestic violence, the social costs are enormous including lost wages, lost educational attainment, unwanted pregnancies, low self-esteem, depression and suicide. Women often blame themselves rather than their perpetrators and can feel humiliated and powerless to prevent violence or to extricate themselves from the situation.

Rapes or other violence often goes unreported and the victims may personally bear the medical costs of a hospital ER exam and sexual assault work up. Fortunately, that sad state of affairs appears to be coming to an end with recent legislation. In addition, there are various local groups including the Faith House, United Way, CAS (Childrens' Advocacy Services) and others who are collaborating to reduce our inappropriately high levels of domestic violence and abuse in CENLA. Soon there will be a Family Resource Center on the grounds of the former Huey P. Long Hospital to serve the needs of abused women (and men). It will provide a one-stop-shop for those seeking material, medical and legal assistance for domestic violence.

Although often hidden behind closed doors, the disgrace of domestic violence, both physical and psychological, should be exposed to the light of day. If you are a victim of abuse, including rape or date rapes, or a witness to domestic violence, please report it! We all have a responsibility to stop this plague in our society.

THE PROM DRESS/ AFTER THE PROM

CAST OF CHARACTERS

>DONNA: Teenage daughter getting ready to go to the prom.

>CAROL: Donna's grandmother. She is in her mid-sixties or a bit older.

SETTING

>Middle class home with a few set elements, a sofa, chairs and a coffee table.

SCENE I: THE PROM DRESS

>*DONNA is in a room with a table and a couple of chairs, a coat rack and nothing more. DONNA is trying on a pair of shoes as CAROL enters. Music is "Moon River."*

CAROL: (*Walks on stage holding a box*) Here it is . . . your prom dress! (*Sets the box on the table and opens it, and then hands a long, elegant prom dress to DONNA*) It's so beautiful. You'll look like a movie star. It's the perfect prom dress for the perfect little girl.

DONNA: (*Looks at the dress*) It's gorgeous. And all the more beautiful because I shed blood, sweat and tears to pay for it. All those hours slaving away for minimal wage at McDonalds, I thought I'd never get enough money.

CAROL: Your grandfather and I volunteered to pay for your dress. So don't blame us for all that after-school work.

DONNA: No, I wanted to buy it with my own money. I wanted it to be a gift to myself, an expression of independence from a grown up woman to herself.

CAROL: That's the nicest part of all. You wanted it to be your dress that you picked out yourself and paid for by yourself. I'm so proud of you. You are certainly a grown up woman, not a little girl anymore. I'm sure your mother would have been just as proud of you. No one can argue with you about that. (*Gives DONNA a big hug and backs away, looking at the shoes.*) And those shoes, they're a perfect match.

DONNA: (*Puts the dress up against her sweat shirt and pants and admires the effect*) It's beautiful. (*Spins around and lets the dress swirl in front of her*) Great dress, great shoes, but I'm just missing one thing to make it truly perfect.

CAROL: I know, you must be talking about jewelry. I have my pearls, or maybe my amber necklace that you admire so much? Or something from your momma?

DONNA: (*Taking on a serious tone*) No, Grandma, I'm only missing my pills. What did you do with them?

CAROL: What pills?

DONNA: My birth control pills, of course. The ones you undoubtedly took out of my dresser when you were snooping around in my room.

CAROL: I. . . .(*does not finish.*)

DONNA: I need those pills. And I need them today.

CAROL: Why? Why will you need them? Where did they come from? Who gave you such a thing?

DONNA: Ah, so you admit you took them. Well, first, I need to take them everyday so I won't get pregnant. That seems pretty obvious, doesn't it? Second, if you must know, I got them from the nurse practitioner at the health unit and she was glad to do it.

CAROL: Why didn't I know about this?

DONNA: Because I'm a grown woman, like you said yourself, and because the health unit is confidential. They do family planning, you know. And they don't have to tell parents or grandparents or anyone about anything if you're older than twelve.

CAROL: Twelve! You can get pills without your parent's knowledge at twelve! That's an outrage!

DONNA: Yeah, and it's pretty outrageous that half my senior class is pregnant before they graduate. Or that they pop out deformed little premies like Melissa Gordon's baby that get stuck on ventilators for weeks before they die anyway. That's pretty shocking, too, isn't it?

CAROL: We're not discussing other people's health; we're talking about you. And that still doesn't answer my question why you need those pills now, just for the prom.

DONNA: Because I plan on having the perfect prom. That seems pretty obvious, too, doesn't it?

CAROL: Are you going to have sex with Greg?

DONNA: (*Pulls off the sweat shirt and pants and tries on the dress*) Help me with this, please.

> *DONNA pulls on the dress and CAROL zips it up in the back and helps adjusts it.*

DONNA: Wow! It looks great! And the answer to your question about having sex with Greg is yes, I do plan on it. We are going to have real sex, just like grown-up people.

CAROL: Where?

DONNA: Where? You mean vaginal or anal, or in whose bed?

CAROL: Don't be disgusting! How can you talk about such things?

DONNA: Well, it is an interesting question. (*Adjusts the shoes*) Anyway, Greg doesn't like condoms. So if I don't have my pills back, I sure won't be able to do vaginal sex, will I? And frankly, I don't like anal sex at all.

CAROL: Stop this! You don't have to have sex anywhere with anyone. You're a young girl, a beautiful young girl. You can wait. There's no rush. There's no obligation to have sex after the prom. You cherish your independence, so don't be like the other girls, and don't give in to peer pressure.

DONNA: You certainly don't know much about boys nowadays, do you? I suppose when you went to the prom you thought a first kiss was a big deal. (*Tries on some earrings*) It's not like that anymore. Most girls at school are already experts at hand and blow jobs. If you're not doing at least that, then you're just not cool.

CAROL: You don't have to be cool! You need to be smart and well-educated and successful, not some sort of lowlife high school whore.

DONNA: Momma would have understood. So, give me back my pills! You're just too old. You just don't understand. I want the perfect prom, with a long romantic evening, ending with fulfilling sex with my boyfriend, who happens to love me.

CAROL: Love? What do you know about love?

DONNA: I'm 18 years old, not eight. I've had periods since I was 12 and have done things you probably never dreamed of (*pauses*) and certainly wouldn't approve of. I want a real prom to remember my whole life, not some fairy tale, hand-holding fantasy like you had.

CAROL: (*Sits down*) Way back then I wanted the same thing that you want now. I wanted a romantic evening with the love of my life, just like you do. We're not as different as you might think.

DONNA: So, did you have sex after the prom, like I want to?

CAROL: Yes.

DONNA: With Grandpa?

CAROL: No.

DONNA: Then with who?

CAROL: With whom.

DONNA: Oh Grandma, you're ridiculous. This isn't an English lesson. Just answer the question.

CAROL: It doesn't matter, but it wasn't your grandfather, and three months later I had an abortion. (*Pauses*) I don't remember too much about the prom because we got drunk. I do remember the abortion. We went to a sleazy place, with a horrible smell of alcohol or Lysol or something. There was a garbage can filled with bloody gauze in the so-called operating room, at least that's what was written on the door. The doctor was so matter of fact, if he even was a real doctor. Back then, it wasn't legal yet, you know. All hush, hush and dangerous. (*Pauses*) I still think about it all the time. And I think about that fancy blue dress I wore to my prom. Your great grandma picked it out for me. It was blue like the Virgin's veil. I still can't see that blue to this day without thinking about that abortion. Every time I look at a statue of the Virgin Mary, I think about that horrible day and the garbage cans full of bloody gauze.

DONNA: (*Long pause*) An abortion! You had an abortion! That's horrible! (*Spins around*) You killed one of my uncles or aunts and you worry about me taking the pill? I don't want to ever go through that sort of thing, even if it is legal. I want happy memories, a beautiful night of young love. I'm sorry for you. I'm sorry for your experience. But I'm not a baby-killer. Now, give me my pills back, for heaven's sake (*extends out her hand.*)

CAROL: Is it too much to expect you to be beautiful, pure and virginal until you get married?

DONNA: Yes, it is!

CAROL: (*Pauses*) You know, back in my high school days, all of the dances, including the prom, always ended with "Moon River." (*Holds out her arms and beckons DONNA*) Come on, take my arms.

DONNA: What on earth are you doing?

CAROL: I want to teach you how to dance the waltz. Everyone needs to know how to do it. That's what "Moon River" was, you know, a waltz. It was the romantic end to every romantic evening at our high school dances.

DONNA: Grandma, this is stupid.

CAROL: No it's not. I'll be the man and you'll be my partner. Now take my arms.

> *DONNA takes CAROL's arm and they assume dance position.*

CAROL: That's right. Now it's very easy. You go backwards and I go forward. One-two-three, two-two-three, three-two-three, four-to-three. That's right.

> *"Moon River" begins to play and the two women dance the waltz with increasing elegance. They dance for several seconds before the music fades. DONNA turns under CAROL's arms and bows. As DONNA straightens up, CAROL hands her the package of birth control pills.*

DONNA: Thank you. (*Clutches the pills*) I doubt whether we will be doing any waltzing at our prom, but I'm still looking forward to dancing with my Prince Charming.

CAROL: I suppose you think doing the waltz is so 70's.

DONNA: Right! 1870!

CAROL: (*Laughs*) Here, let me help you out of that dress. You don't want to mess it up before your perfect prom.

> *CAROL helps DONNA take off the dress. DONNA removes the shoes and is left in her underclothes. They are putting the dress on a hanger and the shoes in a box. DONNA puts on her shirt and pants.*

CAROL: And I think you will still need these (*hands her a small bag.*)

DONNA: I hope it's not your pearls. They looked good on you, but I'm not wearing any vintage jewelry. (*Looks in the bag*) What is it?

CAROL: Condoms.

DONNA: You're worried about me taking birth control pills and you're giving me condoms?

CAROL: Birth control pills don't prevent sexually transmitted diseases. You might not get pregnant, but you can still get herpes or HIV. Better safe than sorry.

DONNA: You're so full of surprises for an old lady! Perhaps I can educate Greg about these things. He can be so stubborn. (*Looks in the bag*) Are these flavored condoms?

CAROL: No! I do have my limits. (*Embraces DONNA*) Have a wonderful prom. And be safe.

BLACK OUT

ACT II: AFTER THE PROM

> *Same room. Two a.m. Music can be "After the Ball is Over" by Charles K. Harris. CAROL is sitting in a chair and is doing some sort of handwork. DONNA, dressed in her prom dress and a bit disheveled, comes in on tiptoe. She is carrying her shoes in her hand.*

CAROL: Back so early?

DONNA: Grandma, what are doing up at this hour? (*Looks at her watch*) And it's certainly not early, it's almost two a.m.

CAROL: You said you were going to dance all night long with Prince Charming. I just wanted to make sure you got home safely. There's a lot of drinking and driving that goes on out there. I don't want you to be some sort of statistic.

DONNA: Help me out of this dress, please.

> *CAROL gets up and begins to help DONNA out of her dress. DONNA is wearing a simple slip so she is not just in a bra and underwear on stage. CAROL holds up the dress with admiration and DONNA snatches it away.*

DONNA: Give me that piece of crap! I'm going to burn it out in the yard along with the shoes and the purse.

CAROL: Burn it?

CAROL: (*Pulls the dress back*) No! You worked and saved for this dress and you are not going to destroy it. You told me yourself that it was a symbol of your personal independence. Why would you want to destroy that?

DONNA: (*Grabs for the dress*) Give it back! It's a symbol all right, but not of independence.

CAROL: (*Clutches the dress and looks at DONNA*) Oh, honey what happened?

DONNA: Prince Charming is a crap head. His name is Greg Hillstrom, by the way, and he's a rotten good-for-nothing asshole.

CAROL: I thought you said you loved him and he loved you. And he's always been a polite, respectful young man with me. Besides, his parents and grandparents are God-fearing, church-going community members and they happen to own the Ford dealership. That's not a bad combination in this day and age.

DONNA: I don't care if his parents are deacons or saints or whatever they are, but their cute little boy raped me!

CAROL: Raped you? How could he rape you?

DONNA: The usual way, by over-powering me and forcing me to have sex when I didn't want to. What do you think?

CAROL: You told me yourself that you were planning on having sex with him tonight to consummate the perfect prom night. So how exactly could he rape you if you wanted to have sex?

DONNA: Yes, I did want to have sex with him, but not in the bed of his Ford pickup on a filthy mattress. (*Pauses.*) He said he wanted to rent a nice hotel room, but that it was just too expensive and that he didn't have the money. Too expensive! He even asked me if I had cash or a credit card. Can you imagine?

CAROL: Oh dear.

CAROL tries to go and comfort DONNA, but she pushes CAROL away.

DONNA: I already told him I was on the pill and that was a big mistake. So he thinks everything's cool. He just assumed that any girl would want to have sex on a mattress in his truck. I told him to stop groping and he just wouldn't stop. And, of course, he wouldn't even think about using a condom. Not him. It's not natural, he says. And when I insisted, he tells me that I'm insulting him. He says he's doesn't have anything dirty and he just kept pawing me.

CAROL: So he forced you?

DONNA: He tried. But I told him he could take his cheap dick and shove it anywhere he wanted, but not in me.

CAROL: So he left you alone? He didn't rape you.

DONNA: NO! He grabbed my face and forced it down into his crotch until I was just over his stiff penis. (*Shudders*) I can't stand that! I can't stand doing what he forced me to do. I wanted to bite his dick off. I swear I did. Then it was in my mouth and then his sperm was in my mouth. (*Screws up her face and wipes her lips*) Yuk! It's disgusting. (*Pauses*) Then you know what he does?

CAROL: What?

DONNA: He offers me a swallow of warm beer to get the taste of his sperm out of my mouth! (*Shakes her head in disgust*) That was Prince Charming's token gesture. Ugh!

CAROL: (*Pauses*) What kind of beer?

DONNA: Grandma! What the hell difference does that make?

CAROL: None, I suppose. It's just that some European beers are meant to be drunk at room temperature.

DONNA: That's a ridiculous thought.

CAROL: I'm sorry. I'm not thinking straight. It's late and this is a lot for my old brain to absorb (*sits down in a chair.*) (*Pauses and fingers the dress*) I told you not to take birth control pills. I told you not to have sex or even think about it or talk about it. I'm sorry for you, but at least you only got a mouthful of sperm instead of a one night stand in some cheap hotel and maybe an STD and bed bugs to boot. It's all too disgusting, but if you have to choose, at least what you did was over in a minute.

DONNA: I didn't choose! Don't you get it! I didn't choose! He did! That's rape, non-consensual sex of any kind. (*Reaches for the dress*) Give it to me! I'm going to burn this dress. I don't want to see a scrap of cloth to remind me of this night. All I want to see is a pile of black ashes and a shoe buckle. That's it. So give it to me!

CAROL: No!

> *DONNA and CAROL struggle with the dress. The battle can be violent, with slapping and grabbing to increase the intensity. Eventually CAROL gives up and DONNA yanks the dress away and clutches it tightly.*

CAROL: That dress is yours. You bought and paid for it. I guess you can do what you want with it. (*Backs away*) Is this really the way you imagined the end of your perfect romantic prom night?

DONNA: (*Still holding the prom dress*) Fighting with my grandmother over a stupid prom dress? Heck no!

CAROL: Maybe you can give the dress to your cousin, Judy. She's about your size and she would never be able to afford such a nice dress. Transform tragedy into a gesture of hope and good will. I would have given my right boob for a dress like that at my prom, not that virgin blue thing your Grandma picked out for me.

DONNA: Yeah, and you would have looked great with one breast. (*Shakes her head.*) No! I can't. It makes me sick to think about it. Greg's tie was the same color as my dress. He picked it out on purpose. Now I'll never be able to look at that color again.

> *DONNA puts the dress on the table between them.*

CAROL: I think we should call the police. It was rape.

DONNA: The police? Who would believe me? I was on the pill by my own choice. I had condoms that I brought myself. I told you I wanted to have sex with him. Who would ever believe me? Every girl in high school wants Greg any way they can get him. (*Pauses*) I got him all right, a whole mouthful. Now he can just move on to Cindy or Roberta or Cathy. (*Starts to cry*) He even told me that he was leaving me because I was such a prude. (*Pauses*) I'm a fool, not a prude.

CAROL: We can all be foolish. I just hate to see you suffer. You wanted a prom to remember your whole life, a wonderful romantic evening.

DONNA: Ending in a forced blowjob? Oh, I'll remember this prom my whole life, that's for sure.

CAROL: (*Takes DONNA in her arms and rocks her*) Think about the future: college, the right young man, the right time, the right place. You are still in one piece. You aren't pregnant. We can fix the dress and. . . (*stops.*)

DONNA: No! It's mine and I really want to burn it. I want to see the fire and smoke and think about Greg, burning in hell. And maybe some of my foolish adolescent notions will go up in flames, too.

CAROL: Just like your innocence?

DONNA: Yes, just like my innocence. (*Looks up and takes on a religious tone and look*) And the smoke will rise up from the altar of my innocence to the high heavens, a signal to all those stupid teenage girls who think that a fancy dress and a scumbag boyfriend will make the perfect prom.

CAROL: Go get yourself cleaned up. Let's get you to bed. Get some sleep and tomorrow the sun will come up, and the world will look so various, so beautiful, so new.

DONNA: I know that poem. (*Pauses and continues slowly*) But hath really neither joy, nor love, nor light, nor certitude, nor peace, nor help for pain.

CAROL: (*Pauses*) So let us be true to one another. (*Takes DONNA's hands*) Let me kiss you before you go off to bed (*bends to kiss her on the lips.*)

DONNA: Not on the lips, please! Not after what they've been through tonight.

CAROL: Your lips will be sweeter than honey, wherever they have been. (*Kisses her on the lips*) Now off to bed with you. I'll clean up here.

DONNA: (*Gets up to leave and turns*) Go ahead and give the dress to Judy. She's a nice girl, even if she's about as homely as they come. (*Pauses*) And that so-called boyfriend of hers, what a Neanderthal nut case.

CAROL: Worse than your Prince Charming?

DONNA: You've got a point there. I'm going to take a shower and go to bed.

CAROL: Don't forget the mouth wash!

DONNA: Thanks, Grandma. I won't forget.

> *DONNA gets up and leaves.*
> *CAROL picks up the dress and*
> *shoes and clutches them to herself.*
> *CAROL puts the dress to herself*
> *and begins to waltz to the melody*
> *"After the Ball if Over," as lights*
> *dim to dark.*

BLACKOUT

SARPS AND SANES: NEW HOPE FOR VICTIMS OF SEXUAL ASSAULT

Public revelations about victims of sexual assault being charged by hospitals for their forensic medical examinations resulted in indignation and the subsequent passage of Louisiana Act 229. While not perfect, the Act addressed these billing practices, as well as other inconsistencies in the current process of dealing with sexual assault victims in some areas of the state.

Act 229 clearly establishes the need for a SARP (Sexual Assault Response Plan) in each of the 9 public health regions of the state. The Act also declares that the parish coroners (or their approved delegate) are responsible for performing the forensic medical exam. These delegated providers may include emergency room doctors or what is known as SANEs (Sexual Assault Nurse Examiners.) These latter are nurses who undergo a rigorous training for such exams and are fully capable of completing the complex process of gathering information, performing the exam and collecting specimens from the victims. They also remain qualified to present the evidence in court where some cases of sexual assault inevitably end.

Parish coroners also designate the facility where the forensic exams take place. Since some coroners who are not physicians, transfer victims to a more appropriate facility, even in another parish. That being said, all ERs must perform an initial screening medical assessment to ensure that victims do not have other injuries that must be treated and stabilized prior to transfer.

Wherever the victim ends up, there should be a victim advocate as well as a representative of law enforcement (when the victim chooses to report the assault.) While many victims have the right to choose whether to report or not, minors, victims of sex trafficking and those unable to give consent must have their cases reported.

Hospitals must have policies and plans to treat victims of sexual assault who cannot be billed for any services related to the forensic medical exam. This non-billing policy must be posted in the emergency room and be made available in pamphlet form to any victim.

Sexual assault kits should be standardized and most of the time will be brought to the healthcare facility by law enforcement. Some facilities keep a limited stock of kits for those victims who choose not to report at the time of the incident. The completed kits are given to law enforcement that transports them to an appropriated crime lab for analysis, after which completed kits are stored back with law enforcement. The hospitals store kits for non-reporting victims in an appropriate location and with a well-defined system of labeling. The hospitals and other providers, including the victim, may apply for reimbursement by the Crime Victim Compensation Fund for up to $1,000/case.

Regional Office of Public Health Medical Directors were mandated to coordinate the development of a regional Sexual Assault Response Plan (SARP), which include, at very least, a list of resources for victims and current policies and practices in the parishes, including how and where assault kits are stored and transported. This plan, created with stakeholder input, will become effective February 1 and be reviewed annually.

The patchwork of policies and practices that characterize the current situation in many parts of the state should give way to a far more systematic approach to sexual assault victims, who should never be penalized (or billed) in the process. For that, Act 229 comes as a welcome incentive, especially to those parishes and regions that have not had comprehensive policies and procedures. The problem of sexual assault (and domestic violence in general) remains a significant one in Louisiana and the United States. Act 229, while amenable to improvement, should provide motivation to move in the right direction for optimal treatment of our many sexual assault victims.

SANE OR INSANE?

CAST OF CHARACTERS

BETTY MILLER: ER Nurse. Woman of any age, probably her 30's. Crisp and efficient.

DOROTHY PRESCOTT: Victim. Young woman of any age from 15 to 25. Bruised. Dressed in a hospital gown with a blood-soaked lower portion suggesting genital violence. May have a regional Southern accent.

MAGGIE STEWART: Sexual Assault Nurse Examiner (SANE NURSE). A young or mature woman. Confident and assertive.

DR. POLLARD: Parish Coroner. Middle-aged or older gentleman with an imperious manner. Dressed in a white coat and a stethoscope hanging around his neck. Can be wearing a tie and polished loafers with slacks.

BRUCE MASTERS: Law enforcement. Only a voice behind a folding screen or even off stage. The audience never sees him.

SETTING

Emergency room. There is a stretcher and a folding screen or other such device. Otherwise the stage can be bare. Extensive props are not required.

DOROTHY is lying on the stretcher with a blood-soaked hospital gown. She may have a sheet discretely draped over the bloodiest portions.

It, too, can be saturated with blood.
BETTY enters and stands before the
DOROTHY.

BETTY: Well, do you want to report the assault or not?

DOROTHY: Report to who?

BETTY: To law enforcement, the Sheriff's Office.

DOROTHY: Damn right, I do! That S.O.B. raped me. Then he beat me up for good measure. Damn sure, I'll report it.

BETTY: You know we will have to perform a forensic medical exam to collect evidence for eventual prosecution of your assailant.

DOROTHY: Assailant! That sounds too good for him. He's a good-for-nothing, cheating, meth popping sorry excuse for a husband. That's what he is!

BETTY: Most victims know their assailants, if that makes you feel any better.

DOROTHY: Better? Why should that make me feel any better? (*Pauses*) Don't you think you need to get on with whatever you're supposed to do here?

BETTY: Of course. Let me notify law enforcement and the coroner's office now. (*Takes a cell phone and calls the Sheriff's Office*) Hello, Brian, is Detective Masters there? (*Pauses*) Yes, please tell him to come down to the ER because we have an assault case to process. (*Pauses*) Yes, I'll be calling the coroner right away.

DOROTHY: Coroner? I'm not gonna die, am I?

BETTY: No, of course not. It's just that we have to notify the coroner and he decides whether to see you in person or delegate the forensic exam to the ER doctor or a SANE nurse.

DOROTHY: Of course I want a sane nurse. What would I want with a crazy one?

BETTY: No, of course not, SANE stands for Sexual Assault Nurse Examiner. They are specially trained for these sorts of exams. They know what's in the assault kits and they know how to do the exam so the evidence holds up in court. Plus, they're usually women and they really know what they're doing.

DOROTHY: I hope they're women. That'd give me the creeps to have some old fart poking around down there. (*Points to the bloody hospital gown.*)

BETTY: (*Calls again*) Hello, is this Dr. Pollard. (*Pauses*) Yes, we have a sexual assault case down here in the ER. (*Pauses*) Thanks. I've already notified the Sheriff's Office and they're bringing down the kit. I'll meet the detective out in the waiting room. If you're upstairs making rounds, we'll see you soon.

> *DOROTHY looks around nearly empty room. There is a screen off to one side. BETTY walks off stage. After a short delay, CORONER walks on stage.*

CORONER: Good thing I was making rounds upstairs. (*To DOROTHY*) Hello, I'm Dr. Pollard, the parish coroner. I've been notified that you were are a victim of an alleged sexual assault.

DOROTHY: Oh no! This wasn't and "a-lleg-ed" assault. This was the real thing. He slapped me around and said he'd kill me if I didn't do it right then and there.

CORONER: Then and there?

DOROTHY: Yeah, in the fucking toolshed. Right there on a pile of dirty old burlap feed sacks. Ugh!

CORONER: (*Smiles*) Doesn't sound too romantic.

DOROTHY: No, it wasn't. And I was having my period and he says he doesn't care because that's a turn-on to him, "like guttin' a pig," he says.

CORONER: (*Makes a face*) Hmmm. (*Pauses and jots down some notes on a pad*) Did you know the alleged assailant?

DOROTHY: (*Yells*) NOT A-LLEG-ED, the real thing and my attacker was my husband, the lousy good-for-nothin' parasite.

CORONER: I'm not the judge or jury, just the coroner. We do have a lot of "gotcha" cases around here, you know.

DOROTHY: Gotcha? Gotcha what?

CORONER: Well, some alleged victims get caught in the act by parents, spouses, family or friends and it's just easier for them to say they were raped than to admit they were having illicit consensual sex.

DOROTHY: (*Explodes*) This was NOT con-sens-u-al! This was rape, pure and simple. He beat me up before the act and he beat me up after the act and he wouldn't take no for an answer in between.

CORONER: It was your husband, wasn't it?

DOROTHY: I don't care! You can't do things like that. You should see how it's all torn up down there. (*Points to the bloody hospital gown*) Blood everywhere, skin hanging off. It's horrible and painful and you're taking to me about my husband and con-sens-u-al sex!

CORONER: Did he use a blunt instrument for penetration?

DOROTHY: (*Crying*) He used a damn axe handle! The whole thing!

CORONER: (*Curious*) The sharp end? With the blade?

DOROTHY: No, you fool! He used the handle, the big, fucking wooden handle!

CORONER: Why?

DOROTHY: (*Exasperated*) Why? Who knows why? Ask that sorry son-of-a-bitch, who I hope's sitting in jail where he belongs. (*Pauses*) I want that special nurse.

CORONER: What special nurse? That one who works in the ER or the SANE nurse, the one the nurse talked to you about without my permission.

DOROTHY: Yes, the SANE nurse.

CORONER: No! I'm doing the forensic exam myself. If I'm already here, there is no point in getting that nurse involved.

DOROTHY: (*Yells*) But I want her!

CORONER: You can't decide, I decide! And I'm here and I'm going to do the exam. In fact, I'm having you transferred over to the Cypress Bend Hospital where we have our own special nurses.

DOROTHY: SANE ones?

CORONER: You mean Certified Sexual Assault Nurse Examiners?

DOROTHY: Yes.

CORONER: Well, not exactly, but they are in training.

DOROTHY: NO! I want the real certified SANE nurse. And I want her here and I want her now!

CORONER: As coroner, I have the legal right and the obligation to do the exam or delegate it to whoever I decide.

DOROTHY: Then delegate it to that SANE nurse, wherever she is, and we'll get this thing over with.

> *BETTY returns with a sexual assault kit in a box. Hands it to the CONONER.*

BETTY: Here's the kit, Dr. Pollard. Law enforcement is here, too and he's behind the screen over there. (*Turns her head and yells.*) You over there, Bruce?

BRUCE: Yeah!

CORONER: Bruce, eh? (*Takes the kit*) Let's get this show on the road. (*To DOROTHY*) There's a lot of paperwork and a very lengthy physical exam. (*To BETTY*) Is the victim advocate here yet?

BETTY: We couldn't get in touch with her. I think she's on maternity leave or something.

CORONER: Is there someone else available for that?

BETTY: No.

CORONRER: (*Dismissively*) Sounds about right. (*Pause*) Well, just make a note that we tried to contact her and she was not available.

BETTY: (*To DOROTHY*) You heard that law enforcement is here?

DOROTHY: Do they have to be here, too? I know most of them guys at the station. They've all been out to our place many times. I think I recognize the name. Isn't he Bruce Masters, related to the Masters over on Row Gully Road?

BETTY: (*Points to the screen*) He's behind the screen. I don't know his relatives, but he only listens to make sure there is nothing weird going on and then he takes the sexual assault kit to the station when Dr. Pollard is done.

DOROTHY: (*To BETTY*) I want the SANE nurse!

BETTY: (*To CORONER*) Is that all right, Dr. Pollard? She wants a SANE nurse.

CORONER: NO! It's not all right. I'm doing this exam myself.

BETTY: But if the patient requests a SANE nurse, don't we have to respect her wishes.

CORONER: NO, WE DON'T! WE don't have to do anything except perform our legal function as coroner.

BETTY: Doctor I already notified the SANE nurse. She should be here any minute.

MAGGIE enters.

MAGGIE: Hello! Is this the right room for the SANE nurse? (*To BETTY*) Hello Betty, nice seeing you. (*To CORONER*) Hello, Dr. Pollard, always a pleasure.

CORONER: (*Coolly*) Hello.

MAGGIE: (*To DOROTHY*) Hello, my name is Maggie Steward and I'm a certified sexual assault nurse here to do your exam.

DOROTHY: I'm Dorothy Parker, nice to meet you. I'm glad to see you here.

MAGGIE: I see that the kit is here. Are we ready to start? (*Looks around.*) No victim advocate?

BETTY: No, she's not available, but law enforcement is behind the screen.

CORONER: WE are not ready to start. But I am.

DOROTHY: (*Points to MAGGIE*) I want this lady to do this exam, not you!

CORONER: Please be quiet. I can and should decide. (*To MAGGIE*) We won't be needing your services today, young lady. Would you please leave, now!

DOROTHY: (*Upset*) I want her to do it! I don't want you. You're an arrogant bully and you talk like my husband. I don't want you touching me, especially down there (*points to the bloody spot between the legs.*)

BETTY: I'm sure we can work this out peacefully.

CORONER: Yes, we can. You can transfer this woman to Cypress Bend Hospital immediately and I'll continue this process in peace.

BRUCE: (*Voice behind the curtain*) Is everything okay over there?

CORONER and BETTY: (*Simultaneously*) YES!

MAGGIE and DOROTHY: (*Simultaneously*) NO!

CORONER: (*To MAGGIE*) Get out of here! You and your SANE program have been a thorn in my side since the beginning and it's only getting worse.

MAGGIE: (*To CORONER*) We're certified after a rigorous training, and we work with almost every other coroner in the state. Most of them don't want to fool around with such complicated cases that end up in court anyway.

CORONER: Most of my other coroner colleagues are fools! Some of them aren't even doctors. And I don't give a rat's ass for your specialized training. I'm the doctor! I'm the coroner! And I don't have to answer to anyone but God and the governor.

BETTY: Doctor, please. (*Looks at DOROTHY*) We're upsetting the patient. Can't we discuss this at another time and in another place?

DOROTHY: No! I wanna hear everything. I wanna know what this pompous ass is gonna decide for me.

CORONER: (*To DOROTHY*) In your best interest, of course.

DOROTHY: No, in YOUR best interest from the sounds of it. Don't you work over there at Cypress Bend Hospital, too?

CORONER: Yes.

DOROTHY: Don't the doctors own Cypress Bend Hospital themselves? I think I heard about that on the news one time.

CORONER: That's none of your business!

DOROTHY: It sure as hell is if you're gonna be transferring me to that particular hospital. . .your private hospital with your private nurses. That's a conflict of interest, isn't it?

CORONER: What are you talking about? Of course it's not a conflict of interest.

DOROTHY: No? (*To BETTY*) Doesn't that sound like a conflict of interest to you? (*To MAGGIE*) Doesn't that sound like a conflict of interest to you? (*To BRUCE behind the screen*) Hey, law enforcement? Bruce? Doesn't that sound like a conflict of interest to you? (*Pauses*) Anyone still back there?

BRUCE: Yeah, Detective Masters here. (*Pauses*) I can't say about conflict of interest.

DOROTHY: Bruce Masters? Harold and Eunice's son? The folks down on Row Gulley Road.

BRUCE: Yeah, the same. But I'm a detective with the Sheriff's Office now.

DOROTHY: I remember you. You and my husband went to high school together. Aren't you married to Celia Bordelon?

BRUCE: Yes, ma'am. But I don't have anything to do with your husband anymore.

DOROTHY: I thought you two were hunting buddies back in the day.

LAW ENFORCMENT: Yes, ma'am, a long time ago. I don't hunt too much lately, too busy with the kids.

CORONER: For God's sake. Stop this chatter and let's get on with it. (*To MAGGIE*) You leave now! (*To BETTY*) You call EMS so we can get this woman transported down the road. (*To BRUCE*) And Mr. Masters, you can go to Cypress Bend Hospital, too, and take possession of the kit when we're done.

DOROTHY: I'm not going anywhere! And you're not gonna touch me. If you do, I'll have you arrested for assault and battery. You're worse than my good-for-nothing husband. You're the one who needs to get out, now!

CORONER: (*Coolly*) You cooperate or you can sign a paper and leave here against medical advice. This is a hospital, not a prison.

DOROTHY: No, this is a three-ring circus, you asshole, not a hospital.

BETTY and MAGGIE: It's a hospital.

BRUCE: It is a hospital!

CORONER, BETTY and MAGGIE: (To BRUCE) Shut up!

DOROTHY: (*Gets off the stretcher*) That's it! I'm leaving!

MAGGIE: Please don't. Someone has to collect the evidence if you want any chance to prosecute your husband.

DOROTHY: How can I prosecute him? I don't have an income or a place to go. I'm too old to learn a trade and too stupid to get my GED. (*Looks around*) I'm screwed.

MAGGIE: No, your husband raped you and we can help you.

BETTY: If you want to stay, we can escort Dr. Pollard out. Detective Masters will certainly help us, won't you, Bruce.

BRUCE: (*From behind the curtain*) Sure, if you need me to.

CORONER: Don't you dare touch me! If anyone lays a finger on me, I'll have them charged with assault and battery and interfering with a public official in the line of duty. You will be in more trouble than you can handle.

DOROTHY: If you can do that, I can do it, too. You touch me, you get the same treatment and neither God nor the governor will be able to help you.

CORONER: (*To DOROTHY*) Shut up! This is all your fault.

MAGGIE: (*To CORONER*) Don't blame the victim, please. (*To DOROTHY*) None of what has happened was your fault, none of it, and certainly not this. (*Makes a sweeping gesture of the ER*) I'm sorry you have to endure this, too.

BETTY: (*To CORONER*) Please, just leave peacefully and we'll take care of this case.

CORONER: Now I'm the victim! I get called in here to do my duty and get assaulted by two. . . (*pauses*). . .no, three angry, resentful women and I'm supposed to just turn my back and walk away?

MAGGIE, BETTY and DOROTHY: YES!

BRUCE: (*After a pause*) YES!

CORONER: Okay, that's it. I can tell when I'm not wanted.

DOROTHY: It's about time.

BETTY: (*To DOROTHY*) Shhhh! Not now, please.

CORONER: I'm outta here. But you haven't heard the last from me, young ladies. The hospital administration and the nursing board are going to get an earful. (*To DOROTHY*) And I'll be damned if I'll testify in any case against your a-lleg-ed assailant (*stomps off stage.*)

> *MAGGIE, BETTY and DOROTHY all sigh deeply in unison)*

DOROTHY: (*Quietly*) So now what?

MAGGIE: Let's start over. I'm Maggie Steward and I'm a certified sexual assault nurse examiner and this is Betty Miller, the Chief Nurse in the emergency room.

BRUCE: (*Still from beyond the screen. Yells*) And I'm Bruce Masters, Detective with the Sheriff's Office. I'll be listening to the exam and picking up the assault kit for transport to a secure spot when it's completed.

MAGGIE: So let's get started. In your own word's, please tell me what happened as best you can remember . . . .

Lights dim.

BLACKOUT

SEXUALLY TRANSMITTED DISEASES IN LOUISIANA

SEXUALLY TRANSMITTED DISEASES: UPDATE FOR LOUISIANA AND CENLA

There are many sexually transmitted diseases, but those that are tracked and quantified in Louisiana and nationally are gonorrhea, chlamydia and primary and secondary syphilis. Although HIV/AIDS is also transmitted sexually, it is often tracked separately.

Louisiana has the dubious honor of ranking in the top 4 states in the U.S. with respect to STDs rates: Primary and secondary syphilis (#1), Gonorrhea (#1), chlamydia (#2) in 2015. If HIV/AIDS is included, we also rank consistently among the top 5 states (#2 in 2015). These extraordinary statistics, which usually lag a year or two behind, translate into significant morbidity and economic loss, both locally and nationally.

CENLA has its share of cases, but does not rank at the top of other public health regions with respect to any of these diseases: 5/9 OPH regions for gonorrhea, 6/9 for chlamydia and 7/9 for syphilis. Although we are doing better than many other parts of Louisiana, we still have tremendous room for improvement when compared with national statistics.

There are some significant demographic differences with respect to STDs both in the nation, the state and our region. In our region, cases for both gonorrhea and chlamydia are more commonly diagnosed in woman, 64% and 73% respectively (not unlike state or national statistics). Some of this relates to "sampling error" since sexually active women are systematically checked in annual gynecological exams (at least in the context of the health units) and men only seek assistance when symptomatic. With syphilis, on the contrary, over 85% of those diagnosed regionally are men (similar to state and national figures), which is skewed by the high incidence of syphilis cases in the population of men having sex with men.

Not only are there disparities with sex, but also with ethnicity. For reasons probably related to low income and low educational attainment rather than race, African-Americans are disproportionately represented in all STDs (and HIV/AIDS) regionally, with 79% of cases of gonorrhea, 60% of chlamydia cases and 69% of those with primary and secondary syphilis. The same holds true with HIV/AIDS, with about 75% of cases in African Americans both regionally and in the state as a whole.

With both gonorrhea and chlamydia, the majority of cases in CENLA (69% and 74% respectively) occur in the 15 to 24 year-old range, hardly a surprise and not different from national statistics. Syphilis, on the contrary, occurs more often in older adults, with 62% of cases in the 25 to 44 year-old group, most of these in men who have sex with men (MSM).

The high rates of STDs (and HIV/AIDs) in our region and in the state should underline the importance of responsible sexual choices. The only sure-fire method for prevention is, of course, abstinence, which is laudable, but not necessarily realistic. While they do not prevent STDs, the practice of "safe sex" with the use of condoms greatly reduces the risk of contracting any sexually transmitted disease, including HIV.

Since young people are the primary recipients and transmitters of at least some STDs, they should receive adequate, realistic education about the risks and consequences of infection in a clear, dispassionate and scientifically accurate manner. While this ideally should come from the family, parents may lack the knowledge or skill to correctly transmit this information. In addition, many people (around 25% for syphilis and HIV) are unaware that they have a STD or HIV, both often asymptomatic. Appropriate testing (and contact tracing by the Office of Public Health for syphilis and HIV) can help reduce the risk of transmission in the general population.

Adolescents, by their neurobiological makeup, are saturated with hormones and yet lack mature development of the frontal lobe where reason and impulse control originate. Their impulsive decision-making and lack of control provides a perfect storm for high-risk behavior, whether it be drug or alcohol use, driving without a seatbelt, or engaging in unprotected sex. Only proper education (from whatever reliable source), avoidance of high-risk environments and role-playing to promote automatic healthy behaviors offer any hope of improving our dreadful STD statistics.

Sadly, attempts to introduce comprehensive STD education at the junior high and high school levels are often opposed by school superintendents, fearful for their jobs, and politicians, fearful of not being re-elected. As far as STDs are concerned, however, ignorance is NOT bliss and silence is NOT golden.

SEX ED AND THE SUPERINTENDENT

CAST OF CHARACTERS

DARLENE JACOBS: School superintendent. Fussy, self-important woman (or man) with frumpy clothing and an exaggerated speech pattern. Possible mild Southern regional accent.

GEORGE FAIRCLOTH: Public Health official. Man or woman, well dressed. Somewhat more educated speech pattern with no regional accent.

HENRIETTA PARKER: Older African-American Woman with an educated speech pattern. Black Southern accent but not overwhelming. Correctly dressed.

SETTING

Superintendent's office. A desk and a couple of chairs. There is no need for an elaborate set. There can be an American flag and a state flag of any chosen Southern state.

DARLENE and GEORGE are sitting or standing in DARLENE'S office. There is a knock on the door.

DARLENE: Yes?

HENRIETTA: (*Pokes her head through a crack in the door*) I'm here to see you. Is this the right time and place?

DARLENE: Yes, of course. Come on in and join us. How are you doing today?

HENRIETTA: (*Enters. Extends her hand to DARLENE*) Nice to see you again, and I'm not doing well at all!

DARLENE: Sorry to hear that. (*To GEORGE*) Mrs. Parker, this is Mr. George Faircloth from the Office of Public Health. I invited him here to meet with you. This is Mrs. Henrietta Parker from the school board

> GEORGE stands and extends his hand. HENRIETTA refuses to take it.

HENRIETTA: I know this man and his filth. My sister over at Garfield Middle Magnet told me how he came in and told a pack of dirty lies to those kids about sex.

GEORGE: Which lies, exactly?

HENRIETTA: That we are number one and number two in this state for all of those nasty sexual transmitted diseases, including HIV. It just can't be true!

GEORGE: I'm afraid it is true. And it has been that way for some time.

HENRIETTA: And what good does it do exactly to fill young, impressionable minds with all sorts of dirty ideas?

GEORGE: Mrs. Parker, with all due respect, if you turn on the television, you have everything you need to know about sex, except the truth.

HENRIETTA: Truth! What you talking about? Truth comes from God, not from disgusting slides about pustule-covered vaginas and dripping penises. Kids don't need to be seeing that sort of thing.

GEORGE: I disagree. Kids need to be seeing that and more on slides before they see the real thing on their bodies.

HENRIETTA: (*Rushing toward GEORGE*) Like porn? Hard core porn? Maybe that'll give them some ideas, too. (*Moves toward GEORGE menacingly*) You and your stupid ideas gave my sweet granddaughter the notion to go and get pregnant and get gonorrhea and syphilis to boot. (*Stops and begins to cry*) I don't know what to do or who to blame.

GEORGE: (*Comforts HENRIETTA*) You must feel very hurt.

HENRIETTA: I raised that child when her own good-for-nothing momma, my own flesh and blood, left her to go running around with drug trash. God only knows where that whore ended up.

DARLENE: That's harsh language for your own daughter, somebody you still love.

HENRIETTA: Love! I adored that little girl. And I adored her daughter too, and now she did the same thing as her momma, she got pregnant at fifteen, dropped out of school, got into drugs so deep that she stole money. . .my money. She stole from her own grandma the way her momma stole from me. And she's run off, too, and I don't even know where she is. (*Sits down and covers her face*) I'm being tested by God, just like Job was, but I don't have Job's strength or his faith. (*To GEORGE and DARLENE*) You gotta help me! You gotta get these kids outta this cycle of disease and drugs and death. (*To GEORGE*) Why didn't your horrible slides keep her away from those nasty boys?

GEORGE: Adolescents are hard wired to take risks. They are awash in hormones and their frontal lobes (*taps the front of his head*), the front part of their brains that makes rational decisions, are not fully developed until they're 24 or so.

HENRIETTA: That's Chinese to me, doc.

GEORGE: (*Stands and explains*) Let's say I'm a teenager. I see a girl and I think, I want to have sex with her. I want pleasure and I'm fully-grown physically and full of hormones. I can do it and I see it on the movies and the TV and on videos. I want that! (*Pauses.*) Now you and I might say "Yes, but if I have sex, that girl might become pregnant. I might get an STD. And that might ruin my chances of going to college." You (*points to HENRIETTA*) and you (*points to DARLENE*) might say that. But Mr. Teenager knows these things intellectually, but his hormones win because he "just can't control himself."

DARLENE: What good does it do for teenagers to take risks like that?

GEORGE: (*Shrugs*) I dunno. Maybe it's to go out and establish new ape colonies, or to challenge the number one alpha ape. Or maybe to try and impregnate the most female apes he can. Who knows? It must have had some evolutionary advantage in cave man days, but certainly doesn't have any evolutionary advantage now.

DARLENE: (*Cringes.*) Can we leave evolution out of this discussion? I think we have enough delicate issues under discussion.

HENRIETTA: (*Pats DARLENE on the arm.*) There, there, dear, I'm not that retrograde. I believe in e-volution.

DARLENE: Nice to hear it.

HENRIETTA: (*Gives DARLENE a mean look*) We don't all have college degrees like you two have, but we are smart and hard-working, intelligent and God-fearing folks who have lived here for generations. And we learned a thing or two in the process.

All pause and move around to different places.

HENRIETTA: So what do we do now? You're the specialist, Mr. Public Health.

GEORGE: (*Assumes an official air*) They are three things we need to do. First, we need to give the kids accurate information, slides and all, so they know the risks and consequences of sex.

DARLENE: No! (*Pauses*) I could do what you propose tomorrow. I could start a new sex ed curriculum with horrible pictures and endless statistics. The problem is that I'd have a dozen angry parents on my case the next day, and a bunch of angry school board members, including the four that already hate me for whatever bad reason. That'll make a majority of the board that wants me out. So they vote to get rid of me and I'll be unemployed. Is that what you want, Mr. Faircloth.

GEORGE: Of course not.

DARLENE: But that's what will happen. I'll get fired.

GEORGE: Blame it on me.

DARLENE: Sure! They'll really believe me. (*Assumes a whiny voice*) "That wicked man from public health made me do it." Sure, that'll work.

HENRIETTA: I'll back you up. I'll get a few other board members to support you. We have to do something, don't we?

GEORGE: Or we throw up our hands and let the children copulate with no protection and get a bumper crop of teenage pregnancies and STD's. (*To DARLENE*) Is that what you want?

HENRIETTA: Like my granddaughter and her mother did.

DARLENE: Of course not! I want healthy, happy children who grow into responsible adults who lead meaningful lives.

GEORGE: Of quiet desperation?

DARLENE: No! With good jobs and stable families and community relevance.

GEORGE: And infertility and congenital syphilis and cervical cancer from HPV exposure?

HENRIETTA: (*To GEORGE*) So what needs to be done? I've failed. You've both failed. You keep your jobs and I lose my daughter and grand daughter.

GEORGE: I'm sorry about how things have worked out for you. But I think education is the first thing and that has to be in schools because it's not happening at home. Second, we do role-playing exercises at school that make the kids give automatic appropriate replies to sexual situations. So then their responses will be prescribed.

HENRIETTA: Like "No means no?"

GEORGE: Precisely. (*Pauses*) We get the responses hard-wired into their brains so they don't have to think about it.

HENRIETTA: Hasn't worked yet. My girls couldn't say no.

DARLENE: (*Sighs*) I'll have to see it to believe it. Pardon my skepticism. And what else?

GEORGE: Third, we keep kids out of unsupervised high-risk situations where drugs and alcohol might be available.

HENRIETTA: (*Groans*) How are you going to do that? Those parents leave their kids and grandkids all alone to run around and get into all sorts of mischief. Especially the rich ones, those kids are the worse. They all steal from their parents . . .drugs, money, alcohol, pills; whatever they can get their hands on. How are you going keep kids supervised?

GEORGE: (*Shrugs*) You do the best you can. And you check to make sure that any all-night party is supervised and not out at somebody's hunting camp, filled with booze and stolen pills.

DARLENE: That's a rich person's problem.

HENRIETTA: What? Unsupervised kids?

DARLENE: No, hunting camps. Not too many poor people I know have hunting camps.

HENRIETTA: And most of the poor folks are black and they got all the problems, too, even worse than whites. (*To GEORGE*) It's true isn't it? STD's and HIV are running wild in the black community, aren't they?

DARLENE: (*To HENRIETTA*) You said it, not me.

HENRIETTA: Somebody got to say it. (*To GEORGE.*) It's true, isn't it? How many more black folks have STD's and HIV than white folks?

GEORGE: At least three to one, and sometimes up to ten to one.

DARLENE: (*Gasps*) Even if it's true, it sounds racist.

HENRIETTA: I've heard that black folks make up a third of the state's population and we have two thirds of the STD's and HIV and two thirds of the men in prison. And more young black men are killing each other than white folks by two to one or more. (*To GEORGE*) Tell me it isn't true, Mr. Public Health.

GEORGE: It is true, completely true.

HENRIETTA: Then tell me why we aren't yelling this information from every pulpit, every schoolhouse, and every dinner table?

GEORGE: (*Sheepishly*) It's a sensitive issue. You'd have to ask your community leaders.

HENRIETTA: No! It's a crime ! (*Pauses*) We got it all: Poverty, crime, failing schools, pregnant teens, STD's, and prisons full of black men. (*Pauses*) Mormons are right; we are the cursed race, at least here in the U.S. (*To GEORGE and DARLENE*) And you two are just part of the problem, the establishment that doesn't care about poor folks or black folks or God forbid, when they're both. (*Sinks down.*) Lord, have mercy on my soul! God strike me down dead so I don't have to see any more injustice. It's a crime and we're not doing anything. (*Pauses*) God's going to get you both! There will be justice some day.

GEORGE and DARLENE: But we're trying!

HENRIETTA: (*Coldly*) Try harder!

DARLENE: We have a lot of folks around hear, black and white, who are not interested in any of this, and who are hostile to anyone who addresses these issues openly and honestly. Community leaders, pastors, priests, business leaders, all of them avoid these topics like the plague, whether they're black or white.

HENRIETTA: (*Screams.*) Damn them! Damn them to hell where they belong. (*Pauses*) This is too important to be afraid. Pray with me! (*Sinks to her knees*) Pray with me.

GEORGE: (*Tries to pull HENRIETTA up*) Please get up.

DARLENE: Mrs. Parker, this isn't the time or the place.

HENRIETTA: No! This is the time and it is the place! (*Looks heavenward*) Where three are gathered In my name, I am there. (*Looks around*) He is here! I know it.

> *Pulls GEORGE and DARLENE down. They form a circle and HENRIETTA prays.*

HENRIETTA: Dear God, Holy Father, Prince of Peace who loves the humble. Open their eyes that they see the truth. And give them the power and the willingness to make changes and the courage to confront your ignorant enemies. Exalt the meek. Let them inherit the earth . . .all of it. Not just the worthless leftover bits and pieces, but the good stuff. And bring your mighty hand down on the wicked that oppose your will. Let them feel your burning wrath and the hot fires of hell where they all belong. (*Pauses*) In your Holy Name, amen.

DARLENE AND GEORGE: Amen.

> *All rise and hug.*

HENRIETTA: (*Pulls away*) Not too close, now. Remember those STD's.

GEORGE: (*Smiles*) That's not the way you catch them, you know.

HENRIETTA: (*Jokes*) I'm not that ignorant, Mr. Public Health. I was just kidding.

DARLENE: (*Raises her hand in supplication*) Enough! I've got an agenda to get together for tonight's school board meeting.

> *GEORGE and HENRIETTA leave together. DARLENE sinks down in a chair and shakes her head.*

DARLENE: STD's, what a pain in the ass. Lord have mercy on us all!

> *Lights dim.*

BLACKOUT

EPILOGUE

If you managed to plow through this volume, or just sampled its contents, you have hopefully learned something. The scientific essays, while they do not pretend to be objective, are at least factual. That being said, the facts in science (and social science) evolve so quickly that some are outdated within a matter of years, if not months.

The plays cover a diversity of subjects, some pleasant and amusing, others horrifying and upsetting. Each play hopes to create a small world in itself, rich with conflict, but also with a dramatic arch and some resolution, however unsatisfactory. Neither the characters nor the reader are expected to be the same at the end as they were in the beginning. While seeing a play on stage is so much more entertaining, there is some merit to reading them. It requires visualizing the characters and their interactions. Some may find that challenging.

In any case, I hope you have taken away something that will inspire you to change yourself and the very imperfect world in which we live.

ABOUT THE AUTHOR

David Jeffrey Holcombe, born in San Francisco, California, in 1949, grew up in the East Bay under the shadow of magnificent Mount Diablo. An idyllic childhood among then country roads lined with pear orchards, he attended local public schools with excellent teachers and few social problems. After high school, he attended the University of California in Davis, from which he graduated with a Bachelor of Science in Agriculture (Applied Behavior Science). He subsequently attended the University of Florida in Gainesville, where he obtained a Master of Science in Agriculture (Poultry Science).

Subsequently, he left for Belgium, where he attended the Catholic University of Louvain in Brussels, Belgium, from which he graduated with an M.D. Summa Cum Laude in 1981.

All during his high school and college years, he continued to paint and write. After returning to the United States in 1983 with his charming Belgian wife, Nicole, they settled in Alexandria, Louisiana where they raised four sons. For twenty years, Dr. Holcombe worked as an internist for 20 years, after which he changed orientation and took a job in public health, a position he has held for the last 10 years.

Medicine and the arts have co-existed, sometimes peacefully and sometimes painfully in his professional career. This ongoing tension and underlying passion have given rise to this work, *PUBLIC HEALTH ON STAGE*, a compilation of published medical essays and self-published plays.

Printed in the United States
By Bookmasters